Y0-DLS-831

EVERY WOMAN'S GUIDE TO PROFITABLE INVESTING

EVERY WOMAN'S GUIDE TO PROFITABLE INVESTING

ELIZABETH M. FOWLER

AMERICAN MANAGEMENT ASSOCIATION

This book is available at a special discount when ordered in bulk quantities. For information, contact Special Sales Department, AMACOM, a division of American Management Association, 135 West 50th Street, New York, NY 10020.

Library of Congress Cataloging-in-Publication Data

Fowler, Elizabeth M.
Every woman's guide to profitable investing.

Includes index.
1. Investments—United States—Handbooks, manuals, etc. 2. Securities—United States—Handbooks, manuals, etc. I. Title.
HG4921.F636 1986 332.6'78'024042 85-48222
ISBN 0-8144-5823-8

Printing number

10 9 8 7 6 5 4 3 2 1

Half for

Frances Thompson Buel,
who gave me an idea for a novel.

Half for my favorite women investors

Catherine Appleton
Betty Cutler
Angela Z. Dailey
Nancy Giffin
Flora Hewett
Helen Holmes
Margaret Menard Price
Vaughn Spilsbury
Mimi Starrett

Contents

1

Happiness Is . . . ***Knowing Investment Fundamentals***

Happiness for a woman is not money, exactly, but money helps. Money is necessary for the most basic sense of security. Everyone thrives on the security that the expectation of money can bring. Being successful is an achievement. But knowing how to invest your earnings wisely will enhance your independence.

It was once said that women can acquire money three ways—make it, marry it, or inherit it. (The ideal, of course, would be to combine all three.) Whether you make your own money, marry well, or inherit money, you should know how to take care of it and how to make your capital grow. That's what investing is all about—using money to make more money. In this book, we'll be talking specifically about investing in securities—stocks and bonds.

Even if you don't own a share of stock now, you probably still are an investor indirectly. Insurance companies in which you have life, fire, and casualty coverage invest their billions of dollars in securities; so do banks. The company for which you or your husband works invests pension fund money in stocks.

Why Invest?

Why invest in securities? One big reason is inflation. More than 43,000,000 Americans, slightly more than half of them women, have found common stocks a sound method of investing, offering growth possibilities against inflation.

In the late 1970s and early 1980s the pace of inflation changed from a fast walk to a run, making careful shopping more important than ever. Consumers did not stage the protest rallies they did in the mid-1960s, but a conservative mood engulfed the country, which demands that political leaders act to stop or at least slow inflation—one reason that President Reagan was swept into office. Since then, inflation has come under control again. However, because of the large federal deficit, there probably will be some increases.

Inflation has created a ragged edge of self-doubt and worry in the minds of most women. Their knowledge of quality often tells them that they must continually be on the lookout against getting gypped—by the supermarket, by the plumber, by the auto dealer, by the television repair shop. Often they feel helpless when they consider how little attention the consumer receives from government and big business.

So, why invest? Because it's a firm, self-protective step into an uncertain future. It gives a woman a feeling that she is taking at least some action. Let's consider the reasons for investing in a less metaphorical way.

It's a Means of Combating Inflation

A woman, working or not, who administers the family's food budget probably feels the impact of inflation much more quickly than her husband. She begins to wonder if she has lost her grip when her $100 weekly food money for a family of four no longer stretches to cover two roasts in a week. Yet it would have done so a few years ago. In fact, $50 would have sufficed ten years ago. Now she needs more. She feels the pinch, too, when she buys children's clothes and shoes. She reads about the ever-rising cost of education at schools and colleges.

Inflation, then, is simply a rise in the cost of living in terms of dollars. They just don't buy as much.

Sometimes, if salaries and other income rise fast enough the impact of higher prices is not felt so keenly. But the trouble is that the first excitement of a raise is usually followed with a rude awakening. What really happens after the first happy thoughts about how to spend the extra money? It all depends on your tax bracket and the rate you pay on state income taxes.

Out of a $2,000 yearly raise, the increase in the family's standard of living amounts to a mere $640 (taking into consideration added taxes and a 5 percent

Table 1-1. What happens to your $2,000 raise?

Taxable income	*$20,000*	*$30,000*	*$40,000*	*$60,000*
Federal tax bracket, 1985 (Rates on additional income)	18%	28%	33%	42%
Total deduction from $2,000 raise for 1985 taxes	$360	$560	$660	$840
5% increase in living costs due to inflation applied to taxable income	$1,000	$1,500	$2,000	$3,000
Take-home pay from raise after taxes and impact of inflation	$640	($60)	($660)	($1,840)

increase in inflation) a year—or $0 if the family income is in the $40,000 range. In fact, it has not even kept pace with the rise in the cost of living. (See Table 1-1.)

By adding the increased living costs and the toll taken by federal income taxes, not to mention the impact of state taxes, you will see that the person in the $20,000 income bracket benefits slightly from a $2,000 raise, possibly $640. The person in the $30,000 bracket goes in the hole slightly. In the higher brackets, the taxpayers are not keeping up financially if they receive only a $2,000 raise.

A wife aware of the importance of financial planning will be less shocked by these figures and hence not so disappointed, especially if she has an investment plan she knows will help their dollars increase in number to help combat inflation's toll.

The difficulty becomes more serious in the case of older people living on retirement income. True, they have some tax advantages that younger persons do not, but their pension money and Social Security payments seldom rise as fast as inflation. The single career woman is in much the same box, and she needs a lift out of it with investment income that rises enough to help her keep climbing financially. In fact, it is hard to think of how a working woman these days can face inflation imperturbably without investing, even at today's somewhat lower rates of inflation. Memory of the double-digit pace of a few years ago should be inspiration enough.

I do know a few women who can face the future with financial equanimity. There's a wealthy widow living in a hotel in New York who every three months receives a personal visit from a young officer of one of the largest banks in New York City. Like a glorified office boy he delivers to her a check for

$250,000. Her income comes completely from tax-exempt mutual funds in a trust set up by her husband. She doesn't worry about money. I know, too, of a few women professors so deeply engrossed in their research that they can be impervious to inflation—and even to what they eat.

The fact that the ranks of investors are growing fast is a sign not only of prosperity but of a widespread realization of the need to build toward financial security. Even more dramatic is the number of women now at work—47 million, and another 4 million between jobs or preparing to enter the job market.

For years liberal economists have claimed that a 1.5 percent increase in the cost of living was a fair price to pay to keep the economy busy enough to ensure virtually full employment. Naturally in a population of more than 237,000,000 persons there will always be several million without jobs because they are looking for work after resigning or being fired, because they are seasonal workers like construction men or berry pickers, because they are mentally or physically incompetent, or because they are in the armed forces or elsewhere.

Twenty years ago, many economists scoffed at the possibility that we might ever have a galloping inflation that could really hurt consumers. Yet 1969 was the ninth year of the gallop, and the fast pace continued. Then came spectacular rises: to 11.5 percent in 1979 and 13.5 percent in 1980, and protests became loud enough to worry politicians. Since then the rise (as measured by the consumer price index) has fallen dramatically to endurable levels below 5 percent in some years.

Some of the reasons for the rise were the expense of the Vietnam war, the nation's balance of payment difficulties (more money flowing out of this country than coming into it from foreign nations), the heavier federal spending on programs to ameliorate ghetto conditions and for the underprivileged, the oil crisis instigated by Arab nations, and the propensity of dollar-happy Americans to lavish money on consumer goods and services.

Another way of putting it is that your cost of living was valued at 100 in 1967, the base year for the government's consumer price index (CPI). Today the same consumer items cost more than three times as much. As of late 1985, the CPI had risen to 324.5. Be sure to take a look at the CPI. It is bound to be even higher.

More than ever, perhaps, inflation became a very real, down-to-earth reason to invest money in progressive or growth-type companies, which can keep ahead of inflation by developing new products or services, increasing prices, creating new needs among customers, serving new markets, perhaps penetrating old ones more deeply. Out of increased sales they can sometimes earn large profits for their stockholders. This money can be passed out in the form of higher cash dividends. Sometimes, however, the companies retain most of their profits for further growth; since their potentials are bright, the price of their stocks still rises.

The classic example of this is IBM—a company that by tradition has retained profits but paid small cash or stock dividends to shareholders. Over the years the price of the stock has soared, reflecting its fast sales growth in an industry essential to modern technology—computers. A schoolteacher who bought 10 shares of IBM at an adjusted* price of only $10 a share in 1950 was not buying for income but because she believed the company would grow fast in its field. By 1974 her investment of $1,000 was worth about $38,000, allowing for stock dividends. In 1979 the shares were split four for one. Today the same investor would have about 1,000 shares worth $130,000 or so.

Mergers will have an important impact on your investment decisions. Many companies today have been caught in a rush to merge or diversify as a quick road to "growth." Hence, you will often read that Company A has offered two shares of its stock for each share of Company B's stock in a merger proposal.

There's nothing new about mergers. Some are carried off quite politely and respectably. Others create much furor and charges and countercharges, often leading to legal actions. Years ago the late John D. Rockefeller, Senior, had the habit of forcing other companies to sell out their oil businesses to his giant Standard Oil in return (sometimes) for Standard Oil shares. If they did not sell pleasantly they might find their company run out of business by price undercutting. Being much larger and more powerful, Standard Oil could afford to lower its prices to ruinous levels in a specific area, in order to drive the other fellow into bankruptcy. Many oilmen did accept stock offers and several became millionaires by holding Standard Oil shares.

In those days there were few ground rules that applied to businessmen like Rockefeller, but today the government's antitrust provisions would prevent such actions as price undercutting and forced mergers. Mergers persist today partly because they apparently help some companies grow stronger financially, and they often can be favorable to stockholders. Investors watched with interest the move by T. Boone Pickens, chairman of Mesa Petroleum, to take over various companies such as Unocal, Phillips Petroleum, Cities Service, and others. Pickens might be described as a raider who forced unwilling companies to take defensive action.

It's Fashionable

Among sophisticated—and not so sophisticated—groups the stock market has become a conversational gambit. Brokers constantly are amazed by the variety of persons who invest.

One day recently I sat on a PATH train, a subway-type operation that runs

*Adjusted means the price has been refigured to reflect payment of stock dividends or splits.

between New York and New Jersey, in front of two roughly dressed workmen carrying lanterns. Their topic of conversation: What was the stock market going to do?

"Do you have any good cheap growth stocks now?" one of the men inquired.

Immediately his friend began to talk about a stock named Research-Cottrell,* describing how well he had done in it, but adding a friendly warning. "Ask your broker. It's a little too high right now."

At that point the train squealed to a halt, the door opened upon the dark tunnel that goes under the Hudson River. In the middle of that nowhere the two workmen clambered off with their lanterns lit, flinging a thanks to the conductor. They were track workers.

Or there is the young suburban matron who has the habit every time she goes to a cocktail party of buttonholing her husband's male friends, and casually but forcefully inquiring what they have been doing in the stock market recently. Her questions are probing but phrased to be complimentary to male egos. By acting much dumber than she really is she collects tidbits of information. Then she tosses the ideas at her broker for his reaction. In that way she has accumulated not only some useful knowledge about investing but occasionally some good opinions that have led her to buy some very successful stocks.

It's No Longer Esoteric

These days Americans have more leisure as well as more dollars than ever before, which means they have more hours to read about the stock market and go to brokers' offices and watch the action on the quotation boards. This is especially true of housewives without careers and of older, retired persons.

Furthermore, tastes have changed. Perhaps the woman who would once have cherished the dream of a mink coat has obtained the coat; or perhaps her sense of values has altered. Cadillacs, to many persons, have lost their appeal as a status symbol, and so have trips to Europe for families who have been there several times. People may not be getting more intellectual, but there certainly is a more noticeable importance attached to intelligence among women—intelligence as to personal finance, as to investments, as to raising children, as to knowing what's going on politically and economically, as to social consciousness. More and more women are going to college or already hold college degrees. Almost half the individuals getting law degrees these days are women, and an ever-increasing number are getting medical degrees and master of business administration degrees.

*Maker of air pollution-control equipment.

To attract new shareholders, companies have been making real efforts to appeal to investors, partly as an indirect but effective method of interesting more consumers in their products. The auto companies, for example, load their stockholders with brochures about new models. The Borden Company asks shareholders to buy its cheeses and other products. Phillips Petroleum sends its shareholders credit cards unasked, urging them to buy gas and have their cars repaired at its string of service stations.

Companies have found that a large, happy family of stockholders can help provide a better credit rating. In fact, many companies attempting to raise money through a new stock or bond issue give their stockholders a chance to buy the securities first, often at a more-favorable-than-market price. This is called a preemptive right.* Often a company is required by its own bylaws to offer shareholders such an opportunity. It's often good business for stockholders, since they get a bargain price.

It's Safer Than in Former Years

Not many years ago, but long enough so that it seems as unbelievable as any fairy tale, it was hard to get access to financial information about companies. For example, a typical earnings report published by the New York, New Haven and Hartford Railroad Company in 1910 gave little information. In that period the New Haven was considered an investment for little old ladies and widows with children to support. Brokers referred to it with glowing pomposity, even though they could obtain little financial information about it, beyond the bare bones of yearly earnings figures. After all, they reasoned, everyone needs the railroad in New England. It carried coal to heat homes; it transported proper and improper Bostonians to and from the hinterlands, even to another city called New York. In the summer it carried thousands to their homes or hotels at the seashore.

What happened? Along with the mismanagement of the railroad, a gentleman in Detroit named Henry Ford helped spoil the outlook by developing a car for mass transportation that even before World War I was becoming a slight competitor. To carry cars, roads were built. Furthermore, electricity and gas began to replace coal as a source of heat for homes and industry. Trucks competed with the New Haven, which was called a short-haul carrier because its lines ran only about 300 miles or so. Result: bankruptcy, not once but several times for the New Haven. For anyone with imagination (or vision) it was far from being a "widow's safe stock."

Yet no one reading the uninformative early reports of the New Haven or

*For a more detailed discussion of preemptive rights, see Chapter 18.

other companies would have guessed that progress and change were afoot to stub the corporate toes of many famous old corporate entities.*

Nowadays such a dearth of information about stocks listed in the New York Stock Exchange or other exchanges is impossible. The government (via its regulatory agency, the Securities and Exchange Commission) and the exchanges themselves have strict rules. Companies must report at length upon their sales and earnings if they are listed on an exchange, not only for each fiscal year as a whole but also, in most cases, on a quarterly basis.† These reports must be signed by responsible accounting firms that have checked the figures and made tests of inventories, accounts receivable, and so on.

Brokerage firms, too, have large staffs of analysts constantly trying to outdo each other and find out more pertinent information about companies. They relate what they find about an individual company to economic factors in the industry as a whole; for instance, in a bad year for auto sales, most auto stocks will go down in price. Another example: Some years ago the paper industry foresaw a huge increase in demand for paper and its products. All those busy typists in your or your husband's office; all that Kleenex children use. Paper companies spent millions on expansion—too many millions, temporarily, because demand did not catch up with their aspirations for a while. Earnings were hurt for almost all companies in the industry, and their shares dropped sharply in price. Some analysts had predicted the decline and urged investors to sell out with profits before the turn came.

Investors still cannot find out all they want, or even need to know, for wise investment decisions, but certainly the trend toward more and more disclosure and deeper analysis favors the shareholder.

The Depression is hardly mentioned any more, although some middle-aged and old people remember it sorrowfully. After all, millions of people suffered because of it; thousands lost their fortunes, even their homes; thousands were never to recover financially. Still, once a depression has passed (as all business cycles do) the tragedy is written more in people's minds than in their checkbooks.

Many of the Great Depression's worst losers were investors, who sold at bargain prices because they were afraid or desperate for cash. Many others lost

*In 1866 the New York Stock Exchange asked the Delaware Lackawanna and Western Railroad for a financial report, and its treasurer responded that the railroad makes "no reports and publishes no statements, and has not done anything of the kind for the last five years."

†Some companies use a fiscal year for reporting, rather than a calendar year. Two familiar examples are Macy's and Sears, for obvious reasons: it takes them a month or so to compile their figures after the year-end rush of Christmas shopping. Other types of companies also have seasonal upswings in activity, such as meatpackers, whose fiscal years usually end in the fall.

because they had bought heavily on margin, which means borrowed money, and they had to sell out when they could not raise more cash. Buying on margin has since lost some glamour and is hedged by restrictions, but it means essentially purchase of securities partly on cash, partly on credit arranged by a brokerage firm, which charges interest for so doing.

Times were different during the Great Depression (see Chapter 3 on business cycles). The government that President Hoover turned over to President Roosevelt had espoused a laissez-faire policy, meaning little interference with business or economic forces and equally little help for citizens in distress. Slowly under the New Deal of the 1930s the role of government increased, and it has been growing more paternal all the time since then, until President Reagan began a policy of deregulation of many industries. The airlines, for example, now can set domestic fares.

Today economists have drummed into the minds of the American people that we are on the upbeat and cannot have depressions. Recessions, yes, they can come with turns in the business cycle; but not deep declines. The reason is built-in economic cushions such as the Federal Reserve system, which pumps money in and out through purchases or sales of government securities very much the way an engineer controls the water level of a reservoir by using the overflow chutes of a dam. Social Security payments, pensions, price floors under some agricultural commodities, government subsidies for some businesses like shipping, insurance funds to pay off depositors if a bank fails; these are some of the other stabilizers. In other words, big government has become Big Brother watching us, maybe not quite so much as a few years ago, but still there. For instance, recently the Securities and Exchange Commission won a case against Paul Thayer, accused of lying and disclosing inside information while a company director. The government helped bail out Chrysler Corporation, which then proceeded to make a dramatic financial recovery under the leadership of Lee Iacocca. The government also has been helping banks—big ones like Continental Illinois and the small-town ones too.

It Can Provide Income

Naturally everyone wants to take action against inflation and see capital grow. But sometimes the need is immediate—steady high income for elderly people, for middle-aged couples with children going to college, for growing families with heavy medical bills. Stocks offering high yields in the form of cash dividends are needed at such times. Stock investment provides the flexibility to meet changing needs.

Here are two stocks well known to most Americans, the first definitely a "growth stock," the second a stock for high income and relative security:

Table 1-2. Two sample stocks.

	1983–Mid-1985 Price Range	*Latest Per Share Yearly Dividend Indicated*	*Yield and Mid-1985 Price*
IBM	$92\frac{1}{4}$–$138\frac{1}{4}$	$4.40	3.3% on 133
Pacific Telesis	$51\frac{1}{4}$–$73\frac{1}{8}$	$5.72	7.8% on 73

Most everyone knows that IBM is the computer giant in a growth industry; Pacific Telesis, one of the former AT&T operating companies, can better be described as a high-income stock with some inflation protection.

Investments can be tailored to the individual's requirements more readily than a woman these days can find a tailor to make her a suit.

It's Easily Understandable

Other forms of investment have prospered in previous years—buying land and houses, collecting antiques, purchasing valuable works of art like Picassos or Renoirs. But such investing requires more specialized, more technical knowledge than the stock market demands, and may involve more time and study. Furthermore, such investments are not as portable as stocks and bonds. The stock market is as close to you as a phone call to a broker; price quotations may be no farther away than your daily newspaper.

While other reasons for investing in stocks can be argued, there is still a final one worth considering—it's fun!

2

Elsie and Dan

The Difference Between Bonds and Stocks

If you remember these two names—Elsie and Dan—and the stories that go with them, you can never forget the basic differences between bonds and stocks.

Elsie's story happened so long ago that it can begin like a fairy tale: once upon a time in the 1620s there was a little girl named Elsken Jorisdochter (meaning Elsie the daughter of George) who owned a bond. Today the New York Stock Exchange has in its archives Elsie's bond, the gift of a Dutch-born broker. Each year it still pays interest—a record of 350 years of cash payments.

In this insecure world Elsie's perpetual bond is quite unusual in itself, but her ownership of it has some notable features, too. Women in Elsie's century did not often own property unless they happened to be queens or nobility who inherited titles and income-producing real estate. But Elsie, who lived so long ago that people did not even have surnames generally, had a prosperous and apparently indulgent father known only as George, who bought her the bond.

The family lived in the lowlands near the city of Utrecht, now part of the

Netherlands. The winter of 1623 witnessed a raging storm on the North Sea, which burst the dikes and flooded the low-lying farms. Since most people in the area depended on farming for their livelihood they quickly banded together to repair the dikes. Living so perilously close to the sea, these Hollanders realized the importance of their dike system to hold back the salt water and the need of canals to irrigate the land. Thus, perhaps more than most nationalities, the Dutch of that period believed strongly in community action.

A bond issue was sold locally to finance the rebuilding of the dike, and each of the handwritten bonds bore on the indenture* the signature of the Catholic canon of St. Mary's Church in Utrecht, indicating not only the significance of the church in local affairs but also a shrewd acknowledgment that a bond issue needed the trapping of prestige and legality. Perhaps the canon was regarded as the most honest person available.

When George bought the bond he apparently had it registered in the name of daughter Elsie—another unusual feature, because most bonds in Europe then and even today are of the unregistered variety, known as bearer bonds, with no person's name on them.† It cost 1,200 gold florins‡, and originally paid 6.25 percent. (See Figure 2-1.)

Still, the most interesting aspect of Elsie's bond is that though national boundaries have changed, governments have fallen, depressions have impoverished Europe periodically, and many wars have beset the area since the early 1600s, the bond has paid interest continually. During one period of financial stringency the bond's interest rate was lowered a little, with the agreement of the bondholder, possibly one of Elsie's descendants.

Most bonds issued these days are not perpetual like Elsie's, but bonds do tend to be issued for a relatively long period of years, often 25 or 30.

Elsie's bond has grown fragile over more than three centuries, and nowadays instead of mailing it to Amsterdam for the interest payment to be recorded on the bond, the New York Stock Exchange mails another document on which

*The indenture of a bond is the written material, which might be called the contract, describing the rights of the bondholder and the duties of the bond issuers such as paying interest, redemption at maturity or before, etc.

†If you buy a bond, be sure to have it registered in your name because it is safer. Then the issuer of the bond will mail the interest on it directly to you. The trend nowadays in the United States is toward registered bonds.

Bearer bonds can be stolen easily or handed over to another person. In Europe, where many people like to keep their finances secret because of onerous taxes or unstable governments, the bearer bonds enable them to preserve a certain amount of anonymity. Such bonds have coupons attached which must be "clipped" or torn off, and mailed or presented in person to the issuer (or a bank handling the payments) for payment of interest.

‡This amount in 1623 was equal in purchasing power to about $150 today.

Figure 2-1. Elsie's bond.

the proper endorsement is made. The check for the interest is donated to the Amsterdam Stock Exchange's employee fund.*

To most investors bonds indicate security, and generally that is a feature they offer in most cases. Elsie's bond is a historic example. But the security of a bond is no better than the stability of the issuer. Consider the case of the impressive bonds issued by the once-prestigious government of imperial Russia, one of the largest nations in the world. Some bonds were issued in 1916, when Russia was in the throes of World War I.

Today an imperial Russian bond is not worth much more than the crisp, impressive-looking paper on which its promises are printed. Gone are Czar Nicholas and his wife Alexandra, and their once-glittering court, swamped by the tidal wave of the Russian Revolution. As might be expected, the Communist government repudiated the imperial bonds, although now and then when the U.S. government and the Russian government make amiable talk through their ambassadors, speculators who apparently will buy almost anything with the hope of a few dollars' profit trade the bonds. For a while they were listed on the American Stock Exchange.

In the 1920s many bonds of South American nations, issued through some major New York banks and brokerage firms, failed to pay bondholders because of upheavals in government, usually dictatorships. Some were totally repudiated; some were redeemed for a few cents on the dollar.

During the Depression in this country in the 1930s some corporate bonds, especially those issued by railroads, were swept away during bankruptcy. Some were redeemed for a few cents on the dollar at face value, or bondholders received stock.

Bond Basics

The basic point about bonds is that, like an IOU, they are a promise to pay. The owner of a bond is thus a creditor of the organization that issues the bond. A creditor has to rely for safety on the stability and trustworthiness of his debtor. Bonds can be as sound as Elsie's or as unsound as the imperial Russian issues.

Naturally there are many types of bonds.

Elsie's bond might be described in modern terminology as a *municipal* since it was issued by a community and backed by its credit. Cities, towns, counties, states, boards of education, bridge authorities, road commissions, all

*The Amsterdam Stock Exchange is the oldest extant stock exchange in the world.

issue municipals. Perhaps the next time you vote you will be asked to give a "yes" or "no" to a proposed municipal bond issue. The purpose might be to raise money for a new school, sewer system, road, city-owned electric light company, incinerator project, or dormitories at state colleges.

One interesting aspect of municipal bonds (which is discussed at greater length in Chapter 16) is that the interest on them has been exempt from federal income taxes for many years. This enviable characteristic is now under attack in Congress by persons who charge that the tax-exempt feature means that many wealthy people can avoid taxation on their income by owning municipal bonds.* But it would probably require a constitutional amendment to do away with this tax exemption completely.

One of the major issuers of bonds is the U.S. government. Its bonds vary widely in maturity dates, interest, and ownership requirements. Some, for example, cannot be owned by individuals; some not by banks. Partly to distinguish them from municipals, the U.S. issues are called *governments.* Income they earn is exempt from state income tax but *not* from federal income tax.

Corporations also issue bonds. For generations bonds have been especially popular with public utility companies, which by tradition and by law try to keep a reasonable balance between bonds, preferred stock, and common stock in their capitalization. The interest on all corporate bonds is subject to federal income tax.

One important variety of corporate bond that should have a place in your investment thinking is called a *convertible* bond. Like the car of the same description, it offers a kind of two-in-one ride for your money. During a stated period the owner of the bond can convert it into common shares of the company. Thus when you buy the bond you have the security of a fixed income investment, with the added lure of participating in the company's earnings growth through the common stock. Convertible bonds are often issued by companies that want to attract investors' interest. The convertible feature acts like a "sweetener"—the same kind of dashing quality that a convertible offers a young man.

As a bondholder you are a creditor, as mentioned before, and thus if the company runs into any trouble you have a claim on the company's assets ahead of stockholders. If the company fares well, the price of the stock probably will rise. At some point you might decide it is profitable and safe to convert your bond into a stated number of shares. At that point you become a stockholder, or an owner of the company. As a stockholder you receive dividends as declared by company directors, in contrast to interest at a stated rate on your bond.

Don't overlook the possibilities offered by convertible bonds in growing

*In fact, tax law now forces individuals living on Social Security payments to be taxed up to a certain level on outside income, including municipal bond interest.

companies; many of them have proved to be worthwhile investments because of the conversion feature.

Some bonds, but not many, are listed on the New York Stock Exchange or the American Stock Exchange. If you turn to newspapers like *The Wall Street Journal* and *The New York Times,* which carry many quotations on securities, you can read the names of bonds listed on the exchanges as well as some sold over-the-counter, a more informal method of trading. As a matter of fact, most bonds are sold over-the-counter.

Bonds generally come in $1,000 denominations—at least for the average investor. For institutions and wealthy individuals, bonds can be obtained in much larger denominations, such as $10,000 or $100,000. A few bonds are offered in $500 certificates.

In quoting the price of a bond, your broker might say it sells at 96 (that is, at a discount), meaning the bond with a face value of $1,000 could be bought for $960. Or perhaps the bond sells at a premium, higher than face value, such as a price of 110, meaning it would cost you $1,100 to buy the $1,000 bond. In other words, bonds are quoted in terms of a hundred dollars.

Many bonds, especially these days, sell below 100, even though issued by prestigious companies like General Motors, American Telephone, E. I. Du Pont. Why?

Remember that bonds, unlike stocks, pay a fixed return clearly stated on the certificate, such as 3.5 percent, 5 percent, etc. A $1,000 bond at 3.5 would pay interest totaling $35; a 5 percent would pay $50 each year.

When a prestigious company like American Telephone issues a bond, it sells it to the public at the going interest rate for a high-quality bond. Naturally, it wants to sell at the lowest current rate of interest for such a security. For example, American Telephone sold some 3.875 percent bonds many years ago with a 1990 maturity date.

But when money is "tight," meaning the cost of money is high, interest rates are high. In 1967 American Telephone issued more bonds, but this time it had to sell them with a 6 percent interest, reflecting interest rates at that time. More recently the company sold bonds at 13.25 percent, due 1991. These bonds are actually called notes by the company because they are shorter term than bonds, which often mature in 30 years. Since interest rates have been moving down in 1985, the company probably will seek to redeem these securities or buy them back in the market.

What happens, then, to the price of the 3.875 percent bonds when current interest rates are much higher? If you check your newspaper under the heading of New York Stock Exchange Bonds you will find that the 3.875 percenters have fallen sharply in price, despite the fine credit rating of the issuer. It has to—no investor in his right mind would buy a $1,000 bond paying 3.875 percent when he could find other more recent issues of the same company paying much higher percent interest. This bond now trades around 78. As it nears its maturity date it will tend to rise in price. Currently it yields about 5 percent, which raises another question: Why would anyone buy a bond yielding 5 percent when interest rates are still much higher than that? The answer is that it offers an appreciation of $22 (or $220 on a $1,000 bond) when it matures in 1990, which is only a few years away. Meanwhile, AT&T's bond carrying 13.25 percent interest sells around 105, a premium price. It yields 12.6% at this level. Thus, some bonds sell at a discount from face value of $1,000, and some sell at a premium.

New investors often find it hard to understand that bond prices basically reflect changes in interest rates. Naturally, a change in the financial status of the issuer can influence a bond's price, along with stock market trends or the supply and demand for a particular bond. But the interest rate situation is the major factor.

Still another technical influence on a bond's price is the closeness of the maturity date, the time when the company must, according to the indenture, redeem the bonds by paying the bondholder the face value of $1,000 in cash. The price tends to move toward that level near the maturity date. If the bond is called for redemption sooner than its maturity date, the indenture usually specifies that a premium over face value must be paid to the bondholder.

For many years after World War II most investors, especially those interested in growth, scorned bonds. Typically, good bonds mean a fixed return and relative safety of principal—a truly conservative investment not for the eager speculator.

Lately, with the unusually high increase in interest rates, bonds have been attracting speculators, along with investors interested in high, safe yields. The reason is simple: bonds offer capital appreciation if held to maturity, provided they have been bought at a discount. Sometimes they can be bought at a discount, and then if interest rates drop further, the bonds' prices tend to rise, offering a chance for a profit. Not only does the person buying such a bond get a good return on his money, but if he holds it the bond will be redeemed at maturity for $1,000, and he will receive capital gains. A speculation? Hardly. A growth situation? Certainly.

To summarize, don't let anyone tell you glibly that a bond never offers a chance for capital gain. "Never" is a word to avoid in the fast-moving world of investments. However, the truism still holds that common stocks generally offer a better way than bonds for capital appreciation.

Don't let anyone tell you that bonds are always "safer" than stocks, either. Like stocks they have to be judged on their merits and their role in your investment planning. The imperial Russian government bonds turned out to be a poorer investment than a supply of caviar. An AT&T bond bought around par ($1,000) and paying 3.875 percent interest did not enable a widow to keep up with inflation, but the same bond bought at a good discount could bring a generous return at redemption time.

Brokers can offer you a new form of security called a *zero coupon bond.* (See Chapter 17 for more information.) This is a bond that pays no interest currently but can be bought at a large discount and then cashed at maturity for its face value of $1,000. Such bonds are good for investors more interested in capital appreciation than yearly income. For example, a parent might want to build up a college fund for children by buying a batch of bonds for $200 each that will pay $1,000 when they mature in ten years or so. They are also good for Individual Retirement Accounts.

Stocks, Preferred and Common

In between bonds and common stocks is an area occupied by another species of investment that typically carries a fixed rate of return and yet is called a stock. Its name, something of a misnomer I think, is *preferred* or *preference stock,* because it has a claim on earnings ahead of common stock.*

In the corporate hierarchy, bonds have the prior claim on a company's income. In fact, interest is paid by a company on its bonds before it reports net income and hence ahead of figuring its income taxes. In other words, bond interest is a deductible payment before calculating federal income taxes—an important feature of their safety, in contrast to stocks. Dividends are paid on preferred and common stock, in that order, after net income is figured. It can be said that net income comes out of earnings after taxes. Sometimes companies pay dividends even when they have no earnings in a particular year, in which case the dividends are paid technically out of an item called surplus, which is nothing more than an accumulation of past earnings not paid out to stockholders but which may have been invested elsewhere (see Chapter 6). In technical jargon, accountants often say that dividends are paid out of this item called surplus, in which they place each year's earnings—a bookkeeping technique. Don't let this technical point confuse you. The important thing to remember is that *interest comes out before income taxes are calculated, and dividends after taxes.* This is much the way you report on your federal income tax form: interest on your debts is deductible as an expense.

Just to make it clear, Table 2-1 shows the effect on a company of paying interest to bondholders compared to paying dividends to stockholders. Company

*There are also convertible preferred stocks that, like convertible bonds, can be switched into so many shares of common stock.

A and Company B both have net operating earnings of $1 million. Company A must pay $100,000 interest on bonds, while Company B must pay $100,000 in dividends on preferred stock. What is left in each case for the common stockholders, if both companies are in the same 46 percent tax bracket (the highest rate in 1985 for companies)? Company A fares better. It has a larger net per share. Table 2-1 helps explain why sometimes companies find it more advantageous to sell bonds than stocks when they need to raise additional funds.

How then is stock different from bonds? Stock is *evidence* (by means of a certificate) *of ownership of a company;* a bond is a promise to pay a debt. Every corporation has to have stock, at least one or a few shares, as evidence of ownership. Often you will hear comments like this, ''Oh, it's a hundred percent-owned family corporation,'' meaning that a family group owns the few shares outstanding. It might be described, too, as a *closed corporation,* meaning there is none available for sale to the public. Other companies are described as *closely held*, meaning their shares are owned by a few people.

Suppose that you and I decide to enter the baby food business—a fine growing field because the population increases continually. We might start out as an informal partnership, doing the cooking and canning in our own kitchens. If we thought we could be successful we might take a forward step and consult a lawyer about setting up a corporation for tax reasons and also with the idea that we might need capital someday and therefore might want to sell some stock. The lawyer draws up the necessary incorporation papers in the state where we live, and thus we have a charter and stock. Let's say we start out with 100 shares divided equally between us. The fact that we are shareholders doesn't indicate how much money we have put into our enterprise or even whether we are making any money. It does indicate we are a corporation subject to state laws with stock outstanding in our two hands.

Over a period of years our business grows and we must expand, hiring more help than our children and husbands can provide, renting a building, and buying some equipment such as large stoves, canning apparatus, a labeling machine, and trucks to deliver our products to supermarkets.

At this point our lawyer or the banker who has lent us money might suggest that we need permanent capital and therefore should sell either bonds or stock or both. We might consult a broker and he might point out that we are too new a company to sell bonds but he will help us sell our stock. He then suggests we split our 100 shares into 100,000 shares and offer 50,000 publicly at a low price, say $5 a share.

We are the same people we were before—with the same enthusiasm, the same amount of money—but now we have offered publicly 50,000 shares and the remainder—50,000 shares—is owned by us. Once the 50,000 shares are sold to the public, we have new cash. The money is spent for a building, equipment, labels, and the purchase of inventories such as meat, raw fruits, and

Table 2-1. Net effect of paying bond interest compared to stock dividends.

	Company A (With Bondholders)	*Company B (No Bondholders)*
Operating earnings	1,000,000	1,000,000
Bond interest	100,000	0
Taxable income	900,000	1,000,000
Taxes owed in 46% bracket	414,000	460,000
Net income	486,000	540,000
Preferred stock dividend	0	100,000
Net available for common shares	486,000	440,000
Net per share on 1,000,000 shares	48.6 cents	44 cents

vegetables. Some goes into the bank for an emergency and for working capital. We're in business in a big way now, and we suddenly have new responsibilities to our stockholders, who will be looking over our shoulders and wanting us to make money as much as we want to do the same. We also pay ourselves a salary.

This is where we come to the story of Dan. A famous company known to almost every American mother began in a simple fashion like that I have just described. Dan Gerber, the founder, often fretted at how long it took his wife to feed one of their babies. He worked on the idea of prepared baby foods to make life easier not only for mothers but impatient husbands, too. Also, prepared foods could be more hygienic. He was not the first to think of it, but one of the most successful. Today Gerber Products Company has more than $800 million in sales yearly.

ReaLemon juice, Minute Maid orange juice, Pepperidge Farm bread, Polaroid cameras, Toni permanent waves, and many other products resulted from some simple ideas and literally grew out of home kitchens or small laboratories or workrooms.

As a part owner of a company, a common stockholder has a right that bond owners generally do not. Stockholders can vote on issues presented to them at annual or special meetings. They are entitled to receive dividends if the directors vote such payments. They can elect the directors.

As mentioned before, preferred stock ranks ahead of common in case earnings are not large enough to pay all stockholders dividends or if the company goes into bankruptcy or must be sold out.

Since preferred stock carries a stated dividend, say $5 preferred or 4 percent preferred, it acts in the market much like a bond, rising and falling in price in line with interest rates. If the company is doing badly or has a year of bad earnings, the price of the preferred stock may be weak along with the price of the common. But generally interest rates play a bigger role in the price of preferred stocks.

The point to remember is that common stock prices are more volatile generally than bonds or preferreds in the same company. Prices of common shares reflect a variety of factors. The supply and demand for the particular stock, for example, is one factor. Some are well known and prestigious; some are new companies or companies barely known to the public. Almost everyone, for example, has heard of the Coca-Cola Company, which has about $7 billion sales each year, but not many persons know the Halliburton Company, which has sales of $5.5 billion a year. It makes equipment for the oil and gas industries.

Other factors that influence common stock prices are general trends in the stock market, economic and political crises or changes, the company's outlook for growth and how it compares with other companies in the same industry. These myriad influences on common stocks are what make investment at once difficult, challenging, and puzzling. It puts the investor in the position of diagnosing the health of any investment she is about to make.

Summary

A bondholder is a creditor of a company. She is paid interest on her bond, usually twice a year, at a stated rate. If bond interest is not paid, the bondholder can start legal action to force the company into reorganization or bankruptcy.

A stockholder is an owner of part of a company, entitled to payments in cash, called dividends, if the directors vote them. Sometimes dividends are paid in shares of stock. Usually dividends arrive quarterly. If the company has a record of stable earnings, it usually has a regular dividend rate, which may be raised when earnings move up. In addition, certain companies pay "extra" or "special" dividends, often at year-end when directors find that the company has done well that year. But directors do not have to vote in favor of dividends; they can choose to retain the cash for corporate uses, a procedure used widely by growth-type companies such as International Business Machines. If the stockholder does not receive dividends, he has little recourse except to sell his shares.

As owners of the company, stockholders have a power that bondholders generally lack: they can vote for directors, they can change company bylaws, they can vote for other management proposals at annual meetings.

Preferred stockholders are entitled to a stated dividend, usually payable if earned, and always payable ahead of any common dividend. If preferred shares are described as "cumulative," then a company unable to pay a dividend one year must make up such a payment in later years when it does have the earnings, and it must do this before it makes payments to the common shareholder. Generally, like bondholders, preferred shareowners have no vote for directors and other company proposals, unless under company bylaws they receive a vote following a period of nonpayment of dividends.

3

*Dismal Thinking Pays Off**

Understanding Economic Cycles

In all recorded history there have been business cycles. Think back to the Old Testament; remember the seven years of plenty and seven famine years?

In those early days the cause of a downswing in an economic cycle might be as simple as a crop failure, resulting from a drought or a plague of insects like locusts. Bread or other basic foodstuffs would become so scarce that families couldn't feed themselves. Commerce might slow to a halt because there was no surplus food to barter with other nations. Then painfully, slowly, the cycle would change with the harvest of a good crop and the granaries would fill again.

*Many years ago economics became known as "the dismal science," partly because in those days the philosophers and sociologists and mathematicians, who became the early "economists," found the world an unhappy place and the outlook quite hopeless. That was especially true of the British political economist T. R. Malthus, who thought population would outrace the ability to feed it. His ideas seemed pertinent in 1984–1985 when so many people died because of drought conditions in Ethiopia and other African nations.

Often in history wars have brought a depression, or at least an unfortunate downswing in the business cycle, in their wake. The land was devastated; trained workers might have been killed or taken from their home areas; government treasuries would be empty, leading to repressive tax actions; trade was interrupted. The result: economic chaos.

For the sophisticated investor, awareness of events of the past is important for present response and planning against the future. Here is a roll call of major depressions or recessions in U.S. history, with some of the important reasons in each case. Anticipation of them, sometimes possible, could have helped investors.

1837. In 1836, the Treasury Department issued its famous Specie Circular requiring that payments in specie—good old hard cash in the form of coins, gold, etc.—be required for all public lands. Previously, notes issued by individual banks were accepted. (Remember, in those days almost any bank could print its own money.) Speculation in land sales dropped sharply. Banks contracted their loans; there was a crop failure in Europe; and a boom in southern cotton speculation ended. The result—a depression.

1857. Another "panic" or depression came in this year; among the causes were overspeculation in the railroads that were being built into the wilderness areas of the West, and tariff problems.

1873. Jay Cooke, the most prestigious financier of the nineteenth century, who almost singlehandedly financed bond sales for the North during the Civil War, fumbled on some railroad speculations. The failure of his firm sparked a downfall in the economy. At the time Europe was in the midst of a depression.

1884. This year brought a brief depression, involving the banking system and the circulation of silver dollars.

1893. In this year a more serious depression started, lasting for about seven years. British investors, who had provided large amounts of capital for expanding railroads and industrial companies, began to unload their securities, catching many speculators unaware. The situation could have become much more serious but fortunately this country had a good harvest that year, at a time when European nations had crop shortages.

1904. The "rich man's panic" occupied headline space in this year, mostly brought about by the attempts of leading financiers to corner markets on some leading railroads and industrial companies. Thus, the "panic" involved mostly overspeculation and paper profits turned into losses.

1907. By this year the nation's banking system had increased to 26,000 banks, with most of them chartered by the states, which were noticeably lax in making banks toe the line. Following a steady decline in stock market prices, the Knickerbocker Trust Company, a prestigious old New York City bank, suspended operations, leading to other bank failures or temporary suspensions. J. P. Morgan tried to help with large loans—$25 million to New York banks.

1920–1921. A not-too-severe post–World War I depression occurred, partly because of overexpansion in agriculture during the war.

1929. The Great Depression, a terrible, memory-searing one.

Since the 1929 Depression, the nation has experienced some relatively mild recessions: in 1948–1949; in 1953–1954; in 1957–1958; in 1961–1962; quite a sharp stock market decline in 1966; the 1969–1971 recession; a sharp drop in 1974; another substantial drop in 1981–1982.

The Depression and Its Aftermath

In this century, and perhaps in world history, the worst economic crisis came in 1929, a vivid memory of many persons still alive. It was terrifying partly because its impact spread so widely through the world and partly because governments seemed to grope in economic darkness to find answers. Answers, even partial ones, came too late for many people.

Some roots of the Depression could be traced to World War I: the devastation throughout most of Europe and the reparations that were required but that could be ill afforded by Germany. In the United States farmers posed a problem, one that was little understood in the early 1920s. Many farmers had borrowed heavily from local banks during the war and bought marginal land for cultivation to meet the nation's heavy demands for food to export. After the war an impoverished Europe could not afford to buy the food, so the surpluses grew, along with the farmers' burdensome debts. Meanwhile many nations built tariff walls high, to protect themselves from foreign goods and to spur domestic industry—an action taken also by the United States. But such retaliatory tariffs can be self-defeating, and in this instance they certainly slowed down economic progress.

In this country millions of people cared or understood little about such problems plaguing the world. They had become used to securities, some finding their investment ideas whetted by the enthusiastic government bond-selling drives during World War I. In the 1920s many investors began to show interest in common stocks, in contrast to their earlier emphasis on bonds and preferred shares paying fixed returns and high yields. They wanted a part of the action in new companies that offered potential—car companies, food chains, electric light companies, and such.

Although based on a somewhat shaky economic foundation, as it turned out, a feeling of prosperity pervaded this country during the 1920s, especially late in the decade.

Observers knew little about or paid no attention to the deepening plight of the farmers weighed down by heavy debt to the small rural banks, whose lending power in turn was dependent on the bigger city banks.

Americans invested heavily in some doubtful foreign government bonds, underwritten by many prestigious New York banks, such as the Chase Bank and the National City Bank.* Such securities paid high rates of interest but entailed risk because of the potential turmoil in dictator-dominated nations in South America and Europe.

Investors also bought shares in good, growing industries. Yet it was a period when many utility empires were being created through a process called pyramiding: a holding company would buy control of an operating company, which then might buy control of many other power companies, resulting in a top-heavy structure easily controlled by a few people in the management. Outside stockholders and bondholders bought the securities, thinking they were buying into a solid, growing venture, not unlike investors in conglomerates today.

But at that time there was no Securities and Exchange Commission to set the ground rules, as there is today. The stock exchanges required little of their listed companies in the way of financial reporting. Banks and brokerage firms, even highly respected ones, actively underwrote securities without much investigation. Thus many investors operated virtually in the dark, buying or selling on the prestige of the company or underwriter, on noticeable price trends, or on rumors.

Even though it was difficult for brokers to analyze companies, they can be criticized in retrospect for being so interested in selling stocks indiscriminately that they did little research. In a typical brokerage firm the job of analysis might be entrusted to one man on a part-time basis.

And lack of knowledge did not deter most investors of the period. Their buying pushed prices higher and higher, culminating in 1929 in a spree of unbridled enthusiasm that the stock exchanges like to forget nowadays. They also like to forget that a president of the New York Stock Exchange named Richard Whitney went to jail for some dishonest transactions—a dramatic fall from a lofty position of prestige, power, and wealth.

A runaway market has to slow down eventually, and in October 1929 it came a cropper. The tumble had to come because the world in the 1920s was running on borrowed time—on overextended credit to farmers and to stock market and land speculators, on stifled world trade, on securities issued by promoters without regard to underlying values, on an unequal distribution of money. Millions of people were poor and a relatively small fraction of the

*Now called the Chase Manhattan and Citicorp.

Table 3-1. The crash in stock prices: October 29, 1929.

	1929 Highs	*Previous Day's High*	*High-Low Range for October 29, 1929*	
American Telephone	310¼	263	230	204
Allied Chemical	354¾	275	218	204¾
Eastman Kodak	264¾	220⅝	186	162
General Motors	91¾	53¼	45½	33½
U.S. Steel	261¾	202½	192	166½

population was rich. One more reason was little comprehension of basic economics by the public and government officials.

How did the stock market crash and the ensuing Depression start? With a series of small events. An Austrian company could not pay bond interest, and a British investment banking firm went bankrupt, partly as a result. Stocks during the year 1929 showed volatile price changes, responding nervously to small news events. Mostly prices trended downward.

There were some who understood. A respected economist named Roger Babson, like a Cassandra, kept giving speeches sounding dire warnings of a crash. A Massachusetts public utility commission refused to permit an electric company to issue more bonds, claiming the corporate structure was shaky. *The New York Times* financial editor warned from time to time about overspeculation.

It could be likened to the modest beginning of an avalanche. After a few stones loosened, there came boulders, followed by the plunge. Even the leading international bankers like J. P. Morgan, the financier, and James Mitchell, chairman of the National City bank, could do nothing to stem the plunge. The official date for the biggest stock price drop in history was October 29, 1929: Black Tuesday.

Table 3-1 shows some of the price drops in leading stocks. Some of the names of the companies caught in the downfall were as well known then as they are today, such as U.S. Steel Corporation, which even made a dramatic and unusual gesture to attempt—in vain—to bolster stockholders' confidence: it announced a short-term increase in its dividend rate before the final big break.

As bad as the Depression was, some good evidently came out of it. Economists doubt that the United States can ever in this century have another really bad depression. We can and do have sharp business upswings and downturns, reflected by sharp price changes in stocks, but nothing quite as grim as 1929.

Why? In the 1930s, for the first time in history, the U.S. government under the leadership of President Roosevelt adopted a philosophy of taking an active role in mitigating economic declines. The government amassed huge deficits by spending money on public works to create jobs; it gave other assistance to the unemployed. It provided complicated crop support programs; it espoused low interest rates to encourage borrowing and the launching of new business. It organized the Securities and Exchange Commission to act as a watchdog of Wall Street and to protect investors. It reformed and strengthened the banking system, so that the small rural banks that financed farmers could not so easily be thrust into bankruptcy as happened in the early 1930s. It insisted that the big city banks divorce themselves from underwriting affiliates, leaving that to investment banking and brokerage firms. It launched Social Security to give most people retirement income.

Finally, late in that decade this country's economy got a boost from another source—an unpleasant one: World War II. With the help of low interest rates, bond sales, and some rationing, the government managed to finance participation in this war more efficiently than in past wars.

At the end of World War II, many onlookers thought that once more we would have a depression or at least a recession because war industries were no longer needed. As before, many farmers had overexpanded, and thousands of returning veterans needed jobs. However, the economic setting was different. World War II had changed people, mentally and financially. Taxation had helped redistribute the wealth more fairly. Many persons had managed to save substantial sums of money from their wartime work, money to invest in businesses and other opportunities or to spend on homes, cars, luxuries. Men returning from the armed forces found they could borrow easily to start new companies. Others returned to college under the GI Bill. They could buy homes at favorable mortgage rates, and a building boom was soon under way. The population had increased, which meant more babies to plan for. Scientists, no longer tied to defense projects, researched and developed new products, and new industries grew to meet ever-increasing consumer needs. Even today, the fortunes of those industries mirror economic growth.

Baby food. Gerber's, for instance, has fared well in sales since World War II.

Cars. Watch the Fords go by in terms of sales increases and in relation to population.

Housing. The building figures for new homes show the upward trend.

Luxuries. The growing number of home computers, motorboats, and VCRs tell a story.

Department store sales. Women do much of the buying, and the trend indicates the health of the nation.

Business technology. Since IBM ranks as the nation's most important company in the computer and office equipment business, its sales growth reflects the growth in this area.

Supermarkets. The chain stores where most people shop for food have a small profit margin but large sales volume.

Airlines. The passenger trains that spanned the country 30 years ago have been largely eliminated as Americans have taken to the air, and the zoom in airlines' revenues indicates that, despite occasional turbulence, this industry has expanded greatly.

Publishing. An exciting new post–World War II development has been the stress on education. We have a new elite, the intelligentsia. Before World War II only relatively prosperous families could afford to send their children to college. Now a college education is a necessity and available to many more millions. Sales growth charts for textbook publishers show the way.

Could It Happen Again?

The United States still does have business cycles and ups and downs in the stock market, but in this fast-changing, bustling world it probably cannot again have a serious depression because of much growth momentum, a wider dissemination of knowledge of economic principles, and our ability to use some of the stabilizers that have been built into the economic system. What are some of them?

A government willing to spend money in an effort to buy its way out of a recession is one stabilizer. The manipulation of interest rates to encourage or discourage lending is another. Large amounts of Social Security and Medicare payments constantly moving through people's hands, plus corporate pension money, have provided cushions. Growing use of life insurance to help widows with children and the elderly has been a factor. Crop support programs and aid to small businesses in the form of loans, expert advice, mortgage financing, and other programs have helped.

No one would venture to say that we won't have substantial swings in stock prices, reflecting investor psychology. The big decline of 1982 is an all-too-immediate example. However, such swings can offer investors opportunities if they know how to take advantage of economic knowledge.

In 1962 there was a sharp drop in stock prices. That price decline came at a time when business profits remained high. However, it had been preceded by a period of rampant speculation when people were sold on the growth-stock idea. They were willing to pay high prices, 50 and even 100 times earnings per share, for the chance to buy stocks in companies whose profits they believed would grow.

Perhaps you recall that during this period when stocks were so overpriced,

President Kennedy sharply rebuked the steel industry and insisted the steelmakers roll back a price increase because he thought it would be inflationary. Stock prices had been drifting down a little in the months prior to this fight between the President and the steel companies. At the end of May the sharp break came, set off apparently by the dispute. But no balloon like this bursts unless it has become overinflated.

Once again, in 1966, there was a sharp decline. But the economic conditions had changed somewhat from 1962. There was tight money, meaning high interest rates, and people had begun to worry about the increasing pace of inflation. Heavy expenses for the Vietnam war caused talk of higher taxes. Business expansion and profits appeared to be slowing down. State and other taxes rose inexorably, especially property taxes.

In 1967 and 1968 the economy righted itself and regained ebullience; but in 1969 and 1970 inflation took an even firmer grip on the economy, with the result that taxes rose (through the imposition of the surcharge) and interest rates moved to record high levels. Social unrest, such as bitterness between blacks and whites and college riots, had shaken people's confidence. Unemployment rose steadily. At last, in 1971, the Nixon administration took the drastic step of a wage and price freeze followed by a year-long "phase two" program involving more moderate economic controls. Thus in a scant four years, the economic situation had changed completely. However, wage and price freezes never have worked well, and they didn't work then. Another sharp drop in stock market prices came in 1974 following the 1973 Arab oil crisis and the resignation of President Nixon.

New ways of thinking about investing evolved during these years of change. Speculators still liked growth-type stocks. Other investors were attracted by the chance to buy high income through purchase of bonds selling at discounts from par value (see Chapter 2). Worried about the outlook, some investors turned again to the blue chips, the shares of well-known, sound, growing companies like Du Pont, AT&T, and others.

The history of stock market prices is well detailed in Figure 3-1, based on prices of the Standard & Poor's Composite Index of 500 stocks. In the year 1982 it shows another sharp drop in stock prices, a time of recession when unemployment rose to a post–World War II high in December 1982. This setback could be attributed partly to consumer buying trends; American goods were being priced out of the market and there was a huge inflow of foreign-made goods, Japanese cars and cameras, for example. A growing trade deficit resulted. At the same time there was an influx of foreign capital seeking investment here at high interest rates. Today we are still suffering the bad effects of the trade deficit and the damage done to many industries like steel and autos. The requirement for heavy defense spending and for social welfare projects has made the situation worse.

Charts like this one show that there are opportunities for investors who are smart enough to buy good stocks in the price troughs and hold them until prices recover, as they inevitably do.

Taking Advantage of the Cycles

These swings in the stock market make it important for the woman investor to keep abreast of changes in investment practices, just as she keeps herself informed about her children's schools, her community's political scene, or the trends in the industry she works in.

All the key business indicators that analysts and economists watch are reported in major daily newspapers, and are easy to read once their significance is understood.

Gross National Product

Despite its complicated-sounding name, the GNP is simply the dollar value of all goods and services in this country, a massive figure the government issues four times a year, equated to an annual rate. Personally, I believe it leaves a wide margin for error and unknown factors.

The point to remember about GNP is that it tends to grow each year partly because we have inflation and partly because the population keeps increasing. However, if the rate of increase slows considerably from one period to another, it can be an indication that a business boom is approaching an end. If the rate of increase rises sharply, a booming economy is present.

Personal Income

This is a component of GNP. It is the dollar average of what you and millions of other Americans receive each year from salaries, dividends, pensions, interest on savings accounts, Social Security payments, etc. If personal income is noticeably on the rise, it shows a strong and growing economy, although one such as we had in the late 1960s and early 1970s also indicates dangerous inflationary pressures.

Figure 3-1. Stock market history since 1926.

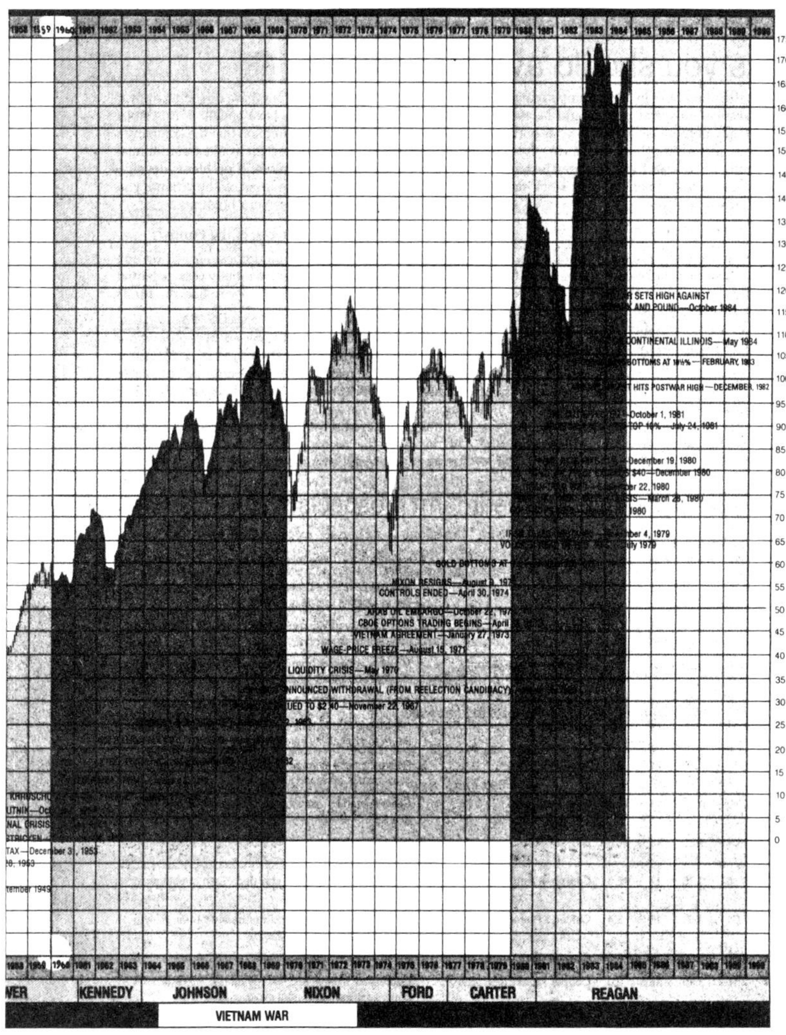
CONTROLS ENDED—April 30, 1974
VIETNAM AGREEMENT—January 27, 1973
WAGE-PRICE FREEZE—August 15, 1971
LIQUIDITY CRISIS—May 1970
KENNEDY
JOHNSON
NIXON
FORD
CARTER
REAGAN
VIETNAM WAR

Table 3-2. Consumer price index trends.

Period	*Average Consumer Prices**	Period	*Average Consumer Prices**
1952	79.5	1969	109.8
1953	80.1	1970	116.3
1954	80.5	1971	121.3
1955	80.2	1972	125.3
1956	81.4	1973	133.1
1957	84.3	1974	147.7
1958	86.6	1975	161.2
1959	87.3	1976	170.5
1960	88.7	1977	181.5
1961	89.6	1978	195.3
1962	90.6	1979	217.7
1963	91.7	1980	247
1964	92.9	1981	282.5
1965	94.5	1982	289.1
1966	97.2	1983	294.8
1967	100.0	1984	315.5
1968	104.2	1985 (through Sept.)	324.5

*Prices are not seasonally adjusted.

Consumer Price Index

The CPI has a basic importance to the average family. From its components you can determine how much the cost of living has risen and where the increases have come, whether in food, services, housing, medical care, appliances, cars, etc.

The government publishes its consumer price index each month, breaking it down into categories. The index is a comparative number, expressed in relation to 100, the "base" price in 1967. A CPI of 300 would indicate a price that has risen threefold since 1967. Table 3-2 gives the story over the span of 33 years.

If the index rises sharply, consumers know that inflation is progressing at worrisome levels. To compensate they may have to withdraw savings, cut back spending, borrow, or obtain more money through salary increases or through investing in securities that appreciate in value or pay higher dividends. Some people habitually seek other sources of investment such as real estate or art objects.

Look at the rise between 1968 and 1970, which was considered sharp. Then cast your eye at the runaway inflation in 1978 through 1981, which ruined the retirement plans of many older persons.

Interest Rates

These rates reflect various forces on the economy at any moment. If consumers are optimistic and willing to spend their money for cars, appliances, houses, and such, interest rates are apt to be high, mirroring the heavy demand for credit from both individuals and corporations. At times of pessimism the interest rates may move lower as banks and the government attempt to stimulate more spending and growth for the economy.

In a sense, interest rates measure the price of money based on the supply and demand for it. However, the Federal Reserve system can, by buying and selling hundreds of millions of dollars' worth of government securities, influence the money market. Money, like most everything else, has a price. Its price in recent years has changed considerably in terms of various types of money, as Table 3-3 illustrates.

Balance of Payments

Anyone who reads a newspaper probably has become aware of and even worried about the U.S. economic position internationally.

A nation like the United States exports billions of dollars' worth of goods each year—machinery, computers, drugs, chemicals, wheat, cotton, and many other items. We import billions' worth in the form of coffee, cocoa, sugar, textiles, shoes, toys, cameras, cars, and other goods. For years we have enjoyed a surplus of exports over imports.

However, in recent years this has changed. We have been sending large amounts of money abroad to maintain troops in Europe and Korea. Billions have also been spent helping underdeveloped nations. Millions of Americans travel abroad, spending dollars. And American business has invested large amounts in building factories and launching new companies abroad. For example, Colgate-Palmolive Company usually makes more sales and earnings from its international operations than it does from domestic plants in this country. American Standard, a large producer of plumbing equipment such as bathtubs and heating units, is another that reports more sales and earnings from foreign operations than from activities at home. As mentioned previously, mar-

Table 3-3. Thirty years of interest rates.*

	Governments *(Short)* *91-day*	*(Long)* *30 yr.*	*Muncipals*	*Corporates*	*Mortgages*†	*Prime*‡
1985 (Oct)	7.15	10.60	9.16	11.48	12.04	9.50
1984	8.16	11.21	9.95	12.47	12.99	11.06
1983	8.96	11.44	9.89	12.87	13.25	11.00
1982	8.01	10.33	9.96	12.15	12.80	11.50
1981	10.93	12.88	12.91	14.38	16.43	15.75
1980	15.66	11.89	10.20	11.30	14.08	20.35
1975	5.50	7.17	7.31	9.59	9.32	7.26
1970	4.86	5.97	5.46	8.13	8.40	6.92
1965	4.36	4.43	3.54	4.92	5.62	4.92
1960	2.27	3.88	3.40	4.94	6.04	4.50
1955	2.56	2.91	2.57	3.27	4.73	3.50

*Rates for 1955–1984 as of December of each year.
†Rates in secondary market.
‡Prime is the rate charged by major banks to large, credit-worthy companies.
SOURCE: Dept. of Commerce, "Business Conditions Digest."

kets for American-produced goods have been lost in such areas as steel, autos, cameras, textiles, and some agricultural products.

The result of all this has been an unfavorable balance of payments for this country: Americans have been lavishing more money overseas than they have received from foreign nations. What is the effect?

The difference used to be made up by payment in gold, since gold has long been the internationally accepted way for nations to settle their balances. We can liken the position to a prodigal man who spends more than he earns each year, and therefore has to use up some of his capital. Worried about the gold drain, the government can ask business to reduce new spending abroad. It can urge travelers to use fewer dollars when they leave the country and can restrict the amount of goods they can bring home free of duty. Troops can be withdrawn from Europe, and government spending can be cut further.

Yet the balance of payment problem continues to grow worse. No simple solution exists: the problem is inextricably meshed with the political and economic life of corporations, of you as an investor, and of the nation and the world at large.

Mindful of the intricacies of basic economics, the clever investor seeks to keep current with the trends, realizing that she can profit by the old adage: "Buy low and sell high."

Where can the average woman find out about basic economics and the rapid changes? Books on basic economics can help. A good newspaper such as *The New York Times* or *The Wall Street Journal,* if read with regularity, will keep anyone up to date. Also helpful are good news magazines like *Time, Newsweek,* and *U.S. News & World Report.*

Many leading banks such as the Federal Reserve Bank of New York, Citicorp, and others publish bank letters, usually monthly, available free to anyone. Leading brokerage firms publish newsletters of a general economic nature, and so do some investment advisory services. Generally, the brokerage firms offer their letters free of charge to persons on their mailing lists, while the advisory services charge fees, although their publications can often be read in brokers' offices or in public libraries.

4

Taking Stock

Start with Self-Knowledge

"Women are different from men." When said by a man, usually with a smile, but sometimes with a smirk, this statement can be very irritating. It's an idea inscribed permanently in men's minds, as deeply engraved as the writing on a stone tablet. True physically and sometimes emotionally, it need not be true intellectually, or in relation to investment ability.

There are wide ranges of personalities among women. Remember cold but passionately ambitious Lady Macbeth, who was the driving force behind her husband, impelling him to kill to obtain the ruling position he wanted? In business we see many successful men at the top partly because their wives are passionately ambitious—although not, one hopes, actually murderous.

There are women who pursue their own careers with a vengeance, intent both on financial security and on self-achievement and independence. And there are women who scrimp a few dollars out of food money year by year to build up estates for themselves in their old age and for their heirs. Hetty Green was an extreme example of a wealthy woman investor who lived penuriously (one black dress so aged that it looked green), and yet by her death she had parlayed $1 million into more than $100 million.*

*$1 billion by today's standards.

There are wives who watch their husbands grow beyond the companionship of the early days of their marriage, who wake up one morning to find their husbands want a divorce to marry someone more in tune with their mental, social, or political aims. There are wives of ever-loving, indulgent husbands who like to keep their wives and children from the harsh realities of life and who never teach them how to handle money. These women can be the most pathetic of all when hardships like death and expensive illnesses befall a family. There are many women who don't get married, or who marry and then find themselves divorced or widowed at young ages.

No woman wants to be lonely in her old age, or to be cut off socially after a divorce. No woman wants to face middle age with little money, especially when her husband has been doing well financially. No mother wants a custody fight with a husband who claims that she cannot bring up the children the way he wants because she will have to go to work or stay home without enough money to support her family.

Every woman can profit by developing a sound approach toward financial planning and investing. Begin by keeping the following guidelines in mind:

1. Make a will. Leave your children some money because their father might marry again, cutting them out temporarily. Make sure that your will also includes a list of the possessions that belong to you alone and that you want to leave specifically to your husband, children, and relatives.

2. Start a savings account as soon as possible in your marriage.

3. Buy as much insurance as you can on your husband's life, because then you will know that you have some protection if he dies during the marriage, or following a divorce. You pay the premiums; make sure you are listed as the owner. At the time of divorce he might change the beneficiary of the policies he owns on his own life.

3. Try to find out from the start of the marriage how much your husband earns each year, how much he has in various retirement, IRA, profit-sharing, and other plans.

4. Join an investment club, or learn about investments from other sources, such as books, friends, and a broker. Start an investment plan; asking relatives to give you money for birthdays, Christmas, Mother's Day, so that you can invest it for your future.

5. Consider, if you do not work, a job on a part-time basis to earn enough to cover the $2,000 needed for an IRA account. Your family can deduct this $2,000 from gross income on its tax return, an advantage. It accumulates dividends, interest, etc., tax free until your retirement. It could be used in an emergency but then a penalty becomes payable.

6. Since most wives sign a joint income tax return each year with a husband, they should make sure they understand the salary, dividends, and interest

[payments] reported, and the deductions the husband takes. Don't ever sign a document without reading it.

Know yourself, said Socrates, calling it the beginning of wisdom. To do well in the stock market, knowing yourself is a cardinal rule for success. Yet many of us find it very difficult to look at ourselves dispassionately. Psychiatrists and psychologists make thousands of dollars from women (and men) who are struggling to develop their identities. The difficulty of knowing yourself apparently has nothing to do with age, financial condition, heritage, or social position.

Yet for a bored, frustrated, or puzzled woman, successful investment could be described as preventive therapy. It's a great ego builder. One of the basic principles is the simple prescription to know yourself financially; and that could be an approach to a larger, more important self-knowledge touching every aspect of yourself.

Your Family's Income Statement

In knowing yourself financially you must consider first the sources of your family's income—salaries, dividends, outside money from gifts, inheritances, royalties, bonuses, and others. The other half of the picture is regular expenses, your family budget plan. (Obviously every woman except the very wealthy or the very insulated should live by a budget, or at least attempt to do so.) The two together—income and expenses—are referred to in financial circles as the income statement.

Usually the largest expense involves housing, whether a family rents or owns its own home, along with maintenance: heat, light, water, telephone, repairs.

A second major expense for many families is one with which most women are well acquainted—the food budget, including a little extra perhaps for peripheral expenses like children's allowances, household supplies and cleaning expenses, the newspaper carrier. These days a family of four probably cannot eat comfortably on much less than $100 a week, not counting the little extras mentioned before. A couple probably has to allot at least $60 a week for comfortable eating, and a single woman cannot manage—and eat well—on much less than $30–$35, and that probably doesn't include her lunches if she works.

Table 4-1 shows a government breakdown of the typical portions of income allotted to various consumer items in three income categories.* (Note that the

*Unfortunately, the government, in a cost-cutting measure, no longer issues such comprehensive figures.

family with $45,000 before taxes spends $30,563. The difference goes largely for Social Security and state and federal income taxes.) If your income is higher than these examples, you should have ample money to start investing. For an investment program out of income there must be some surplus available—the difference between income after taxes and outgo. Cuts often have to be made somewhere to achieve a surplus. But where? Let's take a look at your budget.

Many wives prudently insist that their husbands carry large amounts of life insurance, partly because they are worried about enough money for the financially dangerous years when children have to be sent through college; also for their old age. After all, a married mother of children who returns to the labor force upon the sudden death of a middle-aged husband generally cannot command a very good salary. If she has a profession (accounting, law, medicine) she probably could, but otherwise, no. The rule of thumb these days for sufficient life insurance for a husband might be four times the man's annual salary. The average insurance coverage nationwide is only about $75,000 per family. The husband and wife earning $60,000 should carry about $240,000 between them.

Behind every family should be at least one month's salary in the bank collecting interest and biding time for emergencies.

If the family lives in a house the mortgage payments plus real estate taxes (often included in mortgage payments) and utilities should come to about one-third of family income after taxes. Apartment dwellers can afford a little more, perhaps, because of savings on heat, repairs (most apartments include basic maintenance), and other utilities (if paid by the landlord). In some urban areas rents and home prices are so high that a working woman probably has to have a roommate to share the cost.

Also, many city families can count on another big saving not available to country dwellers or suburbanites—no car and the heavy operating and repair expenses involved. Probably more families underestimate the cost of owning cars than any other item in the family budget. In the first place, most families overlook the item of depreciation. A car ages and sooner or later it must be replaced. Buying a car for most families is a major expenditure, usually financed by monthly payments carrying a high rate of annual interest.

In figuring the annual cost of a car to your family, take the sales price and divide it by five or six years, if you can expect to keep the car that long. Find out how much a five- or six-year-old car will bring when traded in on a similar new car. Ideally, you should be putting some money aside each year for your next car. (Yes, I know that's hard to do!)

Car repairs constitute an operating expense that you have to pay out of income; again, the ideal is to make a rough estimate of repair expenses and budget for them out of income each month. For example, $400–$1,000 a year might be set aside for repairs, including new tires, brake linings, and so

Table 4-1. Average annual expenditures for urban family of three. Interview survey, 1980–81.

Item	*$25,000 Income*	*$45,000 Income*
Total Expenditures	$20,714	$30,563
Food	3,737	4,959
Alcoholic beverages	329	460
Housing	5,810	8,516
Shelter	3,233	4,757
Fuels, utilities, and public services	1,466	1,814
Household operations	250	500
Household furnishings and equipment	860	1,445
Apparel and services	1,075	1,851
Transportation	4,461	6,050
Vehicles	1,593	2,117
Gasoline and motor oil	1,543	1,893
Other vehicle expenses	1,145	1,594
Public Transportation	179	446
Health care	807	1,066
Entertainment	916	1,535
Personal care	178	272
Reading	139	206
Education	200	498
Tobacco	215	217
Miscellaneous	293	482
Cash contributions	562	1,209
Personal insurance and pensions	1,993	3,241

Source: U.S. Department of Labor, Bureau of Labor Statistics, issued December 19, 1984.

forth. Don't forget a sum required almost weekly for basic maintenance, such as gasoline. The first year of the car's life, repairs would be minimal. Much depends on the age of the car, insurance carried, and other factors. Higher-income families with two working members might need two cars. These costs, overlooked by many investors, explain their presence in Table 4-1.

If a budget is tight where can a woman find the money to invest? It's difficult. Very lucky are women who have a little sum of money left over from working days or can accumulate some out of their salaries; luckier yet are those who have inherited money, either a small or large amount. Even so, a woman on an apparently tight but effective budget possibly can find some sources of money. Perhaps the food budget by dint of more careful buying can yield a few dollars a week; perhaps the money being set aside for a new car or other large purchases could be invested for a period of time; perhaps some major spending could be delayed for a while.

A husband might object to such an idea, pointing out that *now* is the time to buy a new car, regardless of what the stock market is doing. A sophisticated wife can give a good answer. If she takes household money and invests in a sound stock like CPC, Ralston Purina, or E. I. Du Pont, she will receive good dividends each year to apply to the purchase of the new car or other major item; and the stock certificates can at any time be taken to a bank and used as collateral for a loan at a lower interest rate than a regular car loan. But more about this in future chapters.

Unfortunately there are still many women who find it hard to make out an accurate budget statement because they are in the dark about family finances. One woman, the wife of a top executive, knows how much her husband earns only because his company has to issue a proxy statement each year before the annual stockholders' meeting that discloses top management salaries. She does know that her husband carries little insurance beyond the coverage his company provides; she knows little else about his finances. But she recognizes the value of investing. She has roughly $100,000 in money she inherited, and this she keeps invested continually in good growth stocks.

Another woman married to a top executive of a major company, also with a large salary, knows that he has set up a trust for her, enough to provide a comfortable income during her lifetime and to pass something substantial on to their children. However, a cautious woman, she has for years saved a little each month out of a generous household allowance and stashed it away, unknown to her family. She now invests these amounts, after they accumulate to about $500, in stocks.

The wife of a middle-level executive, with a good salary of more than $60,000 a year, has long been haunted by memories of the Depression. Shortly after their marriage she urged her husband to start a very sound life insurance program, which has been increased over the years. She can count on about $200,000 from insurance if anything should happen to him. With that accomplished she has been saving small amounts each year to make investments, so that all members of the family, including the children, own stock in their own names. Her aim is to continue and increase the pace of this program.

Another woman has gone back to work as a teacher for two reasons: (1) to help her husband during the heavy expense years when their children will be in college, three of them at about the same time; (2) to build up investments that will help by paying high dividends and offering borrowing power during those difficult years, and also provide a source of capital for retirement later.

A single woman often finds it hard to save, especially if she's young and her salary is low. Clothes, travel, entertainment often appear to be much more important. An Individual Retirement Account helps because it is tax deductible (see Chapter 16). One woman got into the investing habit when her company offered a stock purchase plan and she allotted $20 a week for the shares over a year's period. She found that by tightening up a bit—fewer expensive lunches, more careful buying of food to be eaten at home, less money spent on clothes—she could absorb the difference. Since then she has received a small raise of $30 a week and expects to continue saving, funneling the money into a monthly investment account with a brokerage firm. The money accumulates in a cash management account until she makes an investment decision.

These case histories, all true ones, give an idea of how some women have found money within (or outside of) their budgets for investment. Certainly they couldn't have done this if they had not analyzed their financial status closely and come to a dedicated decision about investing. Like almost anything else worthwhile, it does take dedication.

Your Family's Balance Sheet

Besides the income statement there is a second important aspect of financial planning—the balance sheet.

Most women are so used to budgeting that an income statement is easy to make out and understand. A balance sheet, on the other hand, is something hazy; it looks a little more complicated and the terms used—net worth, earned surplus, current assets—sound difficult. But oddly enough it is even more revealing of a family's progress than an income statement.

Like a page in a diary, a personal balance sheet is a frozen moment in anyone's financial life—and a very telling one, when compared over a period of years. A balance sheet summarizes a person's assets and liabilities at a particular time. Once you have listed your assets carefully on one side of a page and liabilities on the other, you can find a key figure: net worth, namely, the sum of all assets minus all liabilities at a given date. (Most corporations report on a calendar-year basis and thus use December 31—or the last working day of December—as the date for figuring their balance sheet. For an individual this date is also convenient.) Then, year by year, you can compare your financial progress at the particular date.

With inflation rising inexorably each year, your net worth needs to rise at least as fast and preferably faster. This is your target; your balance sheet lets you know how you're doing.

Whereas an income statement revealing that a family is living right up to

Table 4-2. Balance sheet for a family with $50,000 income.

Assets		*Liabilities*	
House	$150,000	Mortgage	$100,000
Furniture, household goods	15,000	Car loans	6,000
Cars (two)	11,000	Car repairs needed	400
Savings account	3,500	Due on department store bills	1,500
Stock owned	15,300		
Cash in checking accounts	3,000	Estimated tax owed above withholding	500
IRA accounts; company savings plan	13,500	Allowances owed children	80
Total assets	211,300	Total liabilities	108,480
		Assets minus liabilities equal net worth of $102,820	

its last penny of income and perhaps going into debt can be disconcerting, a balance sheet for the same family often is surprisingly encouraging. The reason is twofold. Many people do not realize the value of assets until they sit down with pen and paper in hand and think; and many assets have built-in growth factors that often can be overlooked.

Let's make out a typical balance sheet of a middle-income family. Table 4-2 illustrates what a balance sheet might show. Obviously the figures are hypothetical and can vary widely. The table merely illustrates how a balance sheet can be set up. The start is easy; one of the biggest family assets on a long-term basis is a house.

One side of the balance sheet—the assets—adds up to $211,300, perhaps a more impressive figure than you thought. The liabilities total $108,480. The difference between the two is the important one for any family—the net worth. In this case $211,300 minus $108,480 equals $102,820. The net worth belongs to you and your family.

Later, when you start reading corporate balance sheets regularly, you might at first be puzzled because the total assets always equal the total liabilities. However, that is because the net worth belongs to a group outside the company—you the stockholders. In a corporate balance sheet your net worth as a stockholder is often lumped under liabilities, under the headings "available for the common," "earned," and "capital surplus." More about these items later. In other words the stockholders' ownership in the business appears on the liability side of the balance sheet because they own the difference between the total assets and the other liabilities, just as your family owns the net worth involved on the family balance sheet.

Over a period of years the net worth of a family tends to grow. In fact, a balance sheet is the quickest way for you, or anyone interested in your credit standing, to judge your financial progress. Let's see how some assets grow and change.

House. Each year it grows in value to you, possibly for two reasons. Year by year you pay off more of the mortgage debt, so you own a larger part of the house. Second, thanks to inflation the value of many houses has risen in dollars. Also, land values have been increasing faster than the price of houses.

Cash value of life insurance. This is another item that tends to increase each year.

Personal property. Despite wear, some household items like antique furniture, silverware (such as sterling), stamps, and other collections grow in value.

Capital items. Such big items as refrigerators, television sets, air conditioners, and lawnmowers probably decline in value each year owing to usage and the advent of new models.

Pension and profit-sharing plans. Participation in these usually becomes more valuable each year.

Securities. With a rising stock market or additional investments, your securities can be worth more year by year.

Installment debts. As they are paid off month by month such liabilities decline, possibly faster than the depreciation in the items purchased by the loan.

Cars. In the first years of ownership, new cars depreciate sharply in value. A $9,000 automobile might lose about $2,500 in value the first year, if you tried to sell it.

While an income statement tells you how you are faring in managing income in relation to outgo, a balance sheet kept up to date year by year details your financial growth. Certainly anyone finding himself with lower net worth from one year to another should take remedial action.

After you have made out a personal balance sheet and income statement, you should not have as much trouble reading and understanding the corporate financial statements of companies in which you are interested. Several brokerage firms such as Merrill Lynch have brochures telling you how to read financial reports. Practice in reading them also helps.

5

To Auction

How the Stock Market Works

Almost every woman enjoys an auction. There's an air of excitement, even when prices appear to be high in relation to value, or even when the auction goer has no money of her own to spend. At an auction it is interesting to watch the interplay—the agility of the auctioneer as he tries to obtain the highest price for sellers, the pitting of buyers against each other while the tension mounts, the feeling of anticlimactic relief when suddenly the cry "sold" is heard.

The New York Stock Exchange, the biggest center for trading stocks, likes to consider itself an auction market, and so does its smaller and younger neighbor, the American Stock Exchange. Prices, just as at an auction in a gallery or the back yard of a farmhouse, are set by open outcry between brokers who represent sellers or buyers.

Perhaps the best way to understand the exchange and its system of operation, and understand why it continues to be the nation's financial center, is to look at the history of the Wall Street area.

Often described as a canyon amid skyscrapers, Wall Street stretches only about eight hundred man-sized paces from Trinity Church at one end to the East River at the other—or from a scourge of the devil at one end and the not so deep, not so blue sea at the other. Wall Street is crossed at right angles by

Broad Street (which once had a canal running down the center) and by other streets. Solid gray skyscrapers loom over the street levels, quiet and noncommittal; behind them throbs life, along with hopes, dreams, moments of despair in the offices of hundreds of financial firms.

Wall Street got its name because once there was a wooden barricade along it, built by the early Dutch to keep out the Indians—and possibly the British—who coveted the small colony the Dutch West India Company had settled at the tip of Manhattan Island early in the seventeenth century. Thus Wall Street existed before New York. Perhaps today it is a commercial center because of the trade-minded Dutch.

The Dutch settlers, epitomized by peg-leg Governor Peter Stuyvesant who tried to keep order with a kind of fierce and rugged justice, came to this country not for political reasons such as escaping tyranny at home, and not for religious reasons such as the Puritans' desire to find a place to worship in their own way. The Dutch arrived for a very basic reason—to trade and to make money. Their nation in the seventeenth century ranked as a leading commercial power with a strong navy and many merchant ships. Hence the settlement they called New Amsterdam at the tip of Manhattan was soon a bustling seaport and financial center, where more than a dozen languages could be heard in a walk along its dirt streets. Trade and money have long been closely allied because cargoes have to be financed for the long trips abroad and the goods have to be sold.

New York City grew lustily in the nineteenth century and the residential sections gravitated uptown, but the financial center remained largely in Wall Street, partly because of tradition and convenience and partly because people preferred to live away from their businesses.

As the nation grew, putting out fingers of conquest into the wilderness in the West, canals were needed to carry goods and settlers inland, along with roads and later railroads. Ever-growing needs for financing became apparent. In the early years much of the capital came from Europe at high rates of return; but the need for money was always urgent enough that many new financial ventures were begun, to attract capital and funnel it into development. For example, the Bank of the Manhattan Company (later merged with the Chase National Bank) began as a water company founded by Alexander Hamilton. It built wooden pipes to carry water in the city. The Chemical Bank, another early company, was founded, as part of its name implies, to make chemicals. Such organizations often discovered they could make more money as banks lending money to help other new businesses.

The new businesses were many, and when they were formed they often sold shares. In the 1700s, even quite a few years before the Revolutionary War, about two dozen men used to meet regularly under a buttonwood tree on Broad

Street.* A tree makes a logical gathering place, on a hot day as well as on a rainy one. It's also easy to describe; as much so as an office with lettering and a number on the door.

At first only a few stocks were traded under the tree. Most brokers bought or sold for their own accounts or for a few friends busy elsewhere. In those days the general public had no money or time to spend on stocks, or even the credit to do so. In such a simple market many brokers could keep records of their day's trading on a few slips of paper stashed away in their pockets or in their hats.

After a while the traders, perhaps bothered by weather changes or needing privacy to escape from the curious, decided to move their meeting place indoors. A local tavern was a logical choice. Eventually, in 1865, the group, which began to call itself the New York Stock Exchange, moved into quarters in the area where it has remained, with alterations, up to the present.

The Major Stock Exchanges

Over the years the auction idea remained. Billions of dollars of securities are traded each year between brokers, acting for customers or themselves, on verbal acknowledgment alone—the tradition that began under the buttonwood tree. Computers and automation have speeded the process and will change it, but it is still a market where men stick by their word. If mistakes happen, as they do in any business, or differences of opinion arise, the problem is often solved under the eye of a stock exchange committee by the flip of a coin.

How does the intricate stock auction market work for you in this highly computerized, pushbutton age?

Suppose, after consulting your broker, you decide to buy 100 shares of General Motors. Perhaps you are sitting at your broker's desk in a suburban Illinois office of a big brokerage firm, or perhaps you are talking to him by telephone from your home. On his desk or nearby there may be a little machine with buttons; when he presses certain buttons the machine almost instantly either prints out or shows him on a screen the latest price quotation of General Motors. Let's say the last sale was at a price of $68\frac{1}{2}$, meaning \$68.50 a share.

After he tells you the price you might say, "I'll buy it."

"Okay," he replies, "we'll buy at the market—a hundred shares." On a pad he jots down your order. A market order indicates that the shares will be

*There's a plaque marking the spot, which you may see when you visit the New York Stock Exchange. The original agreement to trade was signed by 24 brokers on May 17, 1792.

bought at whatever price is going when the order reaches the floor of the exchange.

Or your broker may suggest that you place the order at 50 cents a share lower: "Let's put the order in at sixty-eight and see if we can get it. I have a feeling the market might go down a little today." He will make the order GTC, which means "good till canceled."

Basically, you should remember three types of orders:

The *market order* means you will get the stock at the price quoted when the order reaches the floor of the exchange. This is the type of order you might use if you don't want to quibble.

The *GTC order*—good till canceled—represents a bid by you to buy the stock when it reaches a specified price. Usually these orders last about six months, and then the broker might ask if you want to renew it.

Or you can put in a *day order,* which is good for that day only. If the stock doesn't reach your price you would have to put in the order again for the next day or the next, and so on. If you are afraid of the market's direction, you might use this type of order.

What happens next to your order still fascinates me, although I've been writing about securities for 35 years. From the broker's desk it goes to his office's order room; perhaps he takes it himself, perhaps an office messenger does the task, or even a conveyor system, or the broker can press a few buttons on a computer terminal. Whatever the method, the order goes directly to the brokerage firm's representative on the exchange floor or through the head office of the firm in New York and then to the floor. Only minutes are involved.

On the floor the order is received by a clerk of the firm, who in turn hands it over to a floor broker for the firm. He walks—quickly—the few dozen steps to the trading post where that particular stock is handled. The exchange, which trades some 2,300 issues of more than 1,500 companies these days, allots the stocks to each of its 14 trading posts.

General Motors is traded at a particular post. At this post your broker joins a group of people around a specialist, a broker who "makes a market" in GM and a few other stocks. This means that at any time he stands ready to buy or sell GM at reasonable prices in relation to recent market quotations. If ever he doesn't make a market, then an exchange committee investigates. It might halt trading if prices get too far out of line temporarily. It might conceivably appoint another specialist to handle the job if he does not perform satisfactorily.

In this group around the specialists brokers come and go, asking the latest price at which the specialist quotes the market. Once they have heard the market price, your broker and others will tell the specialist the price at which they want to buy or sell. This he writes in a little book.

If it happens that the order calls for buying at the market (like your order for 100 shares of GM) then the broker says to the specialist he will take 100 shares at the quoted price. Or there may be another broker in the group willing to sell at the market, in which case your broker can buy directly from him.

However, if the order is a day or GTC order at a price under the market it will go into the specialist's book and will be filled if prices reach that level.

Meanwhile, let's assume the market order has been filled. Your firm's floor broker reports back to the clerk, hands him a little slip noting the filling of the order. The clerk notifies the head office or your brokerage firm or contacts your own broker directly. In a space of a few minutes your broker can tell you that the order has been filled and you have bought 100 shares of GM. The sale has been consummated, but you have five trading days after the date of purchase to present your broker with a check covering the transaction. Usually you will receive a confirmation statement of the trade a day after it took place, although mails might delay it another day.

If the speed of the transaction in this auction market astonishes you, remember it has evolved over a few centuries, based partly on trust. Along the way Wall Streeters have developed shortcuts to speed the process, such as the ticker system, which carries reports on each trade of 100 shares. Almost every brokerage firm in the country has a ticker in its office. If you are in your broker's office you possibly will see your trade appear on the ticker a few minutes after it arrived on the floor. It might look like this:

GM
68

GM is a shorthand symbol, standing for General Motors. When this moves across the tape with a price under it, it means a trade has been completed for 100 shares at this price. If you had bought 200 shares it would look like this:

GM
2s 68

Each stock has a different symbol, which brokers use when they place an order. For example, suppose you are a big buyer and purchase 1,600 shares of Sears, Roebuck at 34. It looks like this on the ticker:

S
1600s 34

In the case of a big order like this the full 1,600 is on it, but the more usual trade involves 100 shares, 200 shares, and so forth. After all, even with 100 shares priced at 68 a lot of money is involved—$6,800.

On your next trip to the Wall Street area pay a visit to the exchange's visitors' gallery and museum on Broad Street. The floor of the exchange has often been described as almost the size of a football field; actually it is about 30,000 square feet.* Scattered around the floor are the 14 trading posts mentioned previously. Instead of having colors and numbers like football players, they post numbers and symbols of stock traded. Stock exchange clerks man the center of the posts to collect and transmit the transactions as soon as received, so that the trade shortly appears on the ticker—clicking out during the trading day in thousands of offices throughout the world. A large numbering board alerts brokers when their clerks, stationed around the edge of the trading floor, need them. Meanwhile, there's a ticker projecting the prices high above the floor, so that visitors can see them from the gallery. The brokers generally are too busy for more than hasty glances.

Until you become well versed in investing—beyond the ABC's—you probably should avoid stocks that are traded on other exchanges, such as the American Stock Exchange, the nation's second largest trading center. If you are old enough you may remember that it was once called the Curb Exchange.

The name dates from the nineteenth century when brokers who traded on the "curb" did so in groups gathered on Broad Street. Often in those days clerks in brokerage firms would call out customers' orders from windows overlooking the street. Just as on the New York Stock Exchange, the business was conducted mainly by word of mouth.

The Amex, however, has always lacked the prestige of the New York Stock Exchange, even after it moved operations indoors in 1926. The reason is that its listing requirements are not quite so strict as the Big Board's. Therefore, the Amex has attracted companies that are not so large or so prestigious as the ones listed on the Big Board, or companies that for various reasons cannot or do not want to report their financial activities as fully as companies listed on the bigger exchange are required to do. Many conservative investors look down their noses at some stocks listed on the Amex, considering them to be much more highly speculative, unseasoned newcomers; these tend to be lower-priced, volatile stocks. Remember that price alone is not a criterion for safety or growth possibilities of a stock, but generally speaking few prestigious companies have stocks that sell for $1, $2, or even pennies a share. Such low-priced stocks usually are traded over-the-counter.

However, every investor, even the novice, should be aware of the Amex and its stocks.† In any market boom many of the higher fliers—the purely

*An official football field is 300 feet by 150 feet, 45,000 square feet.

†There are a few Fortune 500 companies listed on the Amex, such as *The New York Times,* which has two classes of stock—voting and nonvoting. This made it ineligible for NYSE listing.

speculative stocks—have their homes on the Amex. Often small companies that become big and famous season their shares first on the Amex before they move to the Big Board. Trading procedures are very similar in the two markets. Obviously, if your broker makes some suggestions about Amex stocks that sound good and fit your investment ideas, then of course you should consider them.

An interesting point of reference for the average investor, especially one with speculative interests, is to follow the new Amex stock market average. It tends to move up faster during periods of speculative activity than the Dow or other averages such as the S&P 500.*

Over-the-Counter Markets

Shares of a vast number of companies are traded in another market called the over-the-counter market. In fact, what many people do not realize is that it's a much bigger market than those offered by the exchanges. No one, not even the smartest broker equipped with the largest computer, can estimate how many billions of dollars of stock exist in the over-the-counter market.

We can make a pretty fair guess about listed stocks. We know, for example, that the New York Stock Exchange lists about 2,300 company issues currently, the American has 928 listings, and the regional exchanges such as the Midwest, the Pacific Coast, and Boston exchanges list more than 2,000 companies' shares, some duplicating shares listed on the two biggest exchanges. (In recent years regional exchanges have become much more important, especially because of time zone differences between the East and West coasts. For example, when markets close in New York they are still open in San Francisco.) We can roughly measure the value of listed shares traded by multiplying the average price of the shares on each exchange by the number of shares traded.

But the over-the-counter market is impossible to measure. Consider for a moment how many small companies there are in this country, even judging from your own community. Some of them, like the local drugstore, are too small to sell their stock to the public. Perhaps the shares are owned by the pharmacist, his family, and a businessman or two who have supplied him with some capital. Other companies in your home city have grown beyond such family ownership and yet are local in nature—banks in the area and the local electric light company (if not part of a big utility), for instance.

*The S&P (Standard & Poor's) 500 can be seen in Chapter 3, Figure 3-1. It includes the shares of 500 major companies, many more than the 30 leading stocks in the Dow Jones average.

It is obvious that most small, localized companies like these have little desire to become listed on an exchange; in other words, there are many fine, solid companies on the over-the-counter market. And many of the best fast-growth candidates appear in the ranks of over-the-counter securities.

Quotations of the more popular and well-known of the over-the-counter stocks are carried in major newspapers such as *The New York Times* and *The Wall Street Journal*. If such quotations are not readily available in newspapers then they might appear in the sheets published five times weekly by the National Quotation Bureau, and most brokerage offices carry such sheets.

Trading in over-the-counter securities is regulated chiefly by an organization called the National Association of Securities Dealers. Stock quotations for the over-the-counter shares are handled on the NASDAQ* National Market or the NASDAQ Over-the-Counter lists. Membership is held by most brokerage firms, and also by firms that trade solely in the over-the-counter market. Some of these over-the-counter dealers specialize; they might deal only in bank stocks or insurance stocks, for instance.

The method of trading in the market for over-the-counter shares is somewhat different from the auction system of the New York Stock Exchange and the American Stock Exchange. Dealers make the market, standing ready to buy or sell from their inventories. They regularly quote a "bid and ask" price for the stocks which they handle. This means that buyers of shares in the over-the-counter market find that they don't pay commissions in the sense that they do for the listed stocks, but pay a markup.

For example, suppose you have been advised to invest in the local water company of your home community. The area is growing, more water is needed for home use and irrigation, and the company has shown good earnings. You go to your broker, who works for a member firm of the New York Stock Exchange and also has a big over-the-counter trading department, and you ask him to buy the shares for you. He will quote you the latest bid and ask price. This means the price at which dealers will buy shares from you for themselves or for their customers (the bid price); and the marked-up price at which they will sell shares to you (the ask price).

Then he may tell you that the brokerage firm itself makes a market in the issue (that is, keeps it on hand) and that the price at which he can buy it for you is "flat," or net, meaning no commission is involved. If the firm's over-the-counter department does not make a market in the issue, it may have to contact another over-the-counter house that specializes in that stock. In this case, you probably would have to pay a commission above the price quoted.

One problem with over-the-counter shares is that often the market for them

*NASDAQ is the shortened form of National Association of Securities Dealers Automatic Quotation.

is "thin." For example, a woman might inherit several thousand shares of a local company or bank, only to find that it is a little hard to sell the shares, because the market is thin. By "thin," brokers mean stocks that trade in small amounts of shares, often irregularly. In some cases, days might go by without shares being traded. Perhaps there are few shares outstanding; perhaps many have been tied up in portfolios and estates by people willing to hang on to them for years because of family interest, pride, large capital gains, etc. Then the sale of a few thousand shares could take time and might force the price of the shares down.

Still another difficulty encountered by some investors involves bank loans. Generally banks will not lend as much with over-the-counter securities as collateral as they will on stocks listed on the major exchanges. Here again they consider that over-the-counter markets tend to be thin and prices more volatile in the case of sudden liquidation.

In summary, remember that price is no indicator of a stock's value. Shortsightedness has often led some brokers and even more investors to ignore economic forces constantly at work at the edge of the stock market, like the ebb and flow of waves along a beach. Two examples (and there are hundreds of others) help illustrate this point.

I have hundreds of shares in a little company called the Port Ewen Ice Company, a once-profitable venture that has slipped into oblivion. Years ago its operations involved cutting blocks of ice from the Hudson River each winter and shipping them insulated with sawdust by train or barge to New York, where they went to hotels and private homes. Then came the electric refrigerator, which virtually killed the company's one-product market; also, by then icebreakers kept the river open during most of the winter, making it difficult for ice to form in large blocks. Economic progress spelled the end of the company.

A more recent and better-known example involves a company that managed to remain in business despite its failure to move with the trend for many years. Its name: Montgomery Ward. After World War II Sewell Avery ran the company with the singlemindedness of a dictator. An elderly man in the 1940s and a successful business leader when the war ended, he was imbued with the idea that serious depressions always followed major wars. He insisted the company keep millions of dollars in cash and easily liquidated securities such as low-paying government bonds.

Meanwhile, the company's chief rival, Sears, Roebuck, foresaw the growth in the economy, answering the needs of people who had saved up money from good jobs during the war and now wanted to spend on scarce consumer goods. Furthermore, Sears top officials reasoned that the built-in stabilizers in the economy launched during the New Deal years, such as Social Security, unemployment insurance, and public works, would blunt any depression into a mere recession. So they moved ahead and spent hundreds of millions of dollars on improvements, new stores, a wider variety of products for sale, training young executives.

The Sears management judged the economy correctly. There was no depression because the world's needs for consumer goods proved too great, and the war had been better financed so that Americans had money to spend and jobs with which to earn more. Sears moved far ahead in sales and earnings while Montgomery Ward lagged so badly it took a proxy fight to wake up management to the realization that it could not remain out of step with progress. In recent years it was acquired by Mobil Corporation, the big oil company, as a means of diversifying. Now Mobil, disenchanted by this investment, wants to sell Montgomery Ward or spin it off to its shareholders. A spinoff in this instance would mean that each owner of a Mobil share would receive a certain number of Montgomery Ward shares.

Change is the key word in business, and the investor has to be flexible to keep up.

6

Straight Figuring

How to Read Market Quotations

Figures can be as dull as dishwater, but a smart woman investor learns to handle them with discrimination just as she learns to separate the silverware from the kitchen utensils and the good china from the expendable variety. To do this she does have to absorb some boring details but after a while they become a part of her daily investment life.

The first step is to keep up with the stock quotations in newspapers. Soon they will become as easy to read as prices of canned goods in a supermarket or the price sheets from software suppliers.

Figure 6-1 shows a portion of the stock market page taken from the September 13, 1985, *New York Times.* Near the middle, you will note a heading "Volume by Exchanges." That day 107,070,000 shares were traded on the New York Stock Exchange—a reasonably busy day. In 1970, as a point of comparison, brokerage firms broke even or made a little money each day the volume of trading was 12,000,000 shares.

Below that is another section that investors follow: "Volume Comparisons," total trading for the year to date. It shows volume of 18,617,950,006

Figure 6-1. Sample New York Stock Exchange quotations.

New York Stock Exchange Issues

CONSOLIDATED TRADING *

52-Week High	52-Week Low	Stock	Div	Yld %	PE Ratio	Sales 100s	High	Low	Last	Chg.
			A	B	C	D				
24⅜	16	AAR	.56	2.5	15	101	22¾	22¼	22⅜	− ⅜
17⅜	9¾	AGS		...	13	328	16¼	15¾	16⅛	+ ⅜
16½	9⅜	AMCA		...	...	10	10⅞	10¾	10¾	− ¼
21½	13	AMF	.25i	...	96	406	13⅝	13½	13½	...
50¾	25¼	AMR		...	7	6013	42¾	41⅝	41¾	−1¼
23⅜	18⅝	AMR pf	2.18	9.4	...	59	23¼	23	23⅛	+ ⅛
25⅞	23	ANR pf	2.67	11.5	...	27	23½	23¼	23¼	− ½
61⅛	34¾	ASA	2.00	5.3	...	288	38⅜	37¾	38	− ⅜
27	12⅛	AVX	.32	2.8	17	168	12⅝d	11⅝	11⅝	− ⅞
28½	18½	AZP	2.72	11.4	7	2494	24⅜	23⅝	[illegible]	− [illegible]
60	36⅜	AbtLab	1.40	2.5	16	[illegible]	56	55⅝	55¾	− ¼
25⅝	20	AccoWd s	.50	2.3	16	36	21¾	21⅝	21⅝	− ⅜
24¾	12½	AcmeC	.40	2.9	...	45	14	13⅞	13⅞	− ⅛
10½	7⅜	AcmeE	.32b	4.2	11	17	7⅞	7⅝	7⅝	− ⅛
19	15½	AdaEx	1.92e	11.1	...	68	17½	17¼	17¼	− ⅛
20	13½	AdmMl	.32	1.9	7	36	17⅛	17	17	...
17⅞	8⅜	AdvSys	.53t	4.2	18	170	12¾	12½	12⅝	...
40⅜	22⅛	AMD		...	15	4449	26⅜	25½	25¾	+ ⅜
12⅛	6⅞	Advest	.12	1.4	19	224	8⅞	8½	8¾	...
15⅞	9½	Aerflex		...	11	89	13⅜	13⅛	13⅛	− ¼
49⅝	32⅜	AetnLf	2.64	6.2	15	2251	43¼	42⅝	42¾	− ⅛
57½	52⅜	AetL pf	5.79e	10.5	...	112	55	54¾	55	− ¼
37⅜	18½	Ahmns	1.20	3.9	8	1043	31½	30⅞	30⅞	− ⅜
3⅜	2½	Aileen		...	...	67	3	2¾	2¾	− ¼
57	42	AirPrd	1.20	2.3	12	813	52½	52	52⅛	− ⅛
24⅜	15¼	AirbFrt	.60	2.6	13	249	23⅛	22⅞	22⅞	− ¼
2⅛	1⅛	AlMoa s	.10e	5.3	...	78	1⅞	1⅞	1⅞	...
29¼	23⅜	AlaP pf	2.74e	10.0	...	100	27½	27½	27½	− ¼
33⅜	27¾	AlaP pfA	3.92	12.8	...	17	30⅞	30⅝	30⅝	− ⅛
8⅛	6¼	AlaP dpf	.87	11.3	...	20	7⅞	7¾	7¾	...
82	63½	AlaP pf	9.00	11.6	...	z1190	77½	77	77½	+ ½
106¼	96¾	AlaP pf	11.00	10.7	...	z500	102½	102½	102½	...
86	69¼	AlaP pf	9.44	11.8	...	z50	80¾	80	80	− ¾
74	58½	AlaP pf	8.16	11.5	...	z110	71	71	71	+1
75	57	AlaP pf	8.28	11.7	...	z110	70½	69½	70½	+1½
16⅛	11¾	Alagsco	1.04	7.5	10	86	14⅛	13⅞	13⅞	+ ⅛
26⅜	11½	AlskAir	.16	.7	8	301	21⅜	21⅛	21⅜	− ⅛
25	12½	Albrto s	.38	1.7	18	89	23⅜	22¾	22¾	− ⅝
33¼	26⅜	Albtsns	.76	2.8	11	1060	28	27¼	27¼	− ⅜
31¼	23¼	Alcan	1.20	4.6	27	3425	26⅜	25⅞	26	− ⅜
38⅞	27⅛	AlcoSta	1.20	3.5	12	52	34⅜	33⅞	34⅛	− ½
32	21	AlexAlx	1.00	3.7	...	541	27⅝	27⅜	27⅜	...
25½	20⅜	Alexdr		...	21	13	24	23¾	23¾	− ¼
89½	72¼	AllgCp	1.54t	2.0	...	2	77½	77⅜	77½	+ ⅛
26¾	24½	AlgCp pf	2.86	10.8	...	5	26⅜	26⅜	26⅜	...
28¾	20¼	AlgInt	1.40	6.5	...	46	21⅜	21⅛	21⅜	...
20¾	16⅞	AlgIn pf	2.19	12.2	...	7	18	18	18	− ⅛
98	85	Algl pfC	11.25	12.2	...	9	92¾	92½	92½	+ ¼
34⅜	26¾	AllgPw	2.70	9.4	8	2062	29¼	28⅝	28⅝	− ⅝
23½	15¾	AllenG	.60b	2.8	14	183	22⅛	21¾	21¾	− ⅛
46¾	32½	AlldCp	1.80	4.2	8	1915	43	42½	42⅝	− ⅛

MARKET INDICATORS

THURSDAY, SEPTEMBER 12, 1985

N.Y.S.E. Issues

Consolidated Trading

Dow Jones Stock Averages

	Open	High	Low	Close	Chg.
30 Industrials	1317.43	1327.40	1307.01	1312.39	− 7.05
20 Transports	668.54	672.64	660.93	663.27	− 6.09
15 Utilities	154.39	154.75	152.08	152.65	− 2.46
65 Stocks	542.71	546.18	537.33	539.42	− 4.32

S.&P. Index

	High	Low	Close	Chg.
400 Indust	206.54	204.71	204.94	− 1.22
20 Transpt	170.65	168.41	168.69	− 1.70
40 Utilities	81.83	80.43	80.55	− 1.25
40 Financl	21.24	21.01	21.03	− 0.19
500 Stocks	185.21	183.49	183.69	− 1.34

N.Y.S.E. Index

	High	Low	Last	Chg.
Composite	107.16	106.36	106.36	−0.86
Industrial	123.08	122.20	122.20	−0.80
Transport	106.10	105.13	105.13	−1.23
Utility	55.99	55.40	55.40	−0.80
Firance	110.87	110.05	110.05	−1.00

Most Active

	Vol.	Last	Chg.
RockCentr n	9,664,400	19¾	....
WestghEl	2,191,800	38⅜	+ ½
Revlon	1,941,700	43⅞	+ ⅞
MorganJP s	1,858,500	47	− ⅜
KanGasEl	1,414,300	11⅞	−2
Reynln pfC	1,409,200	125	+ ½
IBM	1,388,500	127⅛	− ⅛
BankAmer	1,248,600	13⅜	− ¾
Amer T&T	1,216,800	20⅞	− ¼
MidSouUt	1,209,400	8¾	− ⅜
Beatrice	1,130,800	34⅛	+ ½
Gulf StaUt	1,062,000	12¾	− ¾
AmExpress	1,037,300	42	+ ¾
Arkla	947,000	22	+1¾
Norlnd PS	914,700	11⅞	− ⅛

Changes—Up

	Last	Chg.	Pct.
RiverOak n	3	+ ½	20.0
EmpDE pfB	5⅜	+ ¾	16.2

Volume by Exchanges

Markets	Shares
NYSE	107,070,000
Pacific	4,178,700
Midwest	10,890,900
NASD	6,770,130
Boston	2,190,000
Cinci	179,000
Phila	1,451,700
Instinet	302,100
Total	133,032,530

Volume Comparisons

Day's Sales	107,070,000
Wednesday's Sales	100,380,000
Year Ago	101,360,000
1985 to Date	18,617,950,006
1984 to Date	16,138,438,353

Amex Issues

Consolidated Trading

Market Value Index

High	Low	Close	Chg.
228.35	226.47	226.72	−1.62

Volume Comparisons

Day's Sales	9,926,190
Wednesday's Sales	8,667,800
Year Ago	5,688,570
1985 to Date	1,416,731,335
1984 to Date	1,063,852,330

Market Diary—

	Today	Prev.
Advanced	184	182
Declined	364	344
Unchanged	252	257
Total issues	800	783
New highs	8	2
New lows	23	14

Most Active

	Vol.	Last	Chg.
BAT Ind	2,865,000	3 11-16	.....
HomeGp n	685,900	16¼	− ⅜
WangLabB	291,800	16⅛	− ⅜
Hasbro s	197,300	30¼	+ ¾
Wickes	192,100	4 5-16	−1-16
TexasAirCp	189,500	17⅜	− ⅛
OzarkHldg	177,000	11⅛	+ ⅛
AmExpr wt	161,700	30⅞	+ ⅛
NY Times	136,100	41⅜	− ¼
ChartMdA s	130,700	21¾	+ ¾

Changes—Up

	Last	Chg.	Pct.
Beth Corp	3	+ ⅜	14.3

Over-the-Counter Nasdaq Quotes

Index

Index	Close.	Chg.	Week Ago	Month Ago.
Composite	289.93	−1.50	295.28	298.72
Indust	295.84	−1.24	301.28	306.83
NMS Comp	122.48	−0.64	124.81	126.25
NMS inds	110.07	−0.44	112.10	114.29

Market Diary

Advanced	624
Declined	1,226
Unchanged	2,298
Total issues	4,148
New highs	40
New lows	93
Total sales	71,547,900

Most Active

Name	Volume	Last or Bid	Asked	Chg
Symblic	1,934,900	11		− ½
Intel	1,078,900	25¾		+ ¼
DSC	738,000	12¾		+ ⅜
Mylan s	662,200	16¾		+ ½
Convgt	650,900	8⅛		+ ⅛
ApoloC	632,500	16¾		+ ¼
PriceCo	612,700	54		+ ¾
MCI	584,800	9		....
CrazE s	520,500	12⅞		− ⅜
Gott	518,700	21½		....

Changes—Up

	Last	Chg	Pct
Hemotec	4½	+ ⅞	24.1
Unioil	2¼	+ ⅜	20.0
VanzettiSy	7½	+ 1¼	20.0
HamerCmp un	6⅛	+ 1	19.5
AllSeasR	3⅞	+ ⅝	19.2
Hospos un	4¾	+ ¾	18.8
DairyMrt	19¾	+ 2¾	16.2
DigitlPrd	5⅜	+ ¾	16.2
Kamenstein	2⅞	+ ⅜	15.0
UnivTrad s	4⅞	+ ⅝	14.7

Changes—Down

*Consolidated trading includes volume on regional exchanges.

for the year 1985 to date, well ahead of the previous year. Generally, a strong or rising stock market will go hand-in-glove with heavy volume.

Now for the figures of the "Most Active Stocks," to which you should give some regular attention.

Look at some of the very active stocks that day: Rockefeller Center is a new stock issue. Popular IBM is on the list, as is AT&T.

One day's look at the most active list cannot indicate a trend, usually. It will much more likely show the effect of a specific news item. Earnings, reports, discoveries, or merger talks can stimulate activity in a stock. The important thing is for the investor to keep watching the most active list over a period of time—to spot trends, to develop a feel for what kinds of events have an impact on particular stocks.

Now let's look at the far left column, which gives the current prices of all listed stocks, in alphabetical order by symbol. For example, look at the listing: AbtLab—Abbott Laboratories, a well-known, sound chemicals and pharmaceuticals firm. The first numbers you see are:

52-Week		
High	Low	
60	36¾	Abt Lab 1.40

This indicates simply that the high price for Abbott during the year to date was 60 and the lowest price was 36¾. The figure following the name of the stock refers to the dividend paid on a year's basis—$1.40. It doesn't provide the quarterly rate, unfortunately, so that the investor interested in such a stock must do more research on that. Sometimes the dividend is followed by a small letter referring you to an explanatory footnote. The yield in percent follows, and then a figure called "PE ratio," which I'll explain in a minute.

Next comes a heading dubbed "Sales in 100s," which means the number of round lots (100 shares) traded that day. The figure for Abbott is 1488, meaning 148,800 shares changed hands. Compare this with 9,644,000 shares of Rockefeller Center, the most active stock.

The next headings for Abbott are quite obvious—a high for the day of 56, a low of 55⅜, and a closing price of 55¾, off ¼. It could be described as trading in a narrow range. Furthermore, under the heading "Change" you can see that the price showed little movement in comparison with the closing price the previous day.

A rise of even $1 a share in a stock selling in Abbott's price range would be considered good. Naturally a $1 per share rise in a stock priced at $20 would be even more significant, just on a percentage basis. Just think that if you own 100 shares of a stock that rises $1 you are $100 richer—on paper—than the previous day.

Why virtually no change in Abbott that particular day? It's impossible to say without knowing more about the company itself. The stock market generally tended to be down a little that day, a trend that shows up as your eyes run down all those little plusses and minuses in the right-hand column under the "Change" heading.

By reading the daily news columns of the newspaper you might be able to find a reason for a stock's relative strength on a particular day. Perhaps a brokerage firm has issued a favorable comment about the company; perhaps the company came out with favorable earnings or a new product. Perhaps merger rumors have been surrounding the company. You the investor have to ferret out such news if you want an explanation. Stocks talk to you only through figures and news items. (See Figures 6-2 and 6-3, which will be discussed in more detail a bit later.)

Also note the category called the PE (price/earnings) ratio. This is the closing price of the stock that day divided by the per share earnings. Example: If a stock closes at 20 and the latest 12 months' earnings reported by the company are $2, the PE ratio is 10.

Once you have perused the stock market quotations of companies whose shares you own or in which you might be interested, you will want to find out how the averages fared—namely the Dow Jones industrial average, since that is the best known and most widely quoted. It closed at 1312.39, off 7.05 points; so Abbott, in holding steady with a loss of only ¼ point, fared well.

Then you would scan the other market indicators. You would find that the New York Stock Exchange's industrial average closed at 122.20, down 0.80, and that Standard & Poor's 400 industrials ended at 204.94, down 1.22.

In view of the general stock market trends, you might find the NASDAQ index of over-the-counter issues significant. That particular day the figure was 295.84 for the industrials, down 1.24. An alert investor might conclude that there was a slight swing into the speculative issues on the over-the-counter market if the NASDAQ index moved upward or dropped less than the Dow or the others.

This is the kind of detective work that a smart investor does, and by following such prices, averages, and the news items each day, you can become quite sophisticated about trends.

Figures for the American Stock Exchange issues are quoted similarly to those of the Big Board, although some of the smaller newspapers carry only an abbreviated list of stocks, often limiting their quotations to the Big Board issues.

You may have some investment, or some interest, in a company that is traded over-the-counter. If so, you need to keep up with the lists of over-the-counter issues, regularly carried each day by the major newspapers like *The Wall Street Journal* and *The New York Times*.

Figure 6-2. Sample over-the-counter quotation.

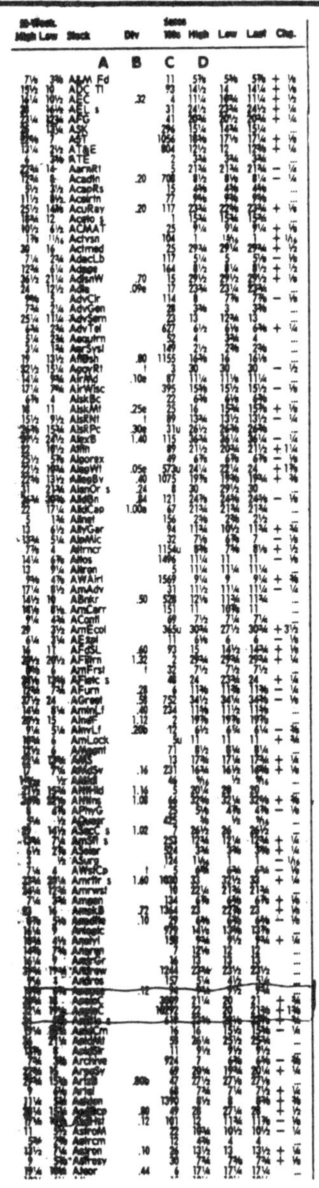

Over-the-Counter Quotations

NASDAQ QUOTATIONS -

52-Week High	52-Week Low	Stock	Div	Sales 100s	High	Low	Last	Chg.
		A	B	C	D			
7⅛	3⅝	A&M Fd		11	5⅞	5⅝	5⅞	+ ⅛
15½	10	ADC Tl		93	14½	14	14¼	+ ⅛
14¼	10½	AEC	.32	4	11¼	10¾	11¼	+ ½
[illegible]	16½	AEL s		31	24½	23¾	24½	+ ¼
23¼	12¾	AFG		41	20¾	20½	20¾	+ ¼
[illegible]	13¼	ASK		276	15¼	14¾	15¼	...
[illegible]	7	AST		1056	18⅜	17⅛	17¼	+ ⅛
13¼	2½	AT&E		804	12½	12	12⅜	+ ¼
6	3⅝	ATE		2	3¾	3¾	3¾	...
27¾	14	AarnR1		5	21¾	21¾	21¾	− ¼
17¾	8	Acadin	.20	708	8½	8⅛	8¼	− ¼
9½	3½	AcapRs		15	4⅝	4⅝	4⅝	...
11½	8½	Acelrtn		77	9⅝	9⅝	9⅝	...
25½	14⅝	AcuRay	.20	117	23¾	22⅞	23¾	+ ⅛
18¾	12	Aceto s		1	15¾	15¾	15¾	...
10½	6½	ACMAT		25	9¼	9¼	9¼	+ ⅛
1⅞	11/16	Actvsn		104	1	15/16	1	+ 1/16
30	16	Actmed		25	29¾	29¼	29¾	+ ½
7¼	2¾	AdacLb		117	5¼	5	5⅛	− ⅛
12¾	6¼	Adage		164	8½	8¼	8½	+ ½
36½	21¼	AdsnW	.70	15	29½	29½	29½	+ ⅛
24	12½	Adia	.09e	17	23¾	23¼	23¾	...
9⅝	5	AdvCir		114	8	7⅞	7⅞	− ⅛
7¾	2¼	AdvGen		28	3⅜	3	3⅜	...
25¼	11¼	AdvSem		23	13	12¾	13	...
6⅜	2¾	AdvTel		627	6½	6⅛	6⅜	+ ¼
5¼	2¾	Aequitrn		52	4	3¾	4	...
3¼	1¾	AerSysl		149	2½	2⅜	2⅜	...
19	13½	AffBsh	.80	1155	16⅜	16	16⅛	...
32½	15¼	AgcyRt	†	3	30	30	30	− ½
14¼	9⅝	AirMd	.10e	87	11¼	11⅛	11¼	...
17¼	7⅝	AirWisc		395	15⅝	15½	15½	− ⅛
6⅞	4	AlskBc		22	6⅜	6⅛	6⅜	...
18	11	AlskMt	.25e	25	16	15¾	15⅞	+ ⅛
15½	9½	AlsRNt	†	89	13¾	13½	13½	− ¼
26⅞	15¾	AlsRPc	.30e	31u	26½	26⅜	26⅜	...
39½	24½	AlexB	1.40	115	36¾	36¼	36¼	− ¼
22	16½	Alfin		89	21½	20¾	21½	+ 1¼
25½	5⅞	Algorex		49	6⅞	6⅞	6⅞	− ⅛
27½	16¾	AlegWt	.05e	573u	24¼	22¼	24	+ 1⅜
22⅜	13½	AllegBv	.40	1075	19⅝	19⅜	19¾	+ ⅜
31	21¾	AlanOr s	.24	8	30	29½	30	...
[illegible]	[illegible]	AlldBn	.84	121	24⅞	24⅝	24⅝	− ⅛
22	17¼	AlldCap	1.00a	67	21¾	21¾	21¾	...
5	1¾	Allnet		156	2⅝	2⅜	2½	...
13	6½	AllyGer		94	11¾	10½	11¾	+ ¾
13¾	5¼	AlphMic		32	7⅛	6⅞	7	− ⅛
7⅞	4	Altrncr		1154u	8⅜	7⅜	8⅛	+ ½
14¼	6⅞	Altos		1496	11¼	11	11	− ⅛
13	9¼	Altron		5	11¼	11¼	11¼	...
9⅝	4⅞	AWAirl		1569	9¼	9	9¼	+ ⅜
17¼	8½	AmAdv		31	11½	11¼	11¼	− ¼
14½	10	ABnkr	.50	528	12⅛	11¾	11¾	...
18⅛	8½	AmCarr		151	11	10⅞	11	...
9¼	4¾	AContl		69	7½	7¼	7¼	...
29	3½	AmEcol		365u	30¾	27½	30¾	+ 3½
6¼	3¼	AExpl		11	6⅛	6	6	− ⅛
16	11	AFdSL	.60	93	15	14½	14¾	+ ⅛
29½	20½	AFlirn	1.32	2	29¾	29¾	29¾	+ ¼
[illegible]	6	AmFrst	†	32	7½	7½	7½	...
28⅜	12⅜	AFletc s		48	24	23¾	24	+ ¼
17⅜	7¾	AFurn	.28	6	11⅜	11⅜	11⅜	− ¼
37½	24	AGreet	.58	752	34½	34¼	34⅜	− ⅛
14⅛	8¼	AmInLf	.40	234	11⅝	11½	11⅝	...
20½	15	AIneF	1.12	2	19⅞	19⅞	19⅞	...
9⅛	5⅛	AmvLf	.20b	12	6½	6¼	6¼	− ⅜
18⅜	6	AmLock		5u	11	11	11	+ ¾
17½	6	AMgmt		71	8½	8¼	8¼	...
27¼	12⅜	AMS		13	17¾	17¼	17¾	+ ¼
17	7⅞	AMedSv	.16	231	16¾	16½	16⅝	+ ⅛
[illegible]	½	AMtld		46	9/16	½	9/16	...
[illegible]	15⅝	ANtHld	1.16	5	20¼	20	20	...
[illegible]	[illegible]	ANtIns	1.08	66	32⅝	32¼	32⅝	+ ⅜
8	4⅞	APhyG		255	5⅛	4⅞	4⅞	− ⅛
[illegible]	½	AQuasr		425	⅝	½	9/16	...
27	14½	ASecC s	1.02	7	26½	26	26½	...
17¾	7¼	AmSft s		253	17¾	17¼	17¾	+ ¼
6½	2⅞	ASolar		524	3¾	3⅝	3⅝	+ ¼
3	½	ASurg		124	1 1/16	1	1	− 1/16
7¼	4	AWstCp	†	5	6⅜	6¾	6¾	− ⅛
33¾	20¼	Amrfir s	1.60	1030	33	32½	33	+ ¼
24⅝	17⅜	Amrwst		10	22¼	21¾	21¾	...
7⅛	3⅜	Amgen		134	6⅞	6⅝	6⅞	+ ⅛
23	16	AmskB	.72	1364	23	22⅞	23	+ ⅛
6⅞	5⅛	Anadite	.10	29	6⅝	6⅝	6⅝	− ⅛
16¼	9	Analogic		970	14⅛	13⅞	13⅞	...
10⅜	4½	Anaryl		158	9¾	9½	9¾	+ ¼
14⅞	7⅜	Anergn		7	12⅛	12	12	...
16¼	9	AnchrGr		16	13	13	13	...
27⅝	17⅜	AnBrew		1244	23¾	23½	23½	...
9⅝	3	Andros		157	5¼	4½	5¼	...
[illegible]	[illegible]	[illegible]	.12	[illegible]	[illegible]	9½	[illegible]	...
[illegible]	16	AppleC		3087	21¼	20	21	+ ¾
27¼	14⅛	ApplC		16072	22	20	21⅜	+ 1⅜
[illegible]	[illegible]	[illegible] s		418	[illegible]	[illegible]	[illegible]	[illegible]
17¼	[illegible]	AplSCm		16	16	15½	15⅝	− ¼
[illegible]	21⅛	ApldMt		58	26¼	25½	25⅝	...
13⅞	8	AppldSir		11	9½	9½	9½	...
7¾	3⅜	Archive		924	7	6⅝	6⅝	− ⅜
27⅜	16	ArgoSy		69	20⅛	19⅞	20¼	+ ¼
27¾	15⅞	ArizB	.80b	47	27½	27⅛	27⅛	...
9	6⅜	Ariel		68	7¾	7¼	7½	+ ¼
11¼	[illegible]	Ashton		1390	8½	8	8⅜	+ ⅜
28¼	15¾	AsdBcp	.80	49	28	27¼	28	+ ½
17⅛	[illegible]	AsdHst	.12	101	12	11¾	11⅞	− ⅛
11	5½	AstroM		22	10¾	10½	10½	− ¼
5⅜	2⅞	Astrcm		12	4⅜	4	4	...
13½	7¼	Astron	.10	26	13½	13	13½	+ ¼
9	5⅞	Astrosy		30	7¾	7⅝	7¾	+ ⅛
19¼	10⅝	Atcor	.44	6	17¼	17¼	17¼	...

Figure 6-3. Typical bond quotations.

N.Y. Stock Exchange Bond Trading

THURSDAY, SEPTEMBER 12, 1985

	U.S. Gov't. Bonds	Other Dom. Bonds	Foreign Bonds	Total All Bonds
Day's Sales	$ —	a$ 28,810,000	$ 10,000	$ 28,820,000
Wednesday's	—	a 28,350,000	90,000	28,440,000
Year to Date	870,000	a 6,359,380,080	22,017,000	6,382,289,080
1984	503,000	a 4,734,984,000	24,217,000	4,759,704,000

a—Includes International Bank Bonds

BOND ISSUES TRADED

	Issues	Advances	Declines	New Highs	New Lows
Sept. 12	847	253	390	24	10
Sept. 11	895	218	461	27	8
Sept. 10	873	314	364	29	4

Bonds	Current Yield	Sales in $1,000	High	Low	Last	Net Chge
A B C D						
AMR 10¼06	12.1	14	84½	84½	84½	...
APL 10⅜97	14.5	5	74	74	74	...
AbbtL 9.2s99	10.4	70	90	88⅛	88⅛	− 3⅛
Advst 9s08	cv	10	82	82	82	...
Aerflx 9⅝05	cv	10	107½	107½	107½	...
AlaBn 9¼99	9.3	10	99⅞	99⅞	99⅞	...
AlaP 9s2000	11.1	5	81¼	81¼	81¼	− ¼
AlaP 7⅞s02	10.9	62	72½	72¼	72½	+ ½
AlaP 9¾s04	11.3	2	86	86	86	+ 1⅛
AlaP 10½05	11.7	2	90	90	90	− 1⅜
AlaP 8⅞s06	11.2	1	79	79	79	...
AlaP 9¼07	11.5	10	80⅜	80½	80½	+ ⅛
AlaP 9½08	11.5	11	83	82¾	82¾	− ¼
AlaP 15¼10	13.8	22	110½	110	110½	+ ½
AlaP 17⅜11	15.0	16	116⅛	116⅛	116⅛	+ 1⅛
AlaP 18¼89	16.1	15	113¼	113¼	113¼	− ¼
AlskA 9s03	cv	4	122¾	122¾	122¾	...
AlskH 16¼94	15.5	98	105½	105	105	...
AlskH 18⅜01	15.7	8	117¼	117¼	117¼	− ¼
AlskH 11½93	11.3	6	101½	101½	101½	+ 1¾
Allgl 10.4s92	13.9	6	75	74⅜	74⅜	− ⅜
AlldC 6.6s93	8.7	10	75⅜	75⅜	75⅜	− ⅞
AlldC zr87	...	19	83¾	83¼	83¼	− ½
AlldC zr92	...	9	46¼	46¼	46¼	− ⅜
AlldC zr96	...	5	31¼	31¼	31¼	+ ½
AlldC d6s88	6.8	6	88⅛	88⅛	88⅛	− ⅛
AlldC d6s90	7.4	20	81¼	80⅞	81¼	...
AlldC zr89	...	50	65¾	65¾	65¾	− 2¼
AlldC zr97	...	40	25⅜	25⅜	25⅜	...
AlldC zr99	...	90	20⅛	20⅛	20⅛	− 1⅜
AlldC zr03	...	50	13¼	13¼	13¼	− 3¼
AlldC zr09	...	15	7¾	7¾	7¾	+ ⅜
AlldSt 10⅜90	10.4	40	100	100	100	...
AlldSt 8⅝09	cv	18	113½	113½	113½	− 1½
AlsChe 16s91	14.5	1	110⅛	110⅛	110⅛	+ ½
Alcoa 6s92	7.9	10	76	76	76	− ⅜
Alcoa 9s95	10.3	6	87½	87½	87½	− 1
AluCa 9½95	10.4	51	91¾	91⅜	91¾	+ ⅜
AMAX 9⅜00	13.6	1	69	69	69	− ⅜
Amax 14¼90	14.4	169	98¾	98½	98¾	+ ¼
Amax 14½94	14.7	30	99	98⅞	98⅞	− ⅛
AHes 7⅛96	8.1	7	87½	87½	87½	+ ¼
ABrnd 11⅛89	10.8	8	103	103	103	...
ABrnd 9⅝87	9.6	10	101⅜	101⅜	101⅜	+ 1⅛
AExC 10.1s90	10.2	25	99½	99¼	99¼	− ¼
AExC 10⅞13	11.5	14	94⅜	94⅜	94⅜	+ 4¼
Alnvt 8⅝s89	9.6	1	90⅞	90⅞	90⅞	...
AmMed 9½01	cv	18	115	115	115	− 1
Chelse 5¼93	cv	31	98	98	98	+ 1
Chmtrn 9s94	11.3	5	79⅞	79⅞	79⅞	+ ⅜
CPoV 8⅝09	11.2	5	77	77	77	− 1
ChvrnC 11s90	10.8	112	101⅜	101½	101⅜	− ⅛
ChvrnC 10⅝95	10.9	45	98⅜	98	98¼	+ ⅛
Chvrn 7s96	9.1	25	77½	77¼	77¼	− ⅜
Chrysl 8s98	10.5	20	76½	76¼	76¼	...
ChryF 7⅝86	7.5	26	99	98⅜	98⅜	− 3/16
ChryF 8.35s91	9.3	4	89⅜	89⅜	89⅜	+ ⅞
ChryF 7.7s92	9.2	1	84⅛	84⅛	84⅛	...
ChryF 9s86	9.0	16	99⅜	99⅜	99⅜	...
ChryF 9⅜87	9.4	18	99¼	99	99¼	+ ¼
CirclK 8⅝04	cv	1	109	109	109	...
CirclK 8¼05	cv	30	102	102	102	...
Citicp 8.90s89t	8.9	15	100	100	100	...
Citicp 5⅜00	cv	5	105	105	105	− 2⅛
Citicp 8⅛07	11.3	5	72⅛	72⅛	72⅛	+ ⅛
Citicp 9.09s98t	9.5	13	95½	95½	95½	...
Citicp 9.9s04t	10.4	80	95⅞	95⅜	95⅜	− 1⅛
Citicp 11⅞88	11.5	65	103¼	102⅞	102⅞	+ ⅜
CitSv 6⅛97	10.0	6	61⅜	61½	61½	...
CitSv 6⅝99	10.6	8	62⅜	62⅜	62⅜	+ ⅜
CitSvc zr85	...	79	97 25/32	97 25/32	97 25/32	− 9/32
CitSvc zr86	...	34	89⅞	89½	89½	− ½
CitSvc zr87	...	64	80¼	79¾	79¾	− ⅝
CitSvc zr88	...	70	71⅞	71½	71⅞	+ ¼
CitSvc zr89	...	54	64⅛	63¼	63¼	− 1
CtyInv 12¾87	12.1	15	105	105	105	− ⅛
ClevEl 9¼09	12.0	6	77	76⅜	77	+ ⅜
ClevEl 9.85s10	12.0	35	82⅜	82¼	82¼	− ½
ClevEl 8⅜12	11.8	8	71	71	71	...
Coleco 14⅜02	14.2	70	101⅜	101	101	− ¾
Dow 8⅝2000	10.8	10	82	82	82	+ ⅛
Dow 8.9s2000	10.9	4	82	82	82	− ½
Dow 8½s05	10.9	2	78	78	78	+ 1⅞
Dow 8½s06	11.1	5	76½	76½	76½	− ⅜
Dow 7⅞07	11.1	3	71	71	71	− ⅝
Dow 11¼10	11.7	32	96	95⅛	96	...
duPnt 8½06	10.8	20	79	79	79	+ 1⅛
duPnt d6s01	9.9	35	61	60½	60⅞	+ ⅛
duPnt 12⅞92	12.0	19	107¼	107¼	107¼	− 1¾
DukeP 7¾03	10.8	20	72	72	72	− 1¼
DukeP 10⅛09	11.4	10	88½	88½	88½	+ ¼
DuqL 8¾00	11.6	10	75¾	75¾	75¾	− 1¼
DuqL 9s06	11.9	9	75¾	75¾	75¾	− ⅛
DuqL 12¼10	12.3	5	99¼	99¼	99¼	− ⅜
E F G H						
EasAir 5s92	cv	28	62¾	62¾	62¾	...
EasAir 4⅞93	cv	5	60½	60½	60½	+ ½
EasAir 11½99	cv	441	96¼	95	95¼	− 1⅛
EasAir 11⅞05	cv	126	108¼	108¼	108¼	...
EasAir 17½97	15.7	4	112	111½	111½	− ¼
EasAir 17½98	15.7	5	111⅜	111⅜	111⅜	− 2⅜
EasAir 16⅛02	14.9	13	108¾	108	108	+ ¼
EKod 8¼07	cv	72	93¼	93	93¼	+ ¼
EKod 12¼15	11.6	10	105	105	105	− 2
Eaton 8½08	cv	20	106½	106¼	106¼	− 1¾
Ens 10s01	cv	66	100	99½	99½	− ½
Enstar 12⅝99	14.3	6	89	89	89	− 4
Equitc 10s04	cv	43	101½	101½	101½	...
Exxon 6s97	8.7	17	69¼	69	69¼	+ ⅜
Exxon 6½98	9.1	76	71⅜	71⅛	71⅜	+ ½
ExxP 9s04	10.7	3	84⅜	84⅜	84⅜	− ⅜
GMA 12s86	11.6	10	103½	103½	103½	+ ½
GMA 12⅜88	11.9	5	105¾	105¾	105¾	+ ⅜
GMA 10½89	10.4	35	100⅞	100⅞	100⅞	− ¼
GMA 9⅜88	9.8	5	100	100	100	− ⅝
GMA 10¼90	10.4	106	99½	99	99	− ¾
GTE 4s90	cv	92	89½	88	88	− 1
GTE 10⅛95	10.9	14	95	93⅛	93⅛	+ ⅛
GaPac 5¼96	cv	15	87¼	87¼	87¼	− ¾
GaPac 10.10s90	10.2	20	99	99	99	+ ¼
GaPw 8⅞00	11.3	1	78¾	78¾	78¾	+ 1¼
GaPw 7⅜01	10.8	10	68	68	68	− ½
GaPw 7⅝01	11.1	23	68¾	68¾	68¾	− ¼
GaPw 7½02J	11.1	10	67¾	67¾	67¾	...
GaPw 8⅝04	11.6	7	74⅛	74	74⅛	− ⅜
GaPw 11⅝00	11.8	18	98¼	97½	98¼	+ ¾
GaPw 11¾05	12.1	18	97	97	97	+ ¼
GaPw 10½09	12.1	11	87¼	87	87	+ ⅛
GaPw 16⅛11	14.7	32	109⅞	108¾	109⅞	+ ⅛
GaPw 16¼11	14.8	75	110	110	110	+ ⅛
GaPw 17½91	15.5	1	112¾	112¾	112¾	− ⅛
GaPw 16¼12	14.9	80	109⅜	109⅜	109⅜	− ⅛
GaPw 13⅛12	12.8	79	103¼	102⅞	102⅞	− ⅜
GaPw 16s14	13.9	9	115	114	115	...
Getty 14s00	13.7	57	102¾	102½	102½	...
GibFn 9¼08	cv	44	92½	91½	91½	− 1
GloMar 12⅞98f	...	40	35	34⅞	35	+ 1¼
GloMr d16s01f	...	165	35	34¼	34½	− ½
GloMar 16⅛02f	...	157	35½	34⅜	34¾	− ¼
GloMar d13s03f	cv	42	32½	32	32	− 1⅛
GdNgt d13½96	13.7	16	98⅞	98¼	98⅞	− ¼
GdNgF d8⅜93	10.7	24	78½	78	78½	+ 1⅜
Grace 4¼90	cv	2	89½	89½	89½	− ¼
GranC 4⅝94	cv	10	64½	64	64½	+ ½
GtNoN 9½13	cv	50	116	115	115	− ¾
GWstFn 8⅞07	cv	5	101	101	101	...
GreyF 9¼92	10.3	10	90⅛	90⅛	90⅛	− ⅜
GreyF zr94	...	3	35⅜	35⅜	35⅜	− 1⅜
Grolier 13s02	14.1	6	92	92	92	...
Grumn 9¼09	cv	26	109½	109	109½	− ½
GifWn 7s03A	11.3	15	63	61¾	61¾	− 1¼
GifWn 7s03B	11.2	1	62⅜	62⅜	62⅜	...
GulfMo 5s56f	8.2	1	61⅛	61⅛	61⅛	− 2⅜
GifRes 12½04	14.0	10	89	89	89	− ⅞
Hallb 16s88	15.0	55	107¼	106¾	106¾	− ¼
Hewn 11¼04	11.4	5	98¾	98¾	98¾	+ ⅜
Hellm 11⅝05	12.1	14	96⅛	95⅞	95⅞	− 1⅛
Hellm zr03	...	62	24¼	24¼	24¼	− ⅛
Hellr 10½86	10.4	1	101	101	101	+ 3/32
Hercul 6½99	cv	11	103⅛	103	103⅛	− ⅛

For space reasons the highs and lows sometimes are not included in the lists of the over-the-counter shares, nor by any means are all unlisted securities quoted. Remember that they constitute an army of thousands of companies, such a vast list that no complete count has ever been made. Only the bigger, more active, and sometimes controversial ones are listed.*

Figure 6-2 shows the over-the-counter market for Friday, May 17, 1985. Let's take a look at a well-known growth stock called AppleC—Apple Computer. That day it closed at a price of 21, up ¾—a good percentage gain.

Now for a look at the bond market quotations carried under the heading of New York Stock Exchange Bonds. Remember that the Big Board lists only relatively few of the leading bond issues; most of them are traded over-the-counter.

Looking down at the list in Figure 6-3 you will find AlldSt 10⅜90. AlldSt

*In some cases, brokers will quote a bid and ask price, especially for over-the-counter securities or securities in which the firm makes a market. Be sure you understand the range between the two quotes and ask what the commissions are. Sometimes the asking price includes the commission.

is Allied Stores Corporation, a large retail store chain that operates Bon Marché, Gertz, and Jordan Marsh, among others. Its sales run about $1.4 billion yearly. The "90" means the year 1990, the maturity date, the year in which the company has promised to pay off the bond—to pay you $1,000 for each bond, in other words. (Most bonds provide for some sort of redemption, unlike Elsie's perpetual bond.) Generally, if a company redeems a bond before the maturity date, the indenture calls for some few dollars of extra payment for the right of "calling" your bond. Allied Stores bond closed at 100 this day.

Remember that since bonds are traded in terms of 100 dollars but come in multiples of $1,000 and up, a quoted price of 94 actually means $940 for the face value $1,000 bond. Every time a bond declines a point in price it means a drop of $10; a $1\frac{1}{2}$ point decline means $15.

Once you become accustomed to reading the price quotations, study the footnotes because they give you helpful additional information. Note the other Allied Stores bond which closed at $113\frac{1}{2}$ is followed by the letters "cv." The notation "cv" after a bond indicates it can be converted into stock. It bears an interest rate of $8\frac{3}{4}$, which means that at a price of $113\frac{1}{2}$ it would pay only 7.7 percent to anyone who bought it at that level. Another important point to notice is the little letter X that often follows a stock. This means that the stock is trading "ex dividend"; in other words, buyers of the stock that day are not entitled to receive the next dividend, possibly because it is about to be mailed. (Usually dividends are declared well in advance of the day they are mailed out.) Sometimes when a stock goes "ex dividend" it will weaken in price, but don't be bothered about that. It's a technicality that has nothing to do with the underlying value of the stock.

How to Read a Company's Numbers

What is happening in the world influences our lives; in the same way what is happening in the stock market affects you as an investor. Still, the company or companies in which you are interested must stand on their own merit as investment prospects. This means that investors should follow closely the figures basic to a company they own or want to own. These basic figures are:

Sales. Most women care very much whether their families have high salaries. Yet, I think, both salaries and sales can be overemphasized. For example, the big supermarket chains have billions of dollars of sales *volume* each year, but they measure their *profits* in pennies—in very small percentages. So, too, the man down the street may be making a much larger salary than you do, but his expenses can take a much higher toll, so that perhaps his family doesn't eat as well as yours, travel as much, or even drive as fancy a car.

In other words, a company with $10 million in sales, growing fast, might be a more interesting investment than a company with $1 billion in sales.

Net income. This figure is most important for you as an investor. It's the amount left over for the common shareholders after all expenses, taxes, interest on bonds, or loans have been paid. In terms of the individual, net would be the money you could put in the bank for savings or use for fun or for self-improvement, like a college course.

You should examine your company's net income in relation to sales. Did sales grow and did net income increase at the same rate? Or did net income increase at a faster rate than sales, usually a good omen? Then a careful investor would study these relationships a step further: how do these figures compare with those of other companies in the same industry? Is your company doing as well as the others, or better?

Price of the stock. How much are you paying in relation to these earnings each year (the PE ratio again) and what kind of a dividend are you getting? If the company is a fast-growing one, it may be plowing back the earnings into new factories and paying a tiny cash dividend, or none at all; yet perhaps the price of the stock is growing at a good pace.

At this point turn to the writeup in Chapter 18 on the magic number 72. It will show you how to relate the return you are getting in your growth stock in terms of any slower-moving stock that pays higher dividends.

Reading a Financial Statement

Take a look at the earnings statement and the balance sheet of Maytag (Figure 6-4, pages 66–68), a relatively small but very profitable company. Maytag has long been noted for one product—washers—but in recent years it has diversified.

Just reading and analyzing financial statements is hardly enough for an investment decision. A prospective investor should also read what the company chairman and president say in the essay part of an annual report. Often their remarks can be revealing. They will comment on the year's results, either indicating satisfaction or explaining why profit and/or sales were not better. They may talk about industry trends, competitive products, labor relations, new developments, and sometimes even the state of the economy.

Meanwhile, your brokerage firm might provide you with its latest analysis of the company, in all probability based on much more expert judgment than you have. For example, the analyst might think that the management of the company was exaggerating its bright future, or possibly in some cases underestimating it. The president or chairman of a company is an individual and often his personality—hopeful, overconfident, cautious, or pessimistic—can come through in the annual writeup. Analysts know, or should know, the particular personality involved.

Because of the information available to him, the analyst has some convictions about the growth rate of the company, and this is vitally important to an investor. In a company that is doing well the current price can be high because the buyer of such a stock is in a sense purchasing tomorrow's earnings.

No analyst can guarantee a company's growth rate, but generally he will be able to make an informal prediction. This is his job essentially—the most important job he can do for you, I think, except provide information as to when you should sell a stock. (Here, I believe, many analysts fall down. They are good at forecasting growth, but are often too slow with sell recommendations.)

Even if he forecasts good future earnings for the company, you must realize this point: the stock's price may not necessarily rise in line with higher net.

Why not, you will ask quite logically. The answer has several facets:

1. Stock prices don't trend up with higher earnings if the stock market itself is in the doldrums, as it was during the reactions following speculative binges in 1962, in 1969, and in 1982–1983.

2. Stock prices might not move upward in line with better earnings if the government is trying to curb inflation, as it has been doing in the last few years. Pressures to halt inflation eventually lead to a company's cutting back on capital improvements, cutting costs, and perhaps losing some sales.

3. Stock prices might not follow earnings upward if the threat of war, civil disturbances, or increasing taxes discouraged investors in general.

4. Stock prices might not move upward if other forms of investment appeared more desirable. In the early 1980s, for example, some investors sold their shares and bought bonds for high yields and real estate as a hedge against inflation.

To summarize, even though an analyst tells you that SuperduperComp-Electronics might increase earnings 20 percent—and be correct in his estimate—the stock's price might not rise by that much if any one or more of the various reasons mentioned above were influencing the thinking of other investors. Remember that the law of supply and demand also rules the market.

Figure 6-4. Sample corporate balance sheet and earnings statement.

ASSETS	December 31 1984	1983
CURRENT ASSETS		
Cash	**$ 6,088,452**	$ 6,576,257
Short-term investments	**41,307,141**	59,144,053
Prepaid pension contribution	**2,500,000**	8,500,000
Accounts receivable, less allowance — $440,000	**47,038,095**	47,891,129
Inventories	**77,683,715**	75,647,997
Deferred federal taxes on income	**2,391,400**	
TOTAL CURRENT ASSETS	**177,008,803**	197,759,436
OTHER ASSETS		
Marketable securities	**15,239,945**	
Prepaid pension contribution	**21,000,000**	15,000,000
Miscellaneous	**4,817,458**	2,749,848
TOTAL OTHER ASSETS	**41,057,403**	17,749,848
PROPERTY, PLANT AND EQUIPMENT		
Land	**2,780,247**	2,596,921
Buildings and improvements	**64,246,744**	60,993,032
Machinery and equipment	**167,214,626**	153,343,151
	234,241,617	216,933,104
Less allowances for depreciation	**122,650,073**	110,342,355
	111,591,544	106,590,749
	$329,657,750	$322,100,033

LIABILITIES AND SHAREOWNERS' EQUITY	December 31 1984	1983
CURRENT LIABILITIES		
Accounts payable	**$ 16,333,385**	$ 20,133,238
Compensation to employees	**12,595,898**	11,546,750
Accrued liabilities	**15,955,585**	14,054,323
Federal and state taxes on income	**6,923,981**	7,896,455
Deferred federal taxes on income		1,772,000
TOTAL CURRENT LIABILITIES	**51,808,849**	55,402,766
DEFERRED FEDERAL TAXES ON INCOME	**24,713,500**	20,383,600
LONG-TERM DEBT	**24,270,834**	24,188,915
SHAREOWNERS' EQUITY		
Common stock (par value $2.50)		
Authorized — 20,000,000 shares		
Issued — 14,382,518 shares (including shares in treasury)	**35,956,295**	35,956,295
Additional paid-in capital	**21,336,836**	21,354,979
Retained earnings	**200,680,564**	178,410,681
	257,973,695	235,721,955
Less cost of shares of Common stock in treasury (1984 — 819,102 shares; 1983 — 489,304 shares)	**29,109,128**	13,597,203
	228,864,567	222,124,752
	$329,657,750	$322,100,033

Figure 6-4. Sample corporate balance sheet and earnings statement (continued).

FINANCIAL HIGHLIGHTS

	1984	1983
Net sales	**$642,560,925**	$596,987,738
Income before taxes	**116,640,557**	113,490,669
Taxes on income	**53,500,000**	52,800,000
Net income	**63,140,557**	60,690,669
Percent to net sales	**9.8%**	10.2%
Per share of Common stock	**$ 4.63**	$ 4.37
Dividends paid	**40,870,674**	37,488,589
Per share of Common stock	**3.00**	2.70
Salaries, wages, pensions and other employee benefits	**154,530,430**	151,316,785
Working capital	**125,199,954**	142,356,670
Ratio current assets to current liabilities	**3.42 to 1**	3.57 to 1
Property, plant and equipment less depreciation allowances	**$111,591,544**	$106,590,749
Total assets	**329,657,750**	322,100,033
Shareowners' equity	**228,864,567**	222,124,752
Per share of Common stock	**16.87**	15.99
Number of shareowners	**16,241**	15,386
Average number of employees	**4,847**	4,703

7

The Man (or Woman) in Your Investment Life

How Brokers Operate

We have seen many changes in our world in the last 20 years, and the world of finance is not unaffected. Today, a female broker, or analyst, or financial planner, is no oddity. Still, the truth is that the majority of brokers are men. Referring to a broker as "he" is in no way intended to ignore the achievements of the women, merely to reflect reality.

And, unfortunately, part of that same reality is that male brokers and female investors, like oil and water, have traditionally not mixed well, unless the women have made some extra effort. Let's face it: many brokerage firms basically don't like female customers—with a few wealthy and knowledgeable exceptions.

Yet the selection of a broker (or brokers) ranks as one of the most important investment decision you make. A good broker interested in your welfare can teach you as you go along, and his advice can make the difference between success and mediocre results in the stock market. The New York Stock Exchange likes to think that no broker working for one of its member firms could possibly guide you into failure, but even that has happened occasionally. And women unfortunately can be more gullible than men because they have less business experience.

Men Brokers and Women Customers

There are several reasons why male brokers tend to treat women customers charily and sometimes contemptuously. First, of course, is the fact that men have the opinion that women often are overemotional. No broker likes to visualize an indignant woman making a noisy scene in the firm's office, if her investments turn sour or mistakes are made in her account. Secondly, male brokers have the deeply ingrained feeling that most women just don't know anything about finance anyway, or care much.

There's another thought that makes them chary about women: it might be categorized as "sentimentality." For example, some years ago officials of Bache & Company (now called Prudential-Bache Securities) laughed ruefully about one of their vice presidents. He was sued by a woman customer who claimed that she gave him her investment account because he led her to believe that he had marriage in mind. Not only was she disappointed in love but she also charged that he had not fared well with her account. The moral is that thoughts of romance should be kept out of a brokerage office relationship. Lonely women should not look upon their brokers as a possible source of companionship or a listening post for their troubles.

Sad to say, there are many lonely women in the world. Many brokerage firms avoid having offices on the ground floor of buildings to discourage customers from dropping in for a social hour or two as they would to a club. Other firms deliberately limit the number of chairs available for board watching.

All brokers encourage customers to do their trading by telephone, and most of it is done in this way. Even so, brokers often claim that women on the telephone talk too much. Whether you like it or not, your broker is in business to make money and he depends for his livelihood on the volume of shares he handles. In some firms he receives a salary; in others he works on straight commission, but in either case what he earns annually is based on a percentage of the commissions received from the trades made for you and other customers. In good volume years popular brokers can earn $150,000 and more a year, making them sometimes more prosperous than the officers of the brokerage firm, who usually receive a straight salary plus bonus out of profits.* In lean years the broker's income can decline sharply. And a customer, male or female, who chats idly on the telephone can exasperate a busy broker. It prevents him from adequately servicing other customers to help him build up his commissions for the year. If you think about it, you would not want anyone to subject you to long conversations during the business day.

The woman who wants to make the most of her relationship with a broker should treat him or her in a businesslike fashion. You might ask when the best time is to call (1) to place actual orders and (2) to talk more generally about the market. Before telephoning, collect your ideas by jotting them down in orderly fashion on paper, including specific questions.

The fickle woman is another variety that brokers fear. She calls up or pays him a visit, and he advises her at some length about what to buy or sell. Then without giving him any straight answer of "Yes, buy it" or "No, I don't want to buy now," she says she will think it over. Or sometimes she says, "Go ahead," and then calls back a few minutes later and asks to change it. But by then the order has been placed, and she is out of luck—she has either bought or sold the stock in question. Remember that brokers—and the stock market—move fast; that's the nature of the business.

All this brings into focus another type of person that brokers find alarming—the reneger. In fact, the New York Stock Exchange made available to brokerage firms a blacklist of renegers and other unsavory types of customers.

Here's a reneger at work: A customer places an order for 100 shares of Ford at the market, meaning the price when the order reaches the floor of the exchange. Let's say the 100 shares are bought for her at $45 a share. Then the next morning the woman reads in the paper that the stock has dropped quite sharply to 42. She tells her broker when the confirmation statement arrives that he misunderstood her, that she definitely remembers she put the order in at 42, not at the market. She probably tries the sweet approach first: her memory was good that day and she knows he must have been very busy and confused her order with another.

If she becomes insistent the broker, to get her out of his hair—perhaps forever—might settle the issue on her terms and then close her account or ask her to use another registered representative in the firm. He probably makes sure that the word goes around that she is a reneger.

*Although exact earnings aren't usually public information, it was disclosed during the 1985 trial of Paul Thayer for passing inside information to his broker that the broker earned $700,000 a year. (Both men received jail sentences. Mr. Thayer passed along the information he received as a director or officer of various corporations and lied about his action, while the broker profited by urging clients to buy shares on the basis of the inside information.)

Knowing that male brokers may look somewhat askance at you, you may prefer working with a female broker. Or you may decide that, thus forewarned, you can work well with anyone. In either case, as a new investor you'll have to do a little selling of yourself to this polite but busy professional.

Getting Acquainted

First, before you approach a brokerage firm to open an account, think about your finances. If you have made out an income statement and a balance sheet as urged in Chapter 4, you will have a good idea of what you can invest. You will be able to answer quickly, without embarrassment, some of the basic questions that the broker will ask.

If you live in a small city and are well known, the broker perhaps will know you by name and income level. Possibly he will know something about your husband and his job, or about your family. Your name might have been on his (or his firm's) mailing list. No doubt he will ask for credit references, such as your local bank.

He will want to ask you about your income status, and possibly whether your family carries adequate life insurance coverage and has some savings in the bank (at least one month's family income after taxes is a good rule of thumb for savings). He will want to know what investments, if any, you already have. The key question, of course, is how much you want to invest at the moment you contact him, or in the future. Some women have a small sum to invest immediately; others count on regular amounts coming in at intervals, perhaps quarterly or once a year.

While his questions may appear to be prying, don't bridle at them. He can advise best if he knows your financial status and aims. The aims are very important.

Recently a leading brokerage firm ran an advertisement that showed a large butterfly. Under it the caption read:

Extinct Species
The no-risk, high-dividend, fast-growth stock

A naive woman investor could be expected to say to her broker something along these lines: "Now I can't take any risk, but I want a high dividend and I must have a quick increase in price—growth, you know."

If there were such an investment "butterfly" you can be sure that investors with much faster nets than yours would have captured it already. Such a statement by anyone indicates he or she knows next to nothing about the stock market.

No risk? There is *always* risk; stock prices rise and fall like a kite, wafted by winds of change in corporate fortunes, in political and economic conditions. What so many women don't understand is that a good stock like General Motors, for example, can drop in price even when car sales do well, as economic or political factors affect the market.

Furthermore, generally speaking, stocks that pay high dividends are not growth issues. They may be very fine stocks for investments, but the fact that they pay high dividends in relation to price indicates that investors are not buying them for growth. This, too, is a fact that many women find hard to understand. For example, they reason that if AT&T pays a good solid dividend without fail, isn't it a growth stock too?

For years after World War II, AT&T was anything but a growth stock. It was the conservative investor's friend: a solid utility offering a basic service to a growing population.

Then came the public's fascination with space age electronics. In the 1950s a few brokerage firms such as David J. Greene & Company "discovered" AT&T. These brokers figured—and rightly so—that AT&T's research and development arm, Bell Laboratories, and its equipment maker, Western Electric, were deep in the exciting new technologies. Thus AT&T, a sound utility company, suddenly switched from being called old Ma Bell into a glamorous go-go girl for a time.

The price of the share rose sharply in relation to dividends because of this new look as a growth stock. The widow who owned AT&T at a price of around $28 a share where it lingered in the early 1950s suddenly found herself with a stock that rose to $40 in 1959, to $70 in 1961, to $75 in 1964, and fell to around the $50 level in 1969. (These figures are adjusted for some stock splits.)

The decline in the years since 1965 came after investment analysts decided that AT&T had lost some of its appeal. One reason was that the government began to threaten antitrust action and also began to give the company trouble about the rate increases. In 1969 the shares were back to a level where they paid high dividends in relation to price, and hence once more were the widow's friend, and not a growth stock with dramatic implications.

In the 1980s the situation has changed again. In 1984, AT&T had to divest its seven regional operating companies according to an antitrust decision. Today it no longer is a stock for widows and orphans but a quasi-growth stock.

The point to remember is that fast-growth stocks usually do not pay high dividends for the simple reason that shrewd investors have found them before their growth potential was widely realized, bought them in quantity, and thus forced the price up, well beyond the point of a favorable yield. Their hope is that earnings will grow fast over a year or so justifying not only today's high price but also higher prices later.

IBM is a prime example of a growth stock that sometimes pays as little as a 2 percent cash dividend return each year, plus an occasional dividend paid in stock. No investor would buy IBM for a high dividend yield the way widows bought AT&T in the early 1950s. The advocates of IBM buy because they have faith that the stock price will rise as earnings increase. So far, IBM has justified their faith in most years.

Therefore before you approach a broker you should know your investment objective. You cannot have high dividends, no risk of price downturns, and assured fast growth in the same stock. You should consider the following three points:

1. Do you want to protect your principal and receive a specific income each year? Then you may want bonds with fixed interest; or you might want to try stocks relatively high dividends with a little expected growth to serve as a sweetener.

2. Can you afford to take more risk and receive low or virtually no cash dividends in exchange for the chances that the price of the shares will increase? Of course this will also mean a capital gains tax (see Chapter 16). Your broker may, quite properly, ask about your tax bracket.

3. Perhaps you need a combination of the two investment approaches, mixed to suit your taste like a good martini. Your broker might suggest some pivotal shares paying satisfactory dividends, and then some fast-growth stocks to help achieve an increase in your total capital that will help combat inflation.

So much for the amount you can invest and your aims. The broker will be sizing you up in other ways: by age range, marital status, and whether you are a homemaker or a career woman, by your psychology (are you prepared to take risks or conservative? are you the nervous, jumpy type?), and by your investment know-how (do you have ideas of your own and pick your stocks yourself, or will you rely on the broker, your friends, or others?).

Such factors—or judgments, since they are based on educated guesses—will enter your broker's estimate of you as a customer and color his ideas about the stocks he might suggest. His suggestions may not turn out to be the investment that you think you should own. Perhaps you have more experience, knowledge of the market, and determination than he credits you with. If so, assert yourself.

These are matters you should think out before you approach a brokerage firm. In fact, it's a good idea to write down your ideas or questions before you sit down at a broker's desk.

What will your broker be like, apart from the obvious physical makeup?

Naturally brokers come in all shapes and sizes, all ages from about 25 up through about 65 when most of them retire. Some are happily married; some divorced. Brokers can be humorous or earnest types, forceful in personality or pleasantly shy. Probably brokers dress quite well, even in the small-town offices. The managers do demand presentable appearances from employees who deal directly with the public, although these days most contact with customers after initial meetings occurs over the telephone.

These days the broker probably has a college education and perhaps has taken some graduate courses. Oddly enough, he or she may also have an unusual working background. People from many different professions switch to the brokerage business, either because they become bored with their jobs or because they believe there is more money to be made in the investment field. The ranks of some recent brokerage firm training programs include former college professors, actors, publishers, engineers, accountants, clergymen, retired army and navy officers, reporters, and business people who had their own firms. What lures them? The fascination of investments and the chance to make a larger income, plus the fact that as brokers they feel that in a sense they work for themselves.

Depending on the firm, a broker can be called a registered representative, an account executive, a customer's man, or some other appellation. To the New York Stock Exchange a broker is a "registered representative," a title the exchange likes because it indicates that the broker has been "signed up," so to speak. It means that he or she has gone through a formal training program given either by the brokerage firm or by an educational organization, has taken formal exams after the training to prove knowledge both of New York and American Stock Exchange regulations, and has acquired some general knowledge and experience. The broker also must take exams indicating knowledge of over-the-counter transactions, under the jurisdiction of the NASD (National Association of Securities Dealers).

The fact that the broker is a registered representative does not mean that he can prevent you from losing money, or even put you into stocks guaranteed to perform the way you expect, especially if you have very elaborate aims such as doubling your money every time you buy a stock. What your broker can do is point you in the right direction in accordance with your investment aims. Remember that he is not necessarily a keen judge of the market, a student of economics, or a creative thinker. To be a really outstanding broker he should combine these qualities with the ability to analyze a particular company. I am sorry to tell you that brokers with such ability are rare, so rare that one of my favorite brokers once said to me: "I know most of the leading brokers in New York, and I can count on the fingers of my two hands the number I think are superior." (Because he is a modest man, in naming them he did not include himself.)

Choosing a Good Broker (or Two)

All this makes it important for you to select your broker carefully, not on his looks, the cut of his suit, his golfing ability, or his friends. It also is another reason why you should learn as much as possible about investments yourself.

If it is so hard to find an exemplary broker, how do you pick one? You should try to select a broker who will fit your ideas comfortably. Naturally you want someone who is pleasant to you, is helpful, and doesn't growl with impatience if you ask questions. You know that some people appeal to you immediately because of their spontaneous enthusiasm about their job and their willingness to be helpful.

You want someone trustworthy and reliable. Most member firms of the NYSE employ only trustworthy individuals as account executives (barring a small percentage of sour lemons or bad apples), and generally you should deal only with a member firm on the New York Stock Exchange. This does provide you with some safety measure, for the exchange has a fund to insure against any losses to customers through the failure or financial embarrassment of a member firm. Also, the exchange regulates its member firms (surprise audits, rules about capital needed, etc.), and when you have a complaint it investigates thoroughly. It also provides for arbitration—an inexpensive way for disputes to be handled by impartial judges without the need for lawyers (see Chapter 18). Member firms must arbitrate a dispute with a customer if the customer chooses, and the decision is legally binding in most instances. The American Stock Exchange also provides for arbitration.

Almost every broker would be vitally interested in a wealthy widow who could invest $1 million, but you want a broker who will show interest in you as a small or novice investor (or both). Many of the big brokerage firms are well geared to handle the small investor; more so than smaller firms who make their money out of a few large accounts. Thus you may fare better with a big firm. All brokers hope that little investors will become big investors because their welfare lies in commissions; and after all, in a few years you might well inherit, receive as a gift, or earn more than the small amount you have to invest at the moment. If your broker does do a good job for you over the years but you yourself cannot bring in a big sum for him to handle, you can always recommend your wealthy friends to become his customers.

Beware of a broker who "churns"—persuades you to buy and sell often; you don't make much money and yet the rapid turnover of stocks in your portfolio brings him big commissions. This is unethical, and as you gain experience you can sense if a broker is advising you to trade too often. Generally the new investor doesn't have to worry about this because she plans to keep her shares for a while, at least for the six months' capital gains period.

You want a broker whose firm has the reputation of turning out good research so that he can provide you with sound material on stocks. Check the highest-rated research firms in *Institutional Investor,* a magazine usually available in public libraries. Generally a broker can be no more effective than the research his firm turns out, for a very simple reason. He has so many customers that he cannot spend much time doing research himself, beyond listening to rumors, reading his firm's research material, and keeping up with what's happening on the ticker and the news service. Good research by a brokerage firm is important to the small, inexperienced investor because she cannot afford or cope with the expensive advisory services available to big investors who can pay fancy fees.

If you are a new investor you probably want advice on specific stocks, on market techniques, as well as on proper timing. You need a little fathering, but that doesn't mean your broker should be an older man. Often very young brokers building up their customer lists can give you more of the type of help you need than an older man who has plenty of wealthy accounts to keep him busy. A broker who is a little hungry for business might be your best bet.

As we pointed out earlier, one of the worst mistakes a new investor can make is to buy the best stock at the wrong time. In other words the smart investor doesn't rush to buy a stock as it hits its record high price. I think this is the biggest mistake that small, unsophisticated investors make—the jump on the bandwagon psychology. If your broker tells you that a good stock like AT&T or Du Pont is too high priced to buy, listen to him. If you insist he might weakly shrug his shoulders and let you buy it without further argument, on the theory that it is a good all-round, all-time stock; but you are making a mistake. A superior broker would give you a good dispute on the point.

Let's take a fine growth stock like IBM as an example. IBM could have been bought at a price of 70 in 1960. It dropped from 150 to 78 in the trough of the 1962 stock market decline—the so-called Kennedy market break (see Chapter 3), obviously a good time to buy it. Then it rose again to reach a new historic high of 375 in 1968: not a good time to buy, since in 1970 it dropped to as low as 218. In 1972, it sold at around 384. A few years ago the shares were split four for one, and today each share sells around 150, indicating a good increase above its presplit price.

Thus in a short space of time good stocks can swing widely in price. The company is the same; its earnings probably (as in the case of IBM) continue to be good. An effective broker would keep you from buying IBM shares at their high point. Yield to his experience. He has a feel for the market, based on experience, which (at the beginning at least) you probably do not.

What about women brokers? The New York Stock Exchange reports that its member firms have 69,960 registered representatives, but doesn't know how many are women; nor does any other organization, apparently. Merrill Lynch, the nation's biggest brokerage firm, has kept tabs of its own, however. In January 1985, it had 11,000 account executives (its name for brokers or registered representatives), and 15.4 percent were women. By these measurements the investment world still is very much a man's domain. However, don't overlook the possibility of having a woman broker. To compete in the business and keep her job a woman broker usually has to be more adept, I think, than the average male broker.

It has long been my contention that the wise woman investor starting out should use *two* brokers. After all, advice from two sources can be better, or at least more educational, than from one. Naturally you should not mention the fact that you have two brokers to anyone because, quite frankly, brokers don't like the idea. But they need never know if you handle the matter with discretion. If your friends ask who your broker is, turn on an enigmatic, Mona Lisa smile.

Suppose you are undecided about investing in a certain stock. You can ask the question of each broker. If both consider the investment wise, then you have the advantage of a double green light, which could mean you are on the right road. If one reacts strongly against such a stock, then the caution light goes on. You should slow down and think before making a move. Which broker is right? Situations like this can happen more often than you think. It wakes the investor up to the fact that investment judgments vary widely, an eye-opener for the novice.

If you remember that the stock market is an auction place where there usually is a buyer for every seller—at a price—you realize that differences of opinion make a market, and win or lose fortunes. It makes investment life that much more interesting. Often you will learn that one mutual fund, supposedly run by experts, is buying a large block of a certain stock, while at the same time another respected mutual fund is selling shares of the same stock. Or two brokerage firms can come out at the same time with diametrically opposite suggestions. For example, number one broker might suggest General Motors, while broker number two says, "Too high," and shows you a chart like the one in Figure 7-1. Then he suggests another company whose stock has not risen so high.

Which do you buy? If you have been a customer of the two brokers for a while, you probably have come to a conclusion about which one performs more efficiently and which one has ideas most suitable to your own.

Also, you can check Standard & Poor's stock comments, usually available at a public library. (Note the S&P writeup on Avon Products in Figure 7-2.) S&P is a leading statistical and research firm whose data are used by most brokers.

Be alert. Develop your own approach to the market. Be creative—and keep changing trends in mind. Let me give you an example. Some years ago Avon Products was considered a good growth stock and a fine buy. Remember it was

Figure 7-1. General Motors' stock action.

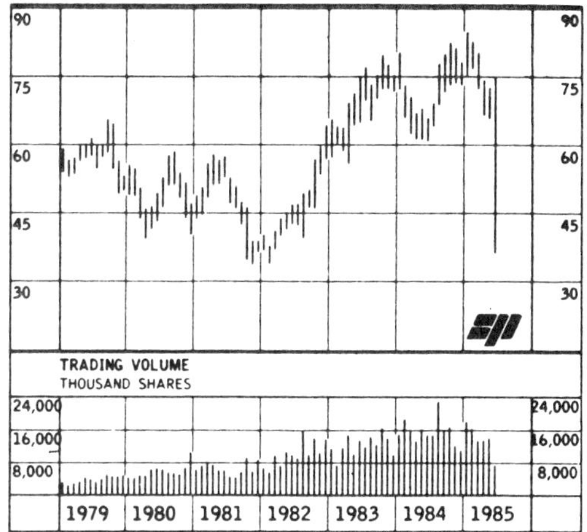

Standard & Poor's Corp.

a door-to-door marketer of cosmetics and jewelry at a time when many women were housewives and stayed home. Today the situation has changed because so many more women are working, away from home during the day, and not buying from home marketers as much as they once did. See Figure 7-2. Note the long decline in price.

One of my friends uses one broker because the firm publishes such fine research material. "As far as I'm concerned," she says, "the broker is only a glorified order taker." She has a second broker who occasionally provides her with interesting, creative ideas for growth-type investments. With two very different brokers she has been successful in her investing. Be like this woman and don't expect too much from your broker, especially at the beginning of your relationship.

There is another good reason to have two brokers—efficiency. Unfortunately most brokerage firms did not computerize early enough to prepare them for the spiraling pace of business, which has led to inefficient operations. Furthermore, the heavy load of clerical work traditionally was relegated to "back office employees" not equipped to do the job. For years brokerage firms hired young and often unmotivated girls and boys right out of high school for the low-paid, dull clerical jobs. Their bright young people were channeled into jobs as registered representatives or as analysts where they could put their college education and personalities and ambition to work for the firm. This situation caught up with many brokerage firms: now they are vying for good back office help and paying much higher salaries, as well as working such employees over-

Figure 7-2. Standard & Poor's chart and writeup on Avon Products.

Avon Products

NYSE Symbol AVP Options on CBOE (Jan-Apr-Jul-Oct)

Price	Range	P-E Ratio	Dividend	Yield	S&P Ranking
Jun. 14'85	1985				
19	23 3/8-17 7/8	9	[2]2.00	[2]10.5%	B+

Summary

This leading door-to-door marketer of cosmetics, fragrances, and fashion jewelry also has interests health care products, mail order and specialty chemicals. In 1984 Avon acquired Foster Medical, a home health care firm, and sold its Tiffany & Co. unit. Earnings in recent years have been hurt by weakness in the direct selling industry and adverse foreign exchange.

Current Outlook

Earnings for 1985 are estimated at about $2.20 a share, up from 1984's $2.16.

Maintenance of dividends at the current $0.50 quarterly rate cannot be completely assured.

Sales for 1985 may be hard pressed to surpass the $3.1 billion of 1984. Although sales of medical products and direct mail operations should be higher, sales of beauty products are likely to remain under pressure from overall weakness in direct selling markets and a reduced sales force. While persisting soft beauty volume will be restrictive, results over the second half should benefit from efforts to improve productivity and higher profits in nonbeauty units. Share earnings should be aided by fewer average shares outstanding.

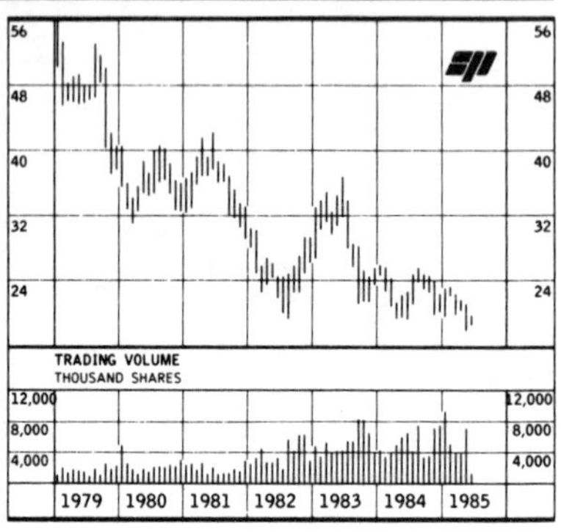

Standard & Poor's Corp.

time when necessary to catch up with the flood of paperwork. In recent years computerization and streamlined techniques have tended to eliminate these headaches. If you use two brokers you might find one more efficient than the other.

Working Well Together

You can help your broker and get better service by learning the ropes—a trite way of saying you should know some of the lingo of investing and the technicalities. Here are some of the basics to remember.

Discretionary accounts. Some of your friends may tell you that they have turned over their money to a broker, Mr. So-and-So, and he has done *so* well with it. He doesn't let them know what he does but just sends them a monthly statement showing the status of the account. It's *so* convenient! Stop right there. What they have is a discretionary account. Don't ever turn your money over to the discretion of a broker. The only possible exception is when you are going to be away for a few months; you could leave written instructions that he could buy and sell certain stocks at his discretion if they are in a certain price range.

Most brokerage firms do not permit their registered representative to handle discretionary accounts except for close members of their family or with special permission. Furthermore, a reliable broker would require you to sign a letter excusing the firm of any responsibilities if he exercises discretion.

In other words, you can take your broker's advice but you must make the decision on a particular investment, since you must accept the final responsibility in any event.

Margin accounts. Buying on margin means buying on credit. The amount of credit a brokerage firm can extend depends mostly on the Federal Reserve system, which sets the margin rate. For some years the margin rate has been 50 percent.

When speculation is rampant, as it was during the early part of 1968, the rate is inclined to be high, perhaps 80 percent. That means you must put up 80 percent of the price of a stock you buy, and the brokerage firm can lend you 20 percent. However, if the price of the stock goes down the broker can call upon you to put up more cash or more securities to back your account. If you do not put up such cash quickly he can sell out your shares and recover the full amount he advanced you, and you have little recourse.

Some firms traditionally require somewhat higher margin rates than those set by the Federal Reserve. Many brokerage firms used to refuse women the right to have a margin account, but that is no longer true. However, you might find that you have to be a good customer of a firm before it will let you open a margin account.

One interesting sidelight is that by means of a margin account an individual can usually borrow money at lower rates of interest because shares act as collateral. The interest rate charged on the account is a few percentage points over the amount the broker pays for his borrowings. Since brokerage firms are large borrowers they get favorable rates.

Types of orders. Your broker probably will ask you what type of order you want when you buy or sell shares, or he may assume that you know the differences. A *market order* means that you want to buy or sell at whatever price is going when your order reaches the floor of the exchange. A *day order* states a specific price to buy or sell, and must be exercised that day, if possible at the stated price or better. It expires at the end of the day; you must contact your broker again if you want to renew the order. And an *open* or *GTC order* carries a specific price at which you want to buy or sell the stock but remains open until canceled (GTC: good till canceled). Usually even a GTC order expires after about six months and then you must renew it if you still wish to buy or sell the shares.

A *stop order* is a useful tool for every investor. Suppose you own a stock and you have decided to sell if it falls a certain number of points; you can order your broker to put a stop order in at that lower price. Suppose you have bought a stock at 50 and in a short time it has risen to 55. You have made a 10 percent gain and you want to protect it. You can tell your broker to sell any time the price drops to, say, 54. Suppose the stock fails to rise further and suddenly drops to 52. On the way down your stop order automatically becomes a market order and is exercised. Often it will sell you out at the hoped-for price of 54, but if the market happens to fall very swiftly and there are other stop orders dated ahead of yours at around 54, your order could be exercised a little lower in price, a disappointment naturally.

Still, the use of a stop order gives an investor a measure of protection against the serious losses and often helps get her out of the market with some profit. As a stock price rises, many wise investors place stop orders a few points below the current market price. As the stock continues moving upward in price they raise the price on the stop order, thus giving them protection.

Other Business Procedures

Your broker will ask you whether you want the stock registered or not. By all means, because of the bookkeeping difficulties these days, ask that the stock be registered in your name. If the shares are registered in your name the company will mail dividends, interim reports, annual reports, and proxy statements directly to your home—all important to keep you alert about your company's progress.

Usually only sophisticated stock traders who buy and sell constantly for quick profits leave their shares with the broker registered in the so-called street names. This means that they are held by the broker in the name of the firm, though credited to the customer's account. The dividends are paid directly to the brokerage firm, which then credits them to the stockholder's account or mails the customer a check. Registration in the street name also means the customer may not receive all the written material the company issues.

Your broker will also ask whether you want the firm to keep the shares or whether you want them delivered to your home. It is much better to leave the registered shares in the custody of your broker. It makes it easier to sell them. Also, unless you have an unusually safe place, like a metal safe or a nearby safe deposit box, keeping stock certificates can be worrisome. (If you are not convinced read in Chapter 18 about the expensive and time-consuming procedure if you lose stock certificates.) And even though the broker holds the physical certificates, all mailings from your company will come to you as the registered owner.

Be sure to keep the statements that you receive each month from the brokerage firm, showing the price at which you bought or sold shares, and the names of the shares, and so on. You will need such statements for tax reasons. Also you should make sure they are correct, so check them carefully each month.

You must also learn the dividend dates for your shares and keep track, checking them off as they are received. Otherwise you might miss some payments, especially these days when the U.S. mail has become so tardy and inefficient. Some dividends arrive in envelopes with windows looking like bills, so don't throw them away by mistake.

The last and perhaps most timely hint for creating good relations with your broker: abide by the five-day rule. He will undoubtedly explain this to you when you place your first order because of its importance to his welfare—and his nervous system.

The rule is that you must pay by check or cash for stock within five business days after the date of purchase. Leeway is permitted for weekends. The five-day rule works like this:

Date of Purchase	*Payment Date*
Monday	Following Monday
Tuesday	Following Tuesday
Wednesday	Following Wednesday
Thursday	Following Thursday
Friday	Following Friday

In other words, you can forget about the weekends since they are not business days. Probably the day you place an order, if it bears a price at or near the market level, the trade of your stock will be consummated—either bought or sold. Your brokerage firm will put a confirmation statement into the mail that day; it should reach you the following morning or a day later. Still, the five-day rule applies no matter how fast or slow Uncle Sam's mail delivery is. So you have to do your own counting.

If you fail to pay by the required time, the broker will telephone you in annoyance. If you continue to be tardy he can sell the shares without letting you know—not a happy situation. Don't try to wheedle extra days from him because it can spoil an otherwise pleasant relationship, get him into trouble with his firm, and even result in your having to pay interest for the late arrival of your money, or losing the stock. He could decline to continue handling your account. Make sure your check arrives by the required date, or take the money in person, which is what I often do. And if you are selling shares and you have them at home registered in your name, you will have to take them to your broker within the five-day limit.

The subject of new corporate stock issues has caused many of the recent difficulties for brokers and bad relations with customers. Many new investors open brokerage accounts with the starry-eyed hope of participating in new issues, the hot-shot stocks they have heard their friends discuss. Don't be fooled. Most new issues are put out by small companies. Let's say Super Atomic Electronics offers 1,000,000 shares of stock at $10 each through a group of 50 leading brokerage firms. Suppose that each brokerage firm agrees to sell 20,000 shares of the stock. A big brokerage house has perhaps 100,000 customers; a moderate-sized one has 50,000 or less. If the 50 firms average 50,000 customers, then they could provide each investor on their lists with only $\frac{2}{5}$ of a share of the new "hot" issue.

Do you get the point? New issues are usually so small that even big brokerage firms have only a few thousand shares to allot among their customers. Therefore they will give their old and large customers the first chance at the new issue. You can be sure that if it is a good issue and if you are a small, new investor you will not be given the chance to buy a single share at the offering day price. Knowing this, you won't be disappointed or angry if your broker shakes his head when you ask. It is not his fault that you cannot buy Super Atomic Electronics at the offering price of $10, even though you might see it rise to $25 in a day or a week.

8

Analysts without Couches

How They Pick Stocks

Behind nearly every excellent broker there are efficient stock market analysts. Good brokers are so busy contacting their customers, watching the market, and making investment decisions that they don't have time to do much basic analysis themselves. Thus they depend largely upon the research departments of their firms. If the firm is too small to have an adequate research department, then a broker can use other investment advisory services for a fee.

Investment analysis has changed greatly over the last fifty years, so much so that the analyst today is quite a different breed from his counterparts before World War II. In fact, today's analyst may well be a woman.

Back in the 1930s, many investors lost a great deal of money, partly because of the Depression, but partly too because companies in those days did not have to provide their shareholders with much information. There were a few leading brokers in favor of tighter governmental reins on securities after the 1929 debacle. One of them, the late Charles E. Merrill, founder of today's largest brokerage firm, Merrill Lynch, Pierce, Fenner & Smith, put into practice several ideas to protect the small investor and help Wall Street regain some of the respect it had lost because of the crash in 1929.

One of his ideas, carrying out the firm's slogan "investigate before you invest," was that a brokerage firm should build up a good research department and offer its services free of charge to small and large investors. Out of this research, of course, should come a large amount of published material, brochures on investing, analysis of various industries and companies, periodical writeups of individual companies. Merrill even launched a magazine for investors called *Investor's Reader,* now defunct.

He also believed that analysts should go through a training program along with young brokers. His firm was among the first to have a formalized training program for young people, usually right out of college or the armed forces, who were interested in making the securities business their profession. The trainees were rotated among departments to get the feel of the business; they attended lectures given by partners of the firm and outsiders; they took a course in public speaking to teach them to think on their feet and develop poise to meet the public; they also passed an exam approved by the New York Stock Exchange. They were encouraged to study outside: to take graduate courses at local universities, for instance, for which the firm would pay the tuition. In other words, the emphasis suddenly became education.

Other large firms took the cue. Those that at first couldn't afford such training programs often hired graduates of Merrill Lynch's program by offering them higher salaries or commissions.

Today, analysts usually go through such a training program. However, I remember as recently as the mid-1950s talking to a partner of a well-known brokerage firm that might be described as medium sized, with a few branches outside New York. The partner told me that only one man in the firm devoted himself to research, and only part time at that, because the analyst was allowed to have some customer accounts.

Handling accounts with one hand and doing research with the other could hardly result in much analysis. Unfortunately, Wall Street brokers until very recently focused much more attention on where the money is—in the hands of investors who can be induced to trade—than on research to help ensure good investments.

The point of this statement, and of the open cynicism it reflects, is that a new investor must make sure that the firm she deals with has a good research department or uses good outside services. Such information can be found by asking business leaders in your community, quizzing the local banker about various brokerage firms, judging for yourself.

The investment industry has taken a big step toward more professional research with the launching some years ago of a program that leads to a degree for analysts called Chartered Financial Analyst (CFA). This move was launched, many years after the death of Mr. Merrill, because some leading analysts thought that the profession needed more prestige and a little more formality. Without a doubt, an analyst with the CFA degree can command a higher salary than one without it. Furthermore it separates the very young analysts, still uneasy with their computers, from the experienced.

The training for the CFA calls for intensive study and the taking of three exams in a period of three or more years. Study doesn't necessarily make a great or even good analyst; there's a little more to it than that, such as creativity and imagination. But if your brokerage firm's analyses are issued by some analysts with CFA after their names, you can be sure that at least they have gone through about the best training that Wall Street offers at present.

The Research Department

The usual big brokerage firm's research department might consist of a large room filled with analysts—perhaps a dozen seniors assisted by another dozen trainees or assistants, plus an assortment of staff: a librarian (who perhaps has some assistants); one or two statisticians who keep charts and work on market averages; an economist who concentrates on general trends (political, economic, world); perhaps some portfolio planners who answer inquiries from the public and analyze individuals' stockholdings; and often a writer or two, attached to the department to edit and improve the abundant publications issued by the analysts. The department probably is headed by a senior partner (or vice president of the firm), assisted by several experienced analysts who also hold titles in the firm. They are the heirs apparent of the top job in the department.

Each analyst is assigned a particular area. Generally, brokerage firms break down the nation's businesses into some major groupings—transportation, public utilities, financial companies (such as banks, investment firms, finance companies, insurance companies) and industrials. One analyst, aided by an assistant, might cover the railroad business. On a comparable level, and probably sitting nearby, would be another analyst assigned to cover other forms of transportation such as airlines, trucks, buses.

At one time the three transportation areas—railroads, airlines, and trucks—might have come under the aegis of one analyst—a busy person. Today the importance of airlines and trucks has grown tremendously in relation to railroads, and the legal, political, and economic factors governing their investment merit have become much more complicated than twenty years ago. At the same time railroads have been undergoing many changes, too. Some have withdrawn almost entirely from the passenger business, generally a losing proposition. Railroads know how to carry cattle profitably and even without making them change trains, but they cannot make money from human cargo in most cases. Some have been forced by states to continue operating commuter trains despite their claims of heavy losses. Mergers have strengthened some railroads. Others have improved their finances by changing into conglomerates like Southern Pacific, which operates a railroad and has some unusual sidelines like oil and real estate ventures. Conrail, as a result of mergers, government financing, and better management, now makes money. It will soon be sold by the government, probably to a railroad.

In other words, railroad stocks these days have become much more like industrial stocks, giving them an entirely new investment look, not to mention the difficulty in analyzing them.

The second major grouping consists of public utilities. They have not changed as much as the railroads; they have not tended to diversify but have stuck pretty much to their own fields, serving consumers with basics like electricity, telephone, gas, and water. Those providing power from nuclear energy have been under attack by consumer groups, and many have been forced to close plants. In the typical brokerage firm a senior analyst would devote himself to utilities, including space-minded AT&T, which does have some elements of a two-headed company—a public utility in one aspect, a scientific instrument company on the other.*

In the third group there are the financially oriented companies, which would also come under the eye of a senior analyst, perhaps with some assistants. These include a wide variety of companies like commercial banks, insurance companies, small loan companies, commercial loan companies, credit unions, pension funds, savings and loan companies—all money oriented. Such companies, including mutual funds, are important in many ways to a brokerage firm. Some offer investment opportunities for the firm's individual customers; all continually make investments themselves; some borrow in the money markets.

By far the largest and most disparate group falls into the all-embracing category of "industrials." These can range from a relatively new company like Kentucky Fried Chicken to General Motors, with $52 billion in assets and 316,482,000 common shares worth $52 billion in 1985.

Twenty years ago it was relatively simple to break down the industrials into subcategories that could be handled by an analyst. For example, one person might be assigned to the automotive companies, such as GM, Ford, and Chrysler, and the many auto equipment-makers ranging from companies who make auto springs, to safety glass, to tires. Another analyst might handle the steel companies—the half-dozen major ones led by U.S. Steel and the more numerous specialized ones—besides the other metal producers like Anaconda and Asarco.

A young analyst might cover the vagaries of cyclical industrial groupings

*Before divestment in 1984 AT&T was ranked the world's largest company in terms of assets because of its heavy investments in power plants, communications equipment, etc. Today Exxon holds the spot as the largest industrial company.

such as the machine and machine tool industry. One of the largest is Cincinnati Milacron, maker of robots as well as machine tools. The sale of machine tools often indicates economic trends since these companies receive the orders months in advance to build machinery for new products, handle new processes, or replace old equipment with more efficient inventions.

Entertainment companies would be another category. Rising interest in them in the past few years indicates that consumers have more leisure and more money to spend than some years ago. Broadcasting companies, moviemakers, and publishers are included in this group. In 1985 we watched a classic battle for control of CBS.

Tobacco and food companies constitute another very important part of any research department coverage, along with department stores, construction companies, etc.

Generally, when a young analyst is assigned to the investment research department he doesn't have a choice but is placed in an available slot. However, later he probably moves to other groups to widen his experience before he takes a final assignment. Often as he progresses in a department he will become restless and look around for a higher-paid or more responsible job elsewhere. There is quite a bit of movement among analysts, who go from firm to firm until they obtain coveted status as senior analysts, or later a chance to head a department as a partner or vice president. As a department head an analyst probably earns well over $100,000 yearly depending on the size of the firm and his share in the profits. The pay is good, though not as good as the commissions a broker can make in an active market.

This, then, is how the research department of your broker's firm works. It is a stimulating place, constantly changing to keep pace with business evolution; it makes for an atmosphere that encourages study and professional growth.

The Analyst's Information Sources

What are some of the tools the analyst uses? First, like you, he reads the annual reports of companies, but many more than you do, since he takes responsibility for a large group in his particular field of specialization. He also has available to him the regular reports published by Standard & Poor's—yellow sheets, they are called—keeping facts about every company updated. Perhaps when you express interest in a certain stock he will hand your broker such a yellow sheet to give you. (See Figure 8-1.) He also has at hand basic manuals published by Moody's and Standard & Poor's, kept up to date by arrival of daily sheets. These provide him with the latest statistical information on the companies he

Figure 8-1. Typical Standard & Poor's stock report.

General Motors

NYSE Symbol GM Options on CBOE (Mar-Jun-Sep-Dec)

Price	Range	P-E Ratio	Dividend	Yield	S&P Ranking
Jun 19'85	1985				
70½	85-66	6	5.00	7.1%	B

Summary

This giant, financially sound company accounts for well over half of all the automobiles assembled in the U.S. In October, 1984 GM acquired for about $2.5 billion Electronic Data Systems Corp., a major computer services company. In June, 1985 GM reached an agreement to acquire for $2.7 billion in cash and 50 million shares of a new GM Class H common stock Hughes Aircraft Co., one of the world's foremost defense electronics companies.

Current Outlook

Earnings for 1985 are estimated at about $12.50 a share, down from 1984's $14.22.

The $1.25 quarterly dividend rate is expected to continue. A stock dividend of one share of Class E common stock for every 20 shares of GM's $1.66⅔ par value common stock also was paid December 10, 1984.

Industrywide car and truck sales in 1985 are expected to slightly exceed the sharply improved total of 1984. GM's share of domestically-built automobile sales in 1985 through June 10 was 56.7%, down from 59.6% a year earlier. Profits in 1985 will benefit from the absence of strikes in the U.S., Canada, and West Germany, continuing efficiency gains, and prospective foreign improvement. However, reorganization costs will be higher in 1985's first half, the $1.34 a share Domestic International Sales Corp. tax benefit of 1984's third quarter will be absent, and amortization of the excess of purchase price over net book value of Electronic Data Systems may penalize GM's profits by as much as $1 a share.

Sales (Billion $)

Quarter:	1985	1984	1983	1982
Mar.	24.18	22.89	16.74	14.72
Jun.	---	21.58	19.40	17.14
Sep.	---	18.54	17.62	14.28
Dec.	---	20.88	20.82	13.88
	---	83.89	74.58	60.03

Total revenues for 1985's first quarter rose 5.6%, year to year, on a 2.8% gain in vehicle unit sales and an initial $271 million from computer systems services. Results were hurt by advanced engineering cost pressures associated with new products and plants. After taxes at 47.9%, against 44.1%, net income fell 34%.

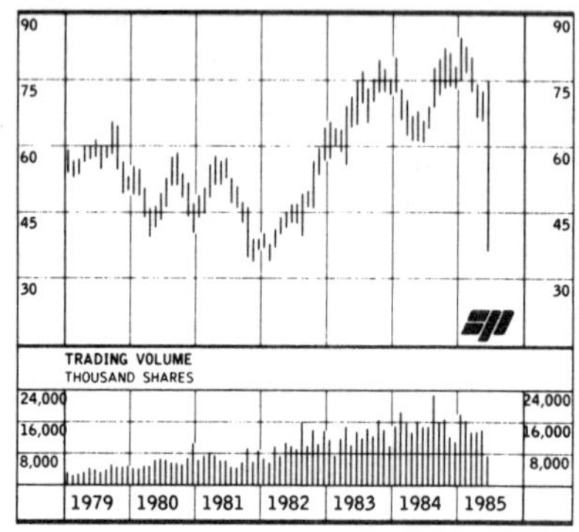

Common Share Earnings ($)

Quarter:	1985	1984	1983	1982
Mar.	3.26	5.11	2.08	0.41
Jun.	E4.00	5.09	3.32	1.82
Sep.	E1.25	1.31	2.33	0.41
Dec.	E4.00	2.71	4.11	0.45
	E12.50	14.22	11.84	3.09

Important Developments

Jun. '85—GM agreed to acquire Hughes Aircraft Co. from Howard Hughes Medical Institutes (HHMI) for $2.7 billion cash and 50 million new GM Class H shares. HHMI should realize $60 a share in three years, but GM's contingent obligation will not exceed $40. Hughes earned $266 million on sales of $5.8 billion in 1984 from satellites, missiles, defense electronics, and other high-technology operations.

Per Share Data ($)

Yr. End Dec. 31	1984	1983	1982	1981	1980	1979	1978	1977	1976	1975
Book Value	**69.80**	65.05	57.75	57.43	59.22	65.30	60.56	54.16	49.18	44.55
Earnings	**14.22**	11.84	3.09	1.07	d2.65	10.04	12.24	11.62	10.08	4.32
Dividends	**[2]4.75**	2.80	2.40	2.40	2.95	5.30	6.00	6.80	5.55	2.40
Payout Ratio	**33%**	24%	79%	224%	NM	53%	49%	58%	55%	55%
Prices—High	**82¾**	80	64½	58	58⅞	65⅞	66⅞	78½	78⅞	59⅛
Low	**61**	56	34	33⅞	39½	49⅜	53¾	61⅛	57¾	31¼
P/E Ratio—	**6-4**	7-5	21-11	54-32	NM	7-5	5-4	7-5	8-6	14-7

Data as orig. reptd.; pertains to $1.66⅔- par common stk. **2.** Plus 0.05 sh. Class E com. stk. NM-Not Meaningful. d-Deficit. E-Estimated.

Standard NYSE Stock Reports
Vol. 52/No. 123/Sec. 9

June 26, 1985

Standard & Poor's Corp.
25 Broadway, NY, NY 10004

covers, including changes in management, dividend rates, etc. When you visit your broker and have a little experience in investing, ask him to show you these manuals, used so regularly by him and the analytical department. (They probably are also available in your public library.)

In addition, the analyst keeps abreast of current changes by following the financial pages of leading newspapers, such as *The New York Times* or *The Wall Street Journal.* If he commutes by train to a big city like New York or Chicago, he probably starts his day with newspaper reading. *The New York Times* is important because of its national circulation, plus company stories, analytical opinion, editorial judgments.

Outside of New York, the analyst for a big brokerage firm probably also reads a leading local paper, in whatever city he works. Since most of the leading brokerage firms operate in New York close to the stock exchanges, their analytical departments generally are in the city, too, so analysts tend to be oriented to the two major newspapers mentioned.

When he reaches his desk the analyst usually finds a pile of mail—research reports from other brokerage firms on the companies he follows, possibly invitations from companies to attend talks by their officials, inquiries from brokers or customers of the firm about certain stocks. During each day he is peppered with news items from the Dow Jones news wire, and from Reuters if the brokerage firm carries it.* Wires from out-of-town offices come in during the day, requiring quick answers about the value of certain stocks.

At the same time the analyst probably is working on some longer-term study of an individual company or an industry he covers, so his desk is apt to be piled with reference books, annual reports, and other reading matter.

He may also have to take an hour out for a talk at the New York Society of Security Analysts, which holds daily luncheons at which speakers from companies present their corporate story and answer questions from the floor.

There is a great deal of local pride in some areas of the country, where growing companies often arouse the interest of investors in the area, and the analyst must be aware of them, too. Unfortunately, since the research facilities in the big brokerage firms are centered in New York, some local ventures do not get the good coverage they deserve. In this case alert brokers in other cities sometimes do their own analyses of such firms. However, many New York-based brokerage firms are now sending their junior analysts on business trips to explore such opportunities. While older analysts do travel, too, much of the legwork falls to the younger people in the department, who then return and write reports.

*Reuters is the leading British news agency with worldwide coverage of news, somewhat like the two major American agencies, Associated Press and United Press International. In New York, Reuters operates separately as a financial news carrier.

To supplement his basic study of the companies he covers, an analyst must talk to the companies' managers frequently and must even try to go through their plants occasionally. Since most corporate presidents and treasurers periodically visit New York, the analysts do have plenty of opportunities to meet the managers. Also many growth-minded companies need periodic infusions of capital, and to tell their story and drum up investor interest they either are happy to talk to analysts or retain public relations firms who help spread the needed information.

The younger analysts' frequent field trips help increase their knowledge of a company or an industry, keep them up to date on new developments. Sometimes the trips are financed by the companies wanting the public to know about their operations; other times the brokerage firms pay the way.

In addition, these days analysts make much use of computers by means of desktop terminals. Some leading firms have sent at least one bright young partner from the research department to be trained in computer programming. Then the research department receives regular time on the computer—time also needed for the handling of orders, bookkeeping, making out payrolls, and other accounting procedures. Small firms, which cannot yet afford their own computer setups for research, use outside computerized research on a rental basis. Standard & Poor's offers services to update analytical information on listed companies that can be processed through a firm's regular equipment. Each day an analyst might receive some of this computerized material about his companies, which he has to analyze and incorporate into his thinking.

Several times each week the analysts of a research department have a staff meeting at which they tell the top officials of the brokerage firm about important changes in the outlook of an industry or of particular companies which they cover. They discuss the reports they plan to make, and exchange information. The economist for the firm may talk about the latest development in the government's economic policies that might affect the stock market. These general exchanges are important because an analyst is busy keeping abreast of his own field and needs the give and take of such a flow of ideas.

Another source of information is the frequent luncheon meetings the analysts attend. Some meetings at which company presidents speak are sterile; the presidents talk more like advertising executives, extolling the company, its management, and its prospects. But some, though only a few, company presidents provide the analysts with the basic data they need. If the speeches are not all that productive, the chance to talk with other analysts from other brokerage firms can be helpful. Some analysts faithfully attend all luncheon meetings devoted to companies in their industries; others send their juniors with questions to ask, and require that they write up reports on the meetings afterward. Often these reports are sent out to customers of the firm.

The Analyst's Recommendations

In general, what are some of the points that an analyst considers before he writes a recommendation to his firm's customer to buy a stock?

Remember first that if he is wrong, and the price goes down, he suffers in reputation not only in his own firm but among other analysts covering the same field. Secondly, the head of his department is not likely to forget a bad error of judgment because the brokers on the firing line—the registered representatives handling the orders—will hear from their customers. Angry customers not only can be unpleasant but they can do a firm's reputation damage.

For one thing, the analyst must look at a company and consider the number of shares available for purchase by the public. A big firm like Merrill Lynch, Pierce, Fenner & Smith, with customers numbering in the hundreds of thousands, isn't likely to suggest to all customers generally that the stock of a small company with few listed shares be bought. A large number of eager buyers could send the price of the shares up too fast. The large firm with many customers has a problem in this respect, whereas the smaller brokerage firm has the advantage.

The analyst will also consider profitability. Is the company making a satisfactory return on its equity capital (the amount of stock outstanding)? Is the rate of profit going up, remaining the same, or dropping? Looking further into the future, the analyst may believe that the company will make an increasing return on equity capital.

For example, Chrysler Corporation is one of the most dramatic recent stories of a debacle and a recovery. Headed for bankruptcy after years of deficits, in 1981 the company was helped by the U.S. government with an infusion of capital wheedled out of reluctant politicians by Lee Iacocca, its chairman.

Iacocca had spent most of his career with Ford Motor Company and was number two man there when Henry Ford, the chairman, fired him after an angry dispute. He moved to Chrysler, where he cut the employee rolls, made a deal for lower wages with the union, stressed quality, developed new cars, and backed up his products with a strong guarantee. From a price of 3 in 1981 when the company was in the doldrums and facing bankruptcy, it rose to 33¾ in 1984.* The company has repaid the government $1.3 billion on some securities the government insisted upon taking at the time of the bailout, and it now pays its shareholders $1 a year in dividend.

The PE ratio (price to earnings) also merits your consideration. This is the current price of the stock related to current earnings, either actual or estimated.

*In the first half of 1983 the price rose as high as 38½.

Suppose, for example, that a stock sells at 50 a share and its annual earnings this year are expected to be $2 a share, then its price earnings ratio is 25 to 1. Next year the analyst figures that the earnings will rise to $2.50 a share. Then the stock's PE ratio will be a more favorable 20 to 1. On the other hand suppose that the analyst figures that the earnings will increase by a large amount to $4 a share, then the price earnings ratio would be about 12½ to 1. It might be a good buy.

Naturally, the PE ratio, if accurate, is meaningful not only to a stockholder interested in a particular company but also in relation to the PE ratios of other companies in the same field. Perhaps there is a good reason for the stock to be selling at a lower or seemingly more attractive ratio than are the stocks of other companies in the same industry: for instance a product losing its competitive place, management disputes, or the possibility of a crippling strike. As a result some investors may be selling the stock—dumping it, in fact—to get their money out. It is possible that the analyst can determine what is happening and advise investors.

Sometimes a stock can be temporarily neglected by investors too busy putting their money elsewhere, with the result that its lower-than-usual PE ratio might indicate it is a good time to accumulate the stock.

Studying a company's management and judging its capabilities are also important to an analyst. It represents a very difficult and intangible part of analysis. Sometimes it comes down to playing golf with or knowing socially some members of the top management of a company.

Some questions an analyst might consider are these:

Is management young enough, aggressive enough, and also experienced enough?

Has it adapted easily and quickly to ever-changing market conditions?

Has it achieved relatively stable labor relations, so that strikes are kept to a minimum?

Has it been willing to invest substantial amounts of money into research and development (R&D), and have these investments paid off with the right results?

Has it spent money to keep plants and equipment at peak efficiency?

How is it considered by competitors? Do other companies try to steal away its top people because they are so able? Has the company been able to make itself financially attractive to its top people so that they will remain? Analysts usually can find out quite a lot about management by contacting a company's rivals. Often they will speak about the quality and fierceness of competition they are getting in the market.

Fortune magazine does some fine stories on individual companies and is a good source for investors interested in growth possibilities and in managerial achievements and unusual approaches to problems.

The Current Research Picture

In recent years some developments have been disconcerting not only to analysts, but also indirectly to investors. These you should know about, because they are changing the emphasis in Wall Street research.

As mentioned before, the trend toward mergers, especially the creating of conglomerates with a wide variety of interests, has made analysis difficult. How do you judge a company that operates in five or six widely different fields, especially if the company doesn't break down its sales and earnings from the component parts? It's even hard to determine sometimes which analyst in a brokerage firm should cover such a company. Example: Mobil, the big oil company, operates Montgomery Ward, the big retailer. Should it be analyzed by both an oil expert and a retail expert? Another example: Textron, Inc., the pioneer conglomerate that started as a textile company, operates in more than half a dozen fields through subsidiary companies. Should a textile analyst cover it? Probably not.

In recent years presidents of corporations have told me that they are so hounded by analysts from many different brokerage firms wanting to talk to them that they cannot grant some interviews. The tendency has been for the president to turn over analysts to the financial officers such as the treasurer or financial vice president. Unfortunately, analysts and newspaper reporters have found that few financial officers can speak with much authority or even know much about what is going on in the productive parts of the company. By nature, treasurers are conservative and willing to talk only about their own small area of a company. Also, they tend to speak warily because they fear offending the president and thus endangering their own chances of promotion to the top spot. The result: inconclusive, lukewarm interviews to analysts and the press.

In the past few years the Securities and Exchange Commission (SEC) has begun to take a stricter view about what companies should tell the public. For example, there was the Texas Gulf Sulphur case in which some insiders including directors and top officers apparently took advantage of their knowledge of a major discovery by the company to buy stock either for themselves or for institutions with which they were associated. The SEC cracked down hard, promulgating some new rules of disclosure.

The whole basis of the Securities Act originally was to help make sure the public received disclosure of facts necessary to make a sound investment judgment. The Texas Gulf case highlighted the importance of immediate disclosure to the public, as fast as humanly possible. There were other significant cases before this one, such as a case involving Curtiss Wright Corporation some years ago. This instance involved a director alerting a broker that the dividend was going to be skipped (a bad sign) before the news made the wire systems of news agencies, which alerted the public.

Disclosure of corporate news apparently means getting the information to the major news services such as Associated Press, United Press International, and Dow Jones, the financial news service.

The rule of immediate and equal disclosure has hurt the relationship of analysts and corporate executives; many executives are now loath to speak freely with their favorite analysts, for fear that they might say something that would violate SEC's strict new rules. Corporate lawyers have had a field day, advising no comments, no speeches, no interviews, etc. Wall Street observers cannot help concluding that these factors have a muzzling effect on analysis.

Another problem is the strict SEC rules about illegal disclosure of inside information. It's founded on the very legitimate concern that "insiders"—directors, officers, or employees—might take advantage of information about impending changes within the company for their personal gain, before the public has access to that same information. Unfortunately, disclosing inside information—which might consist of offhand remarks to friends by people working in a company or chitchat on the golf course or over a drink at a club—cannot be stopped by any regulations. The need to gossip is too deeply ingrained in human nature.

Along with inside information exist false rumors, which abound in Wall Street and which can be used for specific purposes by whoever starts a good one. They can emanate, of course, quite innocently from one person's imagination or from idle talk at lunch—or from deliberate placement. The two—inside information and rumor—are as closely entwined as honeysuckle growing around the branches of small trees. It's hard to disentangle them. Certainly it cannot be done by the SEC.

By strangling legitimate sources of news like the corporation executives, the SEC plays into the hands of the rumor peddlers, I believe. At the same time analysts are relying more on computers and their statistical agility. The result, I think, will be analysis based too much on the computer or too much on rumor, not on the happy in-between that might have been possible if the SEC had taken a more liberal stand.

Such trends make it even more important for the average investor to be aware of economic and political factors at work in the market. She must be aware that with computerization and the SEC rules, analysis will tend to become more static, more technical, less based on actual observation.

The difference between good analysis and superior analysis will come from (1) creativity on the part of the research people searching out special situations or new factors in old companies ahead of other analysts; (2) the quick comprehension of economic and political trends that can influence the stock market;

and (3) the ability to persuade investors to sell—to get out of the market in time. This last has long been a great weakness of Wall Street.

Research departments are always equipped at a given moment with buy suggestions. But once you buy, your broker will seldom tell you when to sell. This is odd because he makes a commission on the sale, too. No investor can make profits while he holds on to a stock because capital gains are created only upon the actual sale. Profits on paper may sound good, look good, and make an investor happy, but they are not a profit in terms of good green dollars until the stock has been sold. Nailing down these profits is important and yet so neglected by most brokers and analysts.

So, once you have opened accounts with a broker or two, prod them regularly to tell you when to sell. This is especially true today because institutions dominate the stock market with their trading. When they unload a large block of stock, the shares you own in that company tend to decline. Therefore you must watch volume figures and try to find out why some big institution might be selling. Your stock might continue to be a perfectly good investment because the large holder could be liquidating to raise cash, to take profits, or for other good reasons.

As good as brokers and analysts are, be sure to do your own homework. The final decision to buy or sell is up to you.

9

The Mysterious Mr. Dow

The Dow Index and Theory Explained

Once you become interested in investing, a shadowy man named Dow will enter your life, along with a companion named Jones. You can forget about Jones, but Dow is inescapable. You will hear his name almost daily if you read the newspapers, listen to the radio, or watch television.

For the rest of your life, in fact, the enigmatic Charles Dow probably will be an influence. Comments like these will become part of your daily investment know-how: "The Dow lost 2 points." "The Dow gained 7 points." "The Dow has dropped 10 percent and Wall Street is worried." "The Dow has edged up to a new record level." (The last statement will make you feel good, although maybe a little apprehensive.) Soon you will notice with regularity whether your stocks tend to go in the same direction as the commentators say the Dow has moved. Generally they will.

The Dow Jones industrial average is not literally an "average" but is the total of the prices of stocks in a certain 30 companies in any given day, weighted to take into consideration stock splits, etc. Trading in these big companies accounts for about 30 percent of the volume on the New York Stock Exchange in a typical day.

Look at the names of the Dow Jones industrials in 1985: Allied Corp.; Aluminum Company; American Brands; American Can; American Express; AT&T; Bethlehem Steel; Chevron; Du Pont; Eastman Kodak; Exxon; General Electric; General Foods; General Motors; Goodyear; Inco; IBM; International Harvester; International Paper; Merck; Minnesota Mining; Owens-Illinois; Procter & Gamble; Sears, Roebuck; Texaco; Union Carbide; United Technologies; U.S. Steel; Westinghouse; Woolworth.

Obviously most of the companies on the list are sound companies whose shares would be good investments. But their movements, grouped together in the Dow average, don't begin to show what some of the fast-growth speculative issues are doing as a group. This, of course, is a basic weakness in the Dow.

In addition to the DJI, as it is called, there is also a Dow Jones railroad average and a Dow Jones public utility average. The Dow Jones industrial is the one you will be aware of most quickly. It gives an indication of the market movement as a whole, not perfect by any means but a measure of direction of basic strength or weakness. It also provides an available yardstick to measure the performance of individual stocks. The investor who can say that his stock is outperforming the Dow on the upside is usually very pleased. The person who watches his favorite stock drop more quickly and more sharply than the Dow knows that something has probably gone awry with his investment judgment.

The thing to remember about the Dow is that by nature it tends to be conservative. Why not? The stocks composing it are those of solid, generally well-heeled companies. Perhaps some have even outlived the years of their fastest growth, like the successful businessman who can't increase his income much on a percentage basis because it is already so high; nor can he grab a much bigger share of the market in his particular business because the government's antitrust sharpshooter would take action.

From time to time some of the Dow component stocks are in the doldrums, such as the steel companies currently.

Though some of the stocks composing the Dow Jones average at any one time are growth-type investments, their pace cannot be expected to match the rate of little growth companies that can double or triple their income and still be small. In other words the investor must not expect Du Pont, though constantly growing, to double its sales; but the investor can perfectly reasonably have such hopes for some newcomers in new fields.

A stock market average like the Dow can be called weighted because the component stocks are changed periodically to reflect stock splits and stock dividends that change the number of shares outstanding. Occasionally stocks are dropped and replaced. A merger might be one reason; lessened industrial status of a company could be another.

The average is calculated several times each market day by—guess who?—Dow Jones, Inc., which also happens to publish *The Wall Street Journal* and *Barron's* and operates a news wire that ticks out the latest news affecting business into almost every brokerage office in the country and in the world.

Who was Charles Dow?

Born in 1851, he was a thoughtful, shy, ambitious man who began his journalistic career in Providence, Rhode Island. Like many newspapermen of the late nineteenth century, he moved around to various towns and cities gaining experience. He worked as far west as Leadville, Colorado. Then, in the year 1880, he came to New York. After working as a financial reporter for the Kiernan News Agency, he organized a service of his own in 1882 with an acquaintance named Edward D. Jones, who had published newsletters for investors. Three years later Mr. Dow bought a seat on the New York Stock Exchange, which gave him a close view of the market and also an entrée into a quite exclusive group. Membership in the NYSE has grown less exclusive in the years since, but it is still costly.*

In the year 1889 Charles Dow took a major step: he started to publish a newsletter called *The Wall Street Journal,* which became the most influential of the financial publications, except for some of the banking letters in the late part of the nineteenth century and the beginning of the twentieth. In those days, remember, the leading bankers (headed by the Morgans) dominated financial thinking, mainly because they controlled most of the major businesses of the country. Their money, prestige, and supposed economic knowledge gave them power, not eclipsed until antitrust laws broke up their empires.

Much of the financial writing in the period was still based on personal judgment, guesswork, and rumor, plus occasional planted news. It wasn't until 1895, for example, that the New York Stock Exchange required that all new companies who wanted their shares listed must publish annual reports. The rule was not retroactive, so the big old-timers could escape such reporting.

A public utility named Kansas City Gas Company became among the first voluntarily to publish its profits "not less than twice a year." Even in the early 1900s a man like Henry Huddleston Rogers, financier, president of several companies, and active speculator, would say haughtily, "Just tell those people [the stockholders] that our way of doing business is to send out reports when we decide it is time for them to be seen." And pretty sketchy reports they were.

*The year Charles Dow bought a seat the price ranged from $20,000 to $34,000: a substantial amount in those days. In 1929 the cost of a seat was a record $625,000. In 1985 the highest price was $480,000.

It doesn't take much imagination to realize the amount of looting of corporate treasuries, the lavish spending, or other improprieties that could occur in those days.

Remember that today you as a stockholder are one of the owners of the company; stockholders were in the same position in 1890 and 1900, too, but managements of corporations so dominated companies that they could ignore stockholders except when they suddenly needed new money for expansion. It has taken years to break down some of this arrogance and indifference, and you will still find it in some companies, especially those owned largely by a family or a few large stockholders.

The breakthrough has come partly because of the rules set by the exchanges and later by the Securities and Exchange Commission (which came into being actively in 1934), and partly because following a series of financial panics (especially 1929) corporations realized they had to live more amiably with the public and raise money from stockholders. Over the years pressure for better financial disclosure had come from some responsible organizations like Dow Jones, Moody's Investors Service, and Standard & Poor's.*

Mr. Dow did not spend all those years in Wall Street (he died in 1902) without developing some valuable ideas about the stock market—namely the so-called Dow theory, of which the Dow averages are an integral part. (See Figure 9-1.) Over the years since his death a cult of Dow theorists has grown up, and many of them have used his ideas successfully in investing or advising others how to invest.

While Mr. Dow was an articulate writer, he never spelled out his theory concisely, which may seem a little odd. But remember he was a pioneer, operating at a time when financial news was not very accurate, up to date, or even available in any quantity. Many investors operated blindly, as did the writers. In fact, he could be likened to a pioneer who went West to discover a gold mine, but didn't quite have the ability or the equipment to dig deep enough for the lodes he hoped to find. That was left to some of his followers. Probably the most able interpretation was made by Robert Rhea, who dug deep to refine and form the raw nuggets of Dow's thoughts into what became a golden theory, probably the most successful in its application to the stock market.

In my early days in Wall Street (as a copyeditor for *The Wall Street Journal* in the 1940s) I kept asking experts where I could find out about Dow's theory from original sources. The answer was always, "Well, you wouldn't understand what Dow was saying, so the best way is to read Rhea." Even that gentleman, however, I found a little vague.

Here in essence is the Dow theory as expounded by Anthony Tabell, a

*Today Moody's is part of Dun & Bradstreet, while Standard & Poor's is a subsidiary of McGraw-Hill.

Figure 9-1. The Dow Jones industrial average.

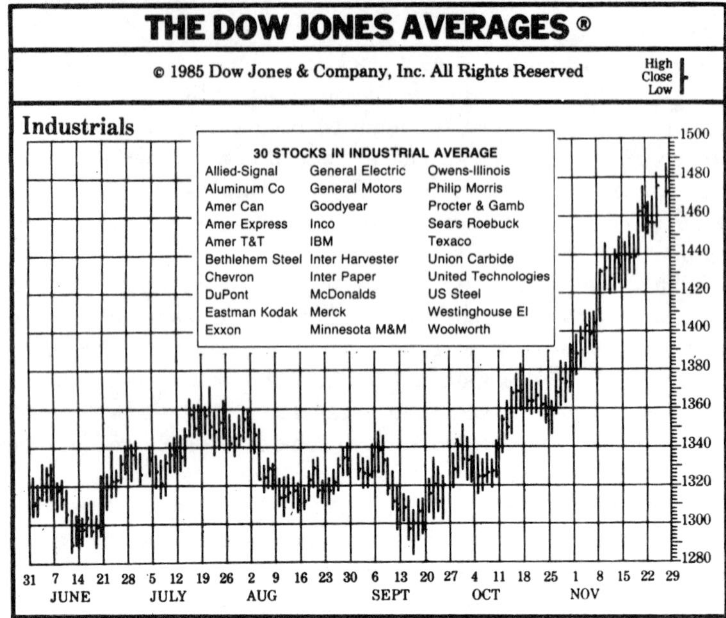

leading Wall Street analyst* who liked to use an analogy about the ocean and the beach.

Imagine standing on a beach watching the waves. As you ponder their ever-changing sameness, you wonder whether the tide is going out or coming in. There are ripples, waves, and then an ebb and flow. To find out what is happening you might pick up a piece of driftwood and poke it in the sand at the edge of the water, and then wait to see whether the waves break and send fingers of water higher on the beach or whether the sand dries because the waves are pulling back.

"Dow's conception," said Mr. Tabell, "of the behavior of the stock market was simply that it was similar to tides—that it was composed of major trends analogous to the tides themselves, intermediate trends analogous to waves, and minor trends analogous to ripples. He believed it was largely impossible to predict the direction of minor and intermediate trends, but that a study of these trends could be used to determine whether the major trend was up or down."

*He was a senior vice president of Walston & Company, a once-large brokerage firm no longer in existence. The description was published in one of his regular monthly reports to investors.

Suppose that after a high point (measured by the Dow industrial average) the prices reacted by falling, then after a while rallied again to a point below the first high and then dropped back to a point below the previous reaction level. The investor might consider this a warning or indication that the tide was ebbing for the market and that a downturn had begun.

Under the Dow theory, the action of the Dow industrial average must be confirmed by similar actions in the railroad averages; and sometimes such similar action would not come at the same time or even near it. In fact, in recent years one of the weaknesses of the Dow has been the railroad average, which has lost much meaning these days because of the decline of importance of the rail industry.

Mr. Tabell summarized his thinking about the Dow theory this way: "Most users would agree, however, that its ability to call major turning points in the market, e.g., 1929, has been extremely good. A moment's reflection will indicate that the theory has its greatest value where long and wide upward and downward moves take place. . . . Regardless of its merit, the Dow theory as applied to the present-day market is of great importance from a historical point of view. The theory was the first systematic recognition of the fact that stock prices follow trends, and that a trend, once established, tends to remain in force. It is this principle that underlies a good deal, though by no means all, of technical work."*

Take a look at the Dow Jones charts in Figures 9-2 and 9-3. The first shows what the Dow had to say in terms of figures from 1929 (the period beginning the Great Depression) through 1971.

If you had been a Dow theorist, when would you have sold your shares in those years? Then take a look at the chart in Figure 9-3. As this book went to press, the Dow Jones Industrial Average had risen above 1565, a record that surprised most analysts.

The bar chart, which looks like the profile of a skyscraper, shows various high points from 1955 to 1985, when the Dow moved well above 1300 to reach a close of 1359.54 in July, a new record.† (See Figure 9-4.) Since that time the market has moved much higher.

The bar chart shows even more effectively that a stock market surge does not come without some downs, along with the ups, just as is shown in the long-term view given in Figure 8-1. Note the quite deep trough in early 1984.

*Mr. Tabell contributed an interesting chapter on forecasting stock prices in a book called *The Anatomy of Wall Street,* edited by Charles Rolo and George Nelson (New York: Lippincott, 1968). The book also contained a chapter by me on the use of stock options—puts and calls. It is out of print but probably obtainable in large public libraries.

†Usually analysts watch the movement of the closing price, not the days' highs.

Figure 9-2. The stock market takes a flyer.

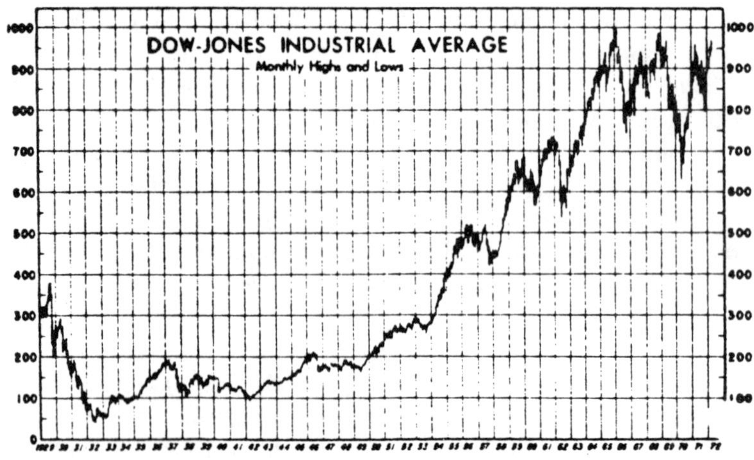

All this may give you an inkling of why Mr. Dow will become such a regular part of your investing life. Often your stocks will rise and fall for no apparent reason, and not even in the same direction as the Dow, like the ripples

Figure 9-3. Market cycles (before the record highs in 1986).

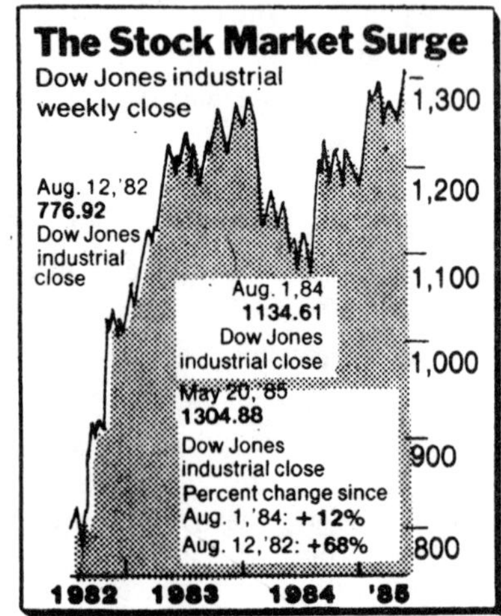

Figure 9-4. Bar chart of the Dow Jones industrial average.

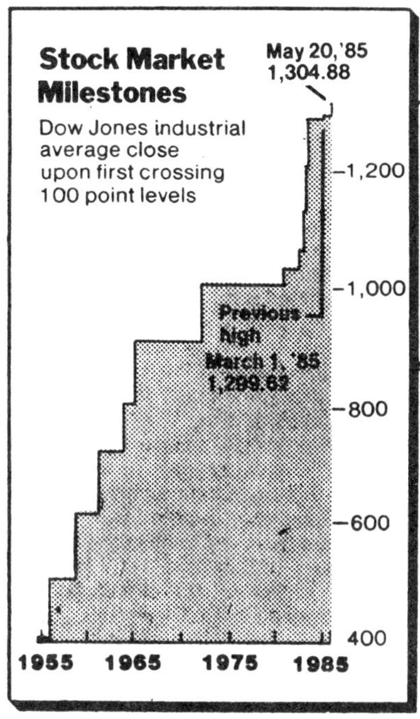

that move on the surface of the water with a fascinating waywardness. At other times there might be specific reasons for your stocks to move by themselves. For example, if suddenly the president of a company in which you owned stock died, the price might drop because some investors might believe that a succeeding management would be less effective. Or if your company suddenly announced a new product, the price might rise suddenly, well above any proportionate rise in the Dow average. Or perhaps over a few months' period you and other investors decide you can do better by selling and investing in another company in the same industry. This might drop the shares of one stock and boost the shares of the other over an intermediate period, all out of proportion to any market trend.

Generally over the long term you will find that if all stocks are moving up in price yours will tend to do the same, and in a long decline all shares will tend to weaken in price, including your issues, even though they may be hot-shot specials.

The best way to follow the action of the Dow is in its own "home"—*The*

Wall Street Journal. Read it every day, or at least once a week, and the charts will soon be telling you their story of market trends.

However, don't become so enamored of the Dow that you forget the growing importance of some other averages. Perhaps one of the most valuable to be used in connection with the Dow is the Standard & Poor's average of 500 stocks, a much larger and more representative group than the companies included in the Dow. (See Figure 3-1.) Since the S&P 500 also includes many small, new companies, it gives an indication of how they are faring.

Thanks to the computer age, the New York Stock Exchange and the American Stock Exchange began to compile their own averages. They include virtually the entire list of stocks listed on the exchange at any given time. They do not have the seasoning of the Dow but they are fast gaining adherents. Eventually, I think, they will emerge as the most useful.

Generally speaking, the investor should be aware that three types of influences affect the market. They might be summarized this way:

1. World events.
2. Economic trends in the United States.
3. Conditions in the market.

Sometimes world events—such as political upheavals, devaluation of some currency, a threat of war—will dominate the market. At other times economic trends within the United States—the business cycle, tightness of money, consumer intentions, etc.—will be the top influence. Then again conditions in the market will be paramount, such as overspeculation, sharp changes in earnings, lack of investment money. These factors, like waves on the ocean, must be considered in the changing tides evidenced by the various averages.

In recent years several types of growth-stock averages have been introduced, and investors in the future probably will follow them more closely as opportunities open up in new fields. Ask your broker, if you are interested in the more speculative type of stocks, which growth-stock average he suggests that you follow.

One important idea has been stressed in recent years; namely that the stock market is not always a good indicator of business conditions. Proof of that came in 1962 when a sharp drop in the booming speculative market (the so-called Kennedy market break) came at a time when business conditions were very prosperous. The reverse can be true, also: the stock market can lag even when business is recovering, such as happened just before World War II and just afterward, and perhaps this can be attributed to mass emotion—investors reacting with the same pessimism.

Generally, however, the fact remains that the Dow and other averages have broken sharply at times of business declines, and usually have given a little forewarning.

Whether you consider yourself a fundamentalist or use a technical approach to the market, the Dow and some other leading averages belong in your thinking. What fascinates me about Mr. Dow is that probably no man connected with the investment world is so well known to so many millions of investors; certainly not the heads of the big brokerage firms or the president of the New York Stock Exchange, not famous analysts, not the head of the Securities and Exchange Commission. Furthermore, I cannot think of any other man whose surname is connected with an important theory and yet who did not actually propound the theory.

Mr. Dow expressed his ideas primarily in editorials, and at one point he made a statement that I think might predict the future: "It is not impossible that with better knowledge, greater wealth and wiser methods the extent of the advance and of the decline may be smaller, but until human nature changes materially there is not likely to be abandonment of the law of expansion and contraction in business and discontinuance of its effects on the prices of stocks."

Happily, if he is right there will always be good swings in the market up and down, offering stockholders opportunities. In future years, however, my guess is that the swings may not be as vigorous as the ones in 1972–74 and 1980–82 and 1985-86, when the average rose to new record highs.

10

The Feeling Isn't Mutual

Mutual Funds Are Fine but You Can Do Better

In recent years two trends have become apparent in Wall Street. Many brokerage firms, harassed by rising costs and bookkeeping snarls, definitely have lost interest in the small investor. Their clerical staffs cannot keep abreast of the sea of paperwork generated by ever-rising trading volume. Consider the figures for trading on the New York Stock Exchange and the American Stock Exchange (see Table 10-1). Not included are the billions traded on smaller exchanges and over-the-counter stocks traded each year—a vast number that has never been counted.

With such volume to keep them busy, many brokers have become less interested in the very small investor and have concentrated on large investors and commercial accounts—pension funds, mutual funds, trust accounts, etc. Today, the big investors dominate the market, accounting for some 75 percent

Table 10-1. New York Stock Exchange and American Stock Exchange trading volume.

Year	*NYSE*	*Amex*
1929	1,124,800,000	476,140,000
1930	810,632,000	222,270,000
1940	207,599,000	42,928,000
1950	524,799,000	107,792,000
1960	766,693,000	286,039,000
1970	2,937,359,000	833,116,000
1980	11,352,294,000	1,626,072,000
1985	27,510,706,353	2,100,815,259

of the trading, in spite of the fact that the 2 million individual investors of the 1940s have grown to an army of 43 million investors today. Some of them were induced to invest years ago mostly because of "be-kind-to-small-investors" policies at some big firms in earlier years. Remember the popular Merrill Lynch slogan "Investigate before you invest"? Now that Sears and American Express, two people-oriented companies, have acquired major brokerage firms, the be-kind-to-the-small-investor theory has taken on new meaning.

At the same time mutual funds have multiplied in number and grown large in size, offering their shares to small investors. Brokers have helped this growth, partly because they receive higher commissions for handling mutual fund sales than they do trading shares for a small investor, who buys odd lots or maybe a round lot of 100 shares occasionally. Furthermore, by putting the small investor into mutual funds the brokerage firm puts no strain on its own research department and lightens its bookkeeping load.

So you can expect that your broker might try to talk you into a good mutual fund. He will, of course, attempt to find out what type of mutual fund will suit your personality—a fast-growth fund, an old liner, or a fund that specializes in certain types of stocks, like science-oriented companies. This is supposed to give you the feeling that you are investing in a fund tailored to your needs or aims.

Frankly, I do not like mutual funds except for the lazy investor who doesn't want to make the effort to do her own searching, or for the frightened investor inhibited about approaching the stock market on her own. Anyone who wants the challenge of investing tends to avoid mutual funds, for several good reasons.

Buying into a mutual fund—buying its shares—usually costs about 8 percent in fees, called the "loading" charge. Some funds have a little lower price tag than that, while some charge more. Generally funds cost quite a bit more than investment in stock. However, to meet competition some funds have eliminated their loading charge and call themselves "no load" funds.

True, you are placing your money in expert hands in a fund, but for this handling each year you also pay a fee. The operating cost is high, to start with. The president, vice presidents, the analysts, the bookkeeper, the transfer agent (usually a bank) receive high salaries. The fund must have an office, usually an impressive one, which means high rent. It also employs experts such as accountants, lawyers, perhaps even a public relations firm. This overhead comes out of the profits or income from securities in which it invests your money and many other people's money.

In other words, with a fund you place a relatively expensive third party between you and your investments. It's like buying prepared potatoes au gratin in a package instead of peeling your own potatoes, cooking them, adding cheese, and baking them in the oven.

With this in mind, let's define exactly what a mutual fund is. It's an investment company, regulated under the Investment Company Act. Generally speaking there are two types of investment companies: the open-end, or mutual fund type; and the closed-end, another species.

The mutual fund is the open-end variety because it issues an unlimited number of shares to meet the demands of buyers. If you, your best friend, and exactly 1,000,000 other people each buy a share in the same mutual fund, the fund will have 1,000,002 shares outstanding. If half the people sell their shares then the mutual fund shares drop back to 500,001. In that sense, the mutual fund creates its shares on demand. Instant creativity, you might say.

The financial sections of major newspapers usually carry a brief listing of the best known of the mutual funds, but there are many others available whose prices can be learned through your broker. A few—those followed by the letters NL—are no-load funds, but most are load funds, as shown in Figure 10-1.

One of the oldest and most prestigious family of funds is the Boston-based Fidelity group; it offers a wide variety, ranging from municipal bond funds, to speculative stock funds, to funds that invest in high-technology stocks or utility stocks. Let's look in Figure 10-1 to the last fund mentioned under the Fidelity heading. It is called the Trend fund, a no-load fund priced that day at $41.28. It showed a drop of $.13 a share from the previous day.

The prices quoted change at least once a day for all funds. The prices are based on the value of the underlying securities in the portfolio on that day. By law a mutual fund must be ready to buy its shares back from a shareholder on demand.

The fund takes your money and invests it in securities, generally common stocks, though there are also bond funds. However, a fund always keeps a certain amount of money in the form of cash in the bank or in quickly negotiable

Figure 10-1. Mutual fund price quotations.

THE NEW YORK TIMES, WEDNESDAY, AUGUST 14, 1985

Mutual Funds

	* N.A.V.	Buy	Chg.
AARP Invst:			
CapGr	17.79	NL	- .06
GiniM	15.32	NL	- .01
GenBd	15.26	NL	- .01
GthInc	17.16	NL	...
TxFBd	15.32	NL	...
TxFSh	15.17	NL	- .01
ABT Family			
Emrg	13.58	14.84	- .08
GthInc	14.90	16.28	- .03
SecInc	10.99	12.01	- .03
UtilInc	16.97	18.55	...
ADTEK	10.60	NL	- .03
Acorn F	34.30	NL	- .09
Afuture	12.28	NL	- .01
AIM Funds:			
CvYld	11.82	12.64	- .03
Grnwy	9.10	9.73	- .01
HiYld	9.89	10.58	...
Sumit	5.83	....	- .01
AMEV Funds:			
Capitl	10.98	12.00	- .02
Grwth	12.52	13.68	- .06
Specl	18.68	NL	- .08
US Gvt	9.63	10.52	- .02
Alliance Cap:			
Chem	9.70	10.60	- .03
HiGrd	10.65	11.27	...
HiYld	9.79	10.36	...
Intl	12.89	14.09	+ .03
Mortg	9.75	10.32	- .02
Survev	13.61	14.87	+ .01
Tech	17.33	18.94	- .21
Alpha F	18.60	20.33	- .01
Amer Capital:			
Corp	7.01	7.66	...
Cmstk	13.65	14.92	- .02
Entrp	12.77	13.96	- .04
Exch	47.45	...	- .17
Fd Am	10.60	11.58	- .01
GvSec	11.69	12.47	+ .03
Grow	25.83	...	- .13
Harbr	12.90	14.10	- .01
Hi Yld	10.16	10.90	...
Mun B	18.85	19.79	- .04
OTC	10.29	11.25	- .08
Pace	20.78	22.71	- .02
Provid	4.45	4.80	...
Ventr	14.84	16.22	- .07
American Funds:			
A Bal	10.60	11.58	- .01
Amcp	8.64	9.44	- .01
A Mutl	15.76	17.22	- .03
Bond	13.35	14.59	- .01
Eupac	15.58	17.03	+ .02
Fd Inv	12.70	13.88	- .03
Grwth	14.39	15.73	- .07
Incom	11.68	12.77	- .01
ICA	11.96	13.07	- .02
NEco	17.05	18.63	- .06
N Pers	8.38	9.16	- .02
TaxE	10.01	10.51	- .02
Wsh Mt	9.68	10.58	- .01
A GthFd	8.36	9.14	+ .01
A Heritg	2.56	NL	- .03
A Invest	7.03	NL	- .02
A Inv In	9.24	NL	...
AmMed	35.77	NL	+ .12
A NlGth	4.02	4.39	+ .01
A NtInc	18.27	19.97	- .01
Amway	6.11	6.53	- .01
Analyt	141.39	NL	- .17
Amstng	7.60	NL	...
Axe Houghton:			
Fnd B	10.71	11.64	- .01
Babson Group:			
Bond	1.57	NL	...
Enterp	12.19	NL	- .02
Gwth	11.31	NL	- .02
UMB St	11.59	NL	- .03
UMB B	10.31	NL	...
BLC Gt	15.69	17.15	- .03
BLC Inc	15.55	16.99	+ .01
BartBV	11.51	NL	+ .03
BartBY	...	...	...
Beac Gth	15.40	NL	+ .01
Beac Hill	20.05	NL	+ .05
Benham Capital:			
CaTFL	10.20	NL	- .02
CalTFI	9.87	NL	+ .01
CapNT	10.43	NL	+ .01
Berger Group:			
100 Fd	15.76	NL	- .08
101 Fd	14.91	NL	+ .01
Boston Co:			
CapAp	28.19	NL	- .03
Modl	11.19	NL	- .01
SpGth	18.98	NL	- .04
Bowser	2.46	NL	...
Bruce	68.55	NL	- .06
Bull & Bear Gp:			
CapitG	14.24	NL	- .02
Equity	10.62	NL	- .03
Golcn	10.49	NL	- .06
HiYld	14.42	NL	- .01
CalMun	10.11	NL	- .05
Calvert Group:			
Equity	17.86	NL	...
Inco	15.69	NL	- .05
Social	19.30	NL	- .02
TxF Lt	10.53	NL	...
TxF Lg	15.65	NL	- .02
Wash Ar	15.28	NL	- .02
WrldW	10.92	NL	+ .02
Delaware Group:			
DMC	10.29	10.71	- .03
Decat	16.38	17.90	- .01
Delaw	21.08	23.04	- .05
Delch	7.61	8.32	...
Tx Fre	7.13	7.49	- .01
Delta	12.54	13.70	- .05
DIT CG	12.18	NL	- .02
DIT AG	19.75	NL	- .11
DIT CI	9.97	NL	...
DG Div	24.89	NL	+ .03
DodCx Bl	28.59	NL	- .02
DodCx St	27.07	NL	- .03
DbleTx	10.65	11.09	- .02
Drexel Burnham:			
Burnh	19.37	20.07	+ .01
Govt	10.60	NL	- .03
Option	10.18	NL	...
Dreyfus Grp:			
A Bnd	13.72	NL	- .01
CalTx	13.76	NL	+ .47
Dreyf	12.94	14.14	...
GNMA	14.96	NL	- .05
Interm	12.85	NL	- .02
Levge	18.85	20.60	- .01
GthOp	10.20	NL	+ .02
NY Tx	14.09	NL	- .04
Spl Inc	7.59	NL	...
Tax Ex	11.58	NL	- .02
Eagl Gth	7.66	8.37	...
Eaton Vance:			
EHStk	13.03	14.05	- .05
GvtOb	11.92	12.78	...
Grwth	6.93	7.57	...
HiYld	4.96	5.32	...
IncBos	9.49	10.18	...
Invest	8.16	8.92	- .03
Nautls	12.92	14.12	- .10
SpEqt	18.63	20.09	- .09
TaxM	17.23	18.83	+ .01
VS Spl	11.93	13.04	- .09
EmpBld	16.13	16.93	+ .02
Evrgrn r	11.30	NL	- .01
EvrgrTtl	16.22	NL	+ .01
FPA Funds:			
Capit	10.40	11.30	- .01
NwInc	8.88	9.35	...
Parmt	14.30	15.63	- .01
Peren	17.55	19.18	...
Fairmt	192.94	NL	- .73
Frm BG	14.77	NL	- .02
Federated Funds:			
CpCsh	11.18	NL	- .02
Exch	39.23	NL	- .03
FT Int	11.41	NL	+ .01
FdlInlr	9.85	NL	+ .02
GNMA	10.92	NL	- .03
Gwth	11.50	NL	- .02
Hi Icm	12.03	12.87	- .01
HiYld	10.43	NL	- .01
Inco	10.66	NL	- .03
St Gvt	10.31	NL	- .01
StkBd	14.32	NL	- .02
Stock	18.19	NL	- .01
Fidelity Invest:			
CalMu	10.54	NL	...
Bond	6.75	NL	- .02
Congrs	60.06	NL	- .14
Contfd	11.06	NL	- .02
Destny	11.18	....	- .03
Discv	20.44	NL	+ .01
Eq Inc	26.13	26.66	- .03
Exch	48.95	NL	- .05
Fidel	16.48	NL	- .04
Fredm	13.63	NL	- .03
Gvt Sec	9.36	NL	- .01
HiInco	9.17	NL	- .01
Hi Yld	11.93	NL	- .01
Lt Mun	8.54	NL	...
Magel	38.74	39.94	- .04
Mun Bd	7.12	NL	- .01
MassT	10.40	NL	- .01
Merc	14.92	15.38	- .02
MtgSc	10.09	10.19	- .03
NYTxS	10.00	NL	...
NYTM	11.05	NL	+ .01
OTC	14.62	15.07	- .07
Ovrse	14.19	14.63	+ .02
Puritn	12.88	NL	- .01
Qual	14.19	NL	+ .01
SelDef	13.48	13.76	- .02
SelEn	10.47	10.68	+ .01
SelFin	24.55	25.05	...
SelHlt	24.48	24.98	- .19
SelLei	15.53	15.85	- .11
SelMtl	9.79	9.99	- .36
SelTch	19.98	20.39	- .18
SelUtil	19.31	19.70	+ .05
SpcSit	13.01	13.41	- .02
Thrift	10.19	NL	- .02
Trend	41.28	NL	- .13
FiduCap	19.94	NL	- .06
Financial Prog:			
Dyna	7.75	NL	- .04
FnclTx	14.22	NL	- .01
HiYld	8.17	NL	...
Indust	4.59	NL	- .01
Incom	8.38	NL	- .01
Select	6.54	NL	...
WrldT	7.10	NL	- .02
NY Mu	10.39	10.82	...
PrecM	10.80	NL	- .25
IRI Stck	8.27	8.66	- .02
IDS Mutual:			
IDS Ag r	6.76	NL	- .05
IDSEq r	6.14	NL	+ .01
IDS In r	5.52	NL	- .01
IDS Bd	4.79	4.97	- .01
IDSEqP	8.50	8.95	...
IDS Dis	6.50	6.85	- .06
IDS Ex	4.90	5.16	- .01
IDS Grt	17.15	18.06	- .08
IDS HiY	4.15	4.36	- .01
IDS Int	5.60	5.89	- .03
IDS ND	9.14	9.62	- .04
IDS Prog	7.02	7.39	- .07
MgtRet	5.33	5.61	- .02
Mutl	11.70	12.32	- .02
IDS Tx	3.61	3.80	- .01
PrecMt	4.71	4.96	- .12
Stock	16.62	17.50	- .02
Select	8.02	8.44	...
ISI Group:			
Grwth	6.66	7.28	...
Incom	3.78	4.13	...
Trst Sh	10.16	11.10	+ .01
Idex	10.20	11.15	+ .02
Industry	6.45	NL	- .03
IntgCap r	10.59	NL	- .02
Int Invst	10.26	11.21	- .28
Invst Portfolio:			
GvtPl	8.28	NL	- .01
HiYld	8.91	NL	...
Optn	8.49	NL	- .01
ITB Group:			
InvBos	10.72	11.56	- .03
HiInco	14.59	15.73	- .04
MaTF	15.19	15.95	- .02
Inv Resh	5.10	5.57	...
Istel *	13.46	NL	- .06
IvyGth	14.17	NL	...
IvyInst	124.93	NL	- .05
JP Grth	14.45	15.71	- .01
JP Inco	8.53	9.27	- .02
Janus Fund:			
Fund	13.09	NL	- .04
Value	11.16	NL	...
Ventur	24.36	NL	+ .01
John Hancock:			
Bond	14.87	16.25	- .02
Grwth	12.93	14.13	- .06
USGvF	8.76	9.57	...
Tax Ex	9.76	10.67	- .01
US GvT	10.30	11.26	...
Kemper Funds:			
CalTx	12.91	13.52	- .03
Incom	8.56	9.11	...
Grow	12.62	13.79	- .01
Hi Yld	10.58	11.35	...
IntlFd	14.03	15.33	- .05
Mun B	8.61	9.04	- .01
Optn	10.79	11.79	- .01
Summ	25.49	27.86	...
Tech	11.56	12.63	- .01
Tot Rt	14.31	15.64	- .02
US Gvt	9.09	9.47	- .02
Keystone Mass:			
Cus B1 r	16.05	NL	- .02
Cus B2 r	18.56	NL	- .01
Cus B4 r	7.97	NL	- .01
Cus K1 r	8.74	NL	...
Cus S3 r	8.47	NL	- .02
Cus S4 r	5.79	NL	- .01
Intl r	5.21	NL	+ .01
KPM r	12.55	NL	- .45
TxFr r	8.01	NL	...
KidPea r	13.73	NL	- .05
LMH	25.29	NL	...
LeggMas	24.02	NL	- .01
LehCap	18.17	NL	- .10
LehInvst	17.75	NL	- .04
Levrge	7.77	NL	- .06
Lexington Grp:			
CLdr fr	12.87	13.81	- .06
Goldfd	3.70	NL	- .01
GNMA	7.70	NL	- .01
Grow	8.88	NL	- .01
Resh	16.61	NL	- .02
Liberty Group:			
Am Ldr	11.48	NL	- .01
Tx Fre	9.38	NL	...
US Gvt	8.69	NL	- .02
LtdTrm	....	....	...
LindDv	23.46	NL	+ .04
Lindnr	18.05	NL	+ .05
Loomis Sayles:			
Capit	22.02	NL	- .12
Mut	18.57	NL	- .09
Lord Abbett:			
Affild	9.79	10.56	...
Bnd db	10.35	11.31	- .01
Dev Gt	7.49	8.19	- .04
Incom	3.16	3.45	...
TaxFr	9.85	10.34	- .01
TxNY	10.11	10.61	- .01
ValAp	10.27	11.22	- .04
Lutheran Bro:			
Fund	15.63	16.45	+ .01
Incom	8.82	9.28	...
Muni	7.30	7.68	+ .01
Mass Financl:			
Grwth	23.20	25.22	- .12
Incom	10.62	11.54	- .03
Ret Eq	20.80	22.61	- .13
TaxEx	7.16	7.50	- .02
Neuberger Berm:			
Enrgy	19.55	NL	- .04
Guard	43.13	NL	- .05
Hemisp	7.05	NL	...
Libty	4.40	NL	+ .07
Manht	7.72	NL	- .02
Partn	15.32	NL	- .05
NY Mun	1.14	NL	...
Newt Gt	27.73	NL	- .09
Newt Inc	8.26	NL	- .01
Nicholas Group:			
Nichol	30.26	NL	+ .05
Nich II	14.77	NL	+ .04
NchInc	3.75	NL	- .02
Nichsn Gt	13.20	NL	- .05
NE InTr	12.37	NL	...
NE InGt	13.18	NL	- .01
North Star:			
Apollo	9.91	NL	- .07
Bond	9.82	NL	- .02
Region	18.21	NL	- .10
Stock	13.37	NL	- .04
NovaFd	14.06	NL	- .07
Nuveen	7.95	NL	- .01
OldDom	21.88	23.91	- .02
Omega	12.57	NL	+ .03
Oppenheimer Fd:			
AIM	16.57	18.11	+ .01
Direct	19.94	21.79	- .10
EqInc	7.47	8.16	+ .01
Oppen	9.60	10.49	- .03
Gold	7.03	7.68	- .21
Hi Yld	17.10	18.34	...
NY Tax	11.26	11.79	- .03
Prem	20.22	22.10	- .04
Rgcy	13.36	14.60	- .38
Specl	19.36	21.16	- .06
Target	17.18	18.28	- .02
Tx Fre	8.42	8.82	- .03
Time	13.71	14.98	- .03
Blue Ch	10.67	11.66	+ .02
Ret Gov	10.56	11.54	- .03
OTC Sec	17.09	18.58	+ .02
Pacific Horizon:			
Agresv	19.02	NL	- .10
Calif	12.80	NL	- .03
Paine Webber:			
Atlas	10.98	12.00	+ .01
Amer	14.05	15.36	- .03
GNMA	9.85	10.29	- .01
HiYld	10.16	10.61	- .01
InvGd	9.91	10.35	- .02
Olymp	9.49	10.37	...
TaxEx	10.01	10.45	- .01
PaxWld	11.98	NL	...
Penn Sq	8.64	NL	+ .01
Penn Mu	6.84	NL	...
PermPrt	11.07	NL	- .02
Phila	8.70	9.51	+ .02
Phoenix Series:			
Balan	11.69	12.78	- .02
CvFd	16.64	18.19	- .03
Grwth	14.41	15.75	- .02
HiYld	9.23	9.92	...
Stock	12.53	13.69	- .01
PC Cp	10.81	NL	- .02
Pilgrim Grp:			
PAR	23.23	23.58	- .01
GNMA	15.62	16.27	- .04
PilMag	7.95	8.57	- .01
PilgHi	8.14	8.48	...
Pioneer Fund:			
Bond	9.26	10.12	- .01
Fund	20.90	22.84	- .07
II Inc	17.15	18.74	- .02
III Inc	14.48	15.83	- .01
Plitrnd	12.93	NL	- .02
Price Funds:			
Grwth	15.50	NL	- .01
GthInc	13.26	NL	+ .04
HiYld	10.47	NL	...
Incom	8.37	NL	- .01
Intl	14.31	NL	- .02
N Era	16.95	NL	- .03
N Horiz	13.46	NL	- .09
TxFrH	10.15	NL	- .01
TxFrSI	5.06	NL	- .01
PrinPTE	9.33	9.77	...
Pro Services:			
MedT	10.08	NL	- .04
Fund	10.77	NL	- .02
Incom	8.36	NL	- .05
Prudential Bache:			
AdjPfd	24.37	NL	+ .01
CalMu	10.72	NL	- .01
Equity	15.77	NL	- .01
Globl r	12.98	NL	+ .04
GvPlu	10.16	NL	- .03
GvtSc	10.31	NL	- .01
Gth Opp	13.13	NL	- .06
HiYld	10.08	NL	+ .01
HYMu	14.74	NL	...
MuNY	10.91	NL	+ .04
OptnG	16.49	NL	+ .03
QtyInc	15.23	NL	- .01
Rsch r	9.15	NL	...
Putnam Funds:			
Balan	10.45	11.42	- .03
Bond	6.39	6.98	- .01
Com S	18.57	20.30	- .04
Grwth	14.34	15.67	- .03
Sequoia	41.04	NL	...
Sentry	11.59	12.60	...
Shearson Funds:			
ATIGt	78.20	NL	- .19
ATIInc	76.43	NL	- .06
AgrGr	11.18	11.77	- .09
Appre	20.37	21.44	- .03
CalMu	14.57	15.34	- .03
FdVal	7.18	7.56	+ .01
Global	22.06	23.22	+ .02
HiYld	18.75	19.74	...
MgGvt	13.04	13.73	- .02
MMun	13.96	14.69	- .03
NYMu	14.93	15.72	- .04
Sherm D	6.15	NL	- .01
Sierra Gt	10.84	NL	- .09
Sigma Funds:			
Capit	14.68	16.04	- .03
Inco	8.03	8.78	...
Invest	8.21	8.97	+ .01
Spcl n	7.59	8.30	- .01
Trust	11.99	13.10	...
Vent	10.53	11.51	- .04
Smith Barney:			
Equt	14.32	NL	- .05
IncGro	9.42	9.99	- .02
USGvt	13.34	14.15	- .03
SoGen In	14.94	15.64	- .03
SthestGt	10.52	NL	- .01
SwInInc	4.93	NL	...
Sover In	21.04	22.15	...
State Bond Grp:			
Com St	5.58	6.10	- .02
Divers	6.45	7.05	- .01
Progrs	8.55	9.34	- .01
StFrm Gt	10.50	NL	...
StFrm Bl	14.73	NL	- .02
StStreet Inv:			
Exch	92.39	NL	+ .03
Grwth r	57.89	NL	- .01
Invst	72.23	72.60	- .19
Steadman Funds:			
Ocean	5.12	NL	- .05
Stein Roe Fds:			
Bond	8.80	NL	- .02
Cap Op	21.25	NL	- .14
Discv	10.19	NL	- .06
HiYld	10.65	NL	- .02
Specl	16.79	NL	- .02
Stock	15.99	NL	+ .01
TaxEx	8.40	NL	- .02
TotRet	23.21	NL	- .01
Univ	17.20	NL	- .04
Strategic Funds:			
Capit	6.28	6.86	- .01
Invst	4.70	5.14	- .34
Silvr	5.53	6.04	+ .13
StratnDv	24.76	NL	+ .10
Strat Gth	18.14	NL	- .03
Strongln	18.03	18.21	- .03
StrngT	17.10	17.27	...
TelInSh	14.44	....	...
Templeton Group:			
Frgn	12.34	13.49	...
Global I	37.41	...	+ .08
Glob II	11.91	13.02	+ .02
Grwth	10.47	11.44	+ .01
World	13.48	14.73	+ .01
Thomson McKinnon:			
Gwth	12.23	NL	- .03
Inco	10.09	NL	- .01
Opor	12.73	NL	- .01
Tudr Fd	20.59	NL	- .12
Trust Portfolio:			
EqGth	10.33	NL	- .01
EqInc	11.35	NL	- .01
Fixed	10.30	NL	- .01
20th Century:			
Gift r	5.61	5.62	- .01
Grwth	14.02	NL	...
Select	25.70	NL	...
Ultra r	7.29	7.32	- .07
USGv	99.29	NL	- .04
Vista r	4.61	4.63	- .04
USAA Group:			
Cornst	10.83	NL	- .13
Gold	7.53	NL	- .28
Grwth	14.50	NL	- .03
Inco	11.42	NL	+ .01
SbIt	15.76	NL	- .10
TxEH	12.37	NL	- .01
TxEIt	11.51	NL	- .01
TxESh	10.49	NL	+ .01
Unified Mgmnt:			
Genrl	8.19	NL	- .02
Gwth	19.53	NL	- .03
Inco	12.48	NL	- .01
Indl	8.10	NL	- .02
Mutl	14.32	NL	+ .04
United Funds:			
Accm	7.91	8.64	+ .01
Bond	5.62	6.14	- .01
GvtSec	5.32	5.54	- .01
IntGth	5.68	6.21	...
Con Inc	16.19	17.69	...
Hi Inc	13.58	14.84	- .01
Incom	14.02	15.32	- .04
Muni	6.77	7.05	- .01
NwCcpt	4.96	5.42	...
Retire	5.88	6.43	...
ScEng	8.62	9.42	+ .01

*N.A.V. means "net asset value." The word "Buy" means the buying price. "CHG" means the change in price from the previous day. As mentioned before, "NL" indicates a "no load" fund. Therefore the price of a "no load" fund is the same as its net asset value that day.

government or corporate issues such as commercial paper* so that it can redeem shares easily.

The mutual fund tends to keep only enough cash on hand to meet required redemption needs or to take advantage of sudden opportunities in the stock market. It likes to keep well invested either for fast appreciation, high yield, or a combination of quality and growth, depending on the aims of the particular fund as outlined in the prospectus it issues.

The mutual fund shareholders receive notices that detail just what the dividend payment (usually paid quarterly) involves in the way of actual dividend income or capital gains, or both.

As mentioned earlier, some funds are the no-load variety sold directly to the public from their offices, and not through brokers or mutual fund salesmen. Hence they do not charge the usual 8 percent loading fee; you can join their ranks as a shareholder, usually without any fee. Naturally, like the load funds, they have overhead expenses that must be paid out of revenues received from their investments, so there is an operational cost involved.

The second major variety of investment companies consists of the so-called closed-end investment trusts. These companies issue stocks just like the regular corporations on the Big Board, and thus they are called closed-end.

One of the largest is Tri-Continental Corporation, listed on the exchange. The shares are bought through brokers just like the stock in any other company listed. Figure 10-2 shows what kind of a record Tri-Continental had during the past few years.

The investment trust, either closed- or open-end, thus offers you the strength of diversity—spreading your investment risk—along with expert handling of your investment. The point is that you are paying quite a high price for this convenience—and in some cases too high a price.

That is why many brokers believe you can do better in the stock market using sound recommendations from a good brokerage firm. One such exponent is Donald Regan, former president of Merrill Lynch, Pierce, Fenner & Smith, the nation's largest brokerage firm, which has grown large by catering to small investors. Mr. Regan now serves in President Reagan's administration as chief of staff. "I think the small investor can do better by himself than he can investing in mutual funds. I think also he can outdo the S&P index of five hundred stocks," Mr. Regan told me in an interview some years ago in response to a question about mutual funds and his firm, Merrill Lynch.

For years Merrill Lynch studiously avoided selling mutual funds because the firm's founder, the late Charles E. Merrill, disliked them and believed his

*Commercial paper comprises short-term issues sold to raise working capital by well-known companies such as General Motors, General Electric, or Exxon. See Chapter 17.

Figure 10-2. Tri-Continental Corp. stock action.

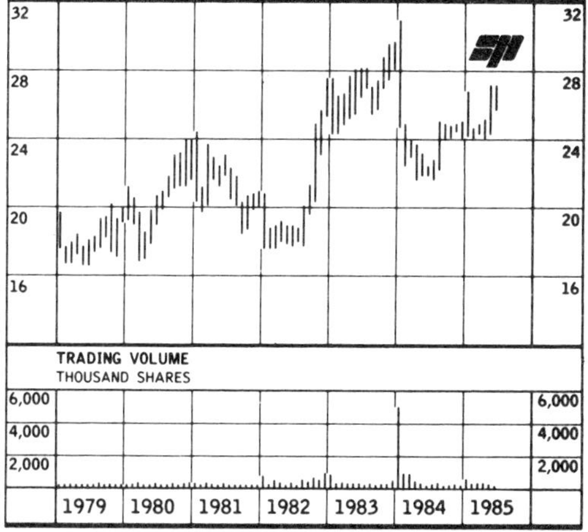

Standard & Poor's Corp.

brokerage firm could do better for the small investor. He emphasized a large research department offering its services—facts and recommendations and portfolio reviews—free of charge.

Then in September 1969, Merrill Lynch finally began to sell funds to its customers; but as Mr. Regan's statement indicates, it made the move with a certain lack of enthusiasm, a kind of "if you can't beat them, join them" philosophy.

Today mutual funds have increased their assets to well over $138 billion, and they have millions of shareholders. Naturally when a fund buys a block of stock as an investment through a brokerage firm, the commissions are large—a business that brokerage firms don't like to do without. Initially Merrill Lynch offered about a dozen selected funds, watched over by a woman analyst in the research department. Figure 10-3 (see pp. 116–117) provides a guide to mutual fund families.

One suggestion for today's woman investor is this: take a small amount of your capital and buy a few shares of a mutual fund or a few shares of a closed-end investment company like Tri-Continental. Keep the shares for at least two years, meanwhile buying shares of some individual stocks with the remainder of your money. Then see if you agree with Donald Regan that the small investor can do better by himself than with the funds. In measuring results, remember to deduct the commissions on the stock and the loading charge for the fund shares.

Other Types of Combined Funds

These days the snowballing rate of inflation has caught up with so many investors that the average family faces the chilling thought that the value of its insurance policies has dropped sharply in terms of today's dollars in recent years. The person who felt secure with $50,000 of life insurance a few years ago realizes that the sum would hardly provide a living income for the surviving family, even supplemented by the Social Security payments they would receive. This unhappy state of affairs has awakened many people to the need for regular investment—including the insurance companies.

The insurance industry has awakened slowly, however. When I wrote a few years ago that a person might do well to buy additional insurance through a term policy and invest the difference between that and the higher premium for ordinary insurance, the president of a large insurance company wrote me indignantly. He made it seem as if I were attacking motherhood by pointing out that insurance does not provide protection against the ravages of inflation. Enclosed with his letter was a brochure he had apparently written years ago citing the danger of investing and the possibility of another major depression. What a lot of nonsense!

As if to indicate that the more alert leaders of the insurance industry have become aware of inflation, most insurance companies are going into the mutual fund business. Some are starting their own funds; more are buying control of going funds or affiliating with them. This should be proof enough that the smooth-talking insurance salesmen realize that Americans know they cannot keep up with inflation just by buying insurance in additional amounts.

Today more and more insurance salespeople (as well as stockbrokers) will be talking to you about mutual funds or insurance with investment aspects, sometimes with fancy names like universal life. As a variation on the theme of combining insurance and mutual funds in a package deal, some companies have been formed to lend you the money—at high rates of interest—to set up long-term programs that you "pay" for monthly.

A much better way, I believe, is to make sure you have enough life insurance on your husband, and if you need more buy additional term insurance while you build up an investment program. But keep the two separate. In other words, first make sure you have sufficient insurance coverage and, second, invest regularly in stock—but bypass the mutual funds.

The new trend in Wall Street is for brokerage firms to sell life insurance as well as mutual funds and stocks. For example, Prudential Insurance Company acquired Bache & Company, a large brokerage firm a few years ago, and now its representatives can offer securities and insurance—virtually complete financial planning. However, I suggest that you avoid getting involved in package deals. Buy insurance from insurance salespeople; buy stocks from brokers. Package programs can sap your initiative.

Furthermore, don't sign up for any contractual plans that tie you up for regular monthly payments, because they usually involve some sort of penalty if you cannot keep up with the program.

If you have only a small amount to invest, there is a good way to accumulate money for investment, while having cash readily available—a new product called money market funds. The funds invest your money in short-term securities, usually government issues. When an investor sells stocks, the money can find a haven in a money market fund automatically, so that interest is not lost before the money is reinvested in stocks again. It is a nice service.

If you still feel that you must buy a mutual fund, a point to remember is that insurance salespeople usually will not be able to give you a wide choice. And they will of course be biased in favor of the funds affiliated with the insurance company (or companies) they represent. In contrast most big brokerage firms are prepared to handle a larger variety of funds. Also, since the brokerage firms' research departments have been studying funds for a much longer period than the insurance companies, they will have the edge in analysis (I believe), for a few years at least. Also, if you are interested in super growth-type funds, another point to consider is that insurance companies tend to be much more conservative in their investment outlook than do most brokerage firms. The fast-growth fund you might hear touted by your friends probably will not be handled by insurance salespeople.

Besides, for those persons who don't want the trouble or the excitement of investing for themselves, there is another way to relieve themselves of responsibility—a method known to many, many widows: let a bank's trust department take over your affairs. It can be done by several methods.

Commercial banks offer investment advisory services, combined if you wish with taking custody of your funds and sending you dividends, etc., from your investments. It's like the bus company slogan of "leave the driving to us."

Many large banks, starting with the big ones and more recently the medium-size ones, have common trust funds. They combine sums of money ($250,000 or possibly as little as $50,000 in the case of smaller banks) into funds, and put them into stocks and other securities along with other trust funds. This master portfolio is managed continually by the bank's investment department. Some banks have several types of such funds—one for growth, another for investment safety through bonds, etc.

The idea of centralized investing of trust funds resulted from a desire of the banks to handle customers' money with greater efficiency and offer them a broader basis of investment. The trend has been growing, and within the next few years probably many small banks will make available common trust funds for relatively small sums of money. The fees for such funds generally are much lower than the loading charges of mutual funds.

Still another method of shifting investment responsibility is to hire an investment adviser. These advisers need not be as expensive as you might think: usually their service entails a small basic fee, plus a percentage of the capital gain achieved each year on your shares. The way such an arrangement ordinarily works is that you place your shares in the hands of your own brokerage firm, and your broker sells or buys the stocks recommended by the investment adviser. Thus you have the peace of mind of knowing your shares are held in safekeeping by the broker. If he thinks that the investment adviser is doing a bad job or trading you in and out too much he might warn you. On the other

Figure 10-3. Mutual fund families.

If recent history is any guide, about one out of every six dollars placed in Individual Retirement Accounts this year will go into mutual funds. Only commercial banks and S&Ls are larger repositories for IRA money.

A major chunk of this tax-deferred money will be earmarked for mutual funds belonging to a family of funds operated by an investment management company. Typically, each member of a fund family is designed for a different investment objective, ranging from high yield and safety to aggressive growth. Most of the large fund groups, such as T. Rowe Price or Fidelity, have growth funds, bond funds, money-market funds and funds that emphasize a combination of capital growth and income.

If you select a fund within a fund family, you can readily switch your money as frequently as you like, either because of a changing assessment of economic conditions or personal financial considerations. Switching between independent funds that are not part of a "family" can become costly, especially if the funds have a sales charge and redemption fee.

Conservative investors, for example, may opt to distribute their capital among two or three funds with

†Principal Objective	Fund	Performance Record — % Change in Per-Share Assets▲ — Annual Data 1985	1984	1983	1982	1981	1980	‡Value on 12/31/85 of $10,000 Invested 12/31/79	**Rank	Yield %
	American Capital Group (800) 231-3638 P.O. Box 1411 Houston, TX 77251									
IS	***Corporate Bond**	+23.6	+ 8.2	+10.7	+32.6	+ 0.4	− 2.9	$19,315	C	10.8
G	***Comstock**	+20.4	− 2.7	+18.1	+37.6	+ 9.1	+31.2	27,250	D	2.8
ISG	***Harbor**	+23.2	− 3.7	+26.0	+39.3	− 4.9	+32.7	26,280	B	5.5
	American Funds Group (800) 421-0180 333 S. Hope St. Los Angeles, CA 90071									
ISG	***American Mutual**	+28.2	+ 5.6	+22.8	+25.1	+ 2.4	+34.9	28,728	B	3.6
G	***AMCAP**	+21.3	− 1.3	+18.9	+28.1	+ 5.5	+28.0	24,626	D	2.4
I	***Income Fund of America**	+25.8	+13.3	+16.6	+34.0	+11.0	+ 9.4	27,042	C	6.6
	Dreyfus (800) 645-6561 767 5th Avenue New York, NY 10153									
GIS	**Growth Opportunity**	+29.4	−11.1	+31.1	+ 1.6	−14.1	+49.0	19,612	D	1.5
GIS	**Dreyfus Fund**	+23.2	+ 3.0	+17.1	+12.1	+ 4.3	+28.3	22,291	E	4.9
IGS	**Special Income**	+21.8	+ 6.4	+20.4	+14.1	+ 0.2	+16.2	20,846	D	7.7
	Federated Securities (800) 245-2423 421 Seventh Avenue Pittsburgh, PA 15219									
GI	***American Leaders**	+26.7	+13.1	+24.9	+27.2	+ 2.3	+21.0	28,181	B	4.4
I	**Fund for U.S. Gov't Secur.**	+15.8	+10.7	+ 9.7	+39.5	− 1.8	− 3.5	18,595	D	11.1
I	***High Income Securities**	+19.2	+ 8.7	+13.8	+29.5	+ 3.5	+ 2.6	20,483	C	11.6
	Fidelity Group (800) 544-6666 82 Devonshire Street Boston, MA 02109									
IG	***Equity Income**	+24.1	+ 6.9	+27.6	+29.9	+ 8.4	+28.8	30,069	B	4.6
SI	**High Income**	+24.1	+ 8.5	+17.8	+32.2	+ 7.2	+ 4.2	23,451	C	12.2
G	***Magellan**	+41.4	+ 0.7	+39.0	+44.8	+16.5	+67.8	56,026	B	0.8
	Franklin Custodian (800) 632-2350 155 Bovet Road San Mateo, CA 94402									
G	***Equity**	+30.5	+ 7.7	+18.4	+15.7	− 9.6	+34.9	23,480	D	2.5
I	***Income Series**	+17.2	+14.1	+15.0	+33.3	+ 1.1	+19.1	24,683	C	11.1
IS	***U.S. Gov't Securities**	+18.6	+11.6	+ 7.7	+30.4	+ 6.3	−12.2	17,348	C	11.5
	IDS (800) 437-4332 IDS Tower Minneapolis, MN 55402									
IS	***Bond Fund**	+22.7	+ 5.7	+14.3	+33.6	+ 0.1	+ 1.3	20,082	D	8.7
G	***Growth Fund**	+36.1	−18.4	+14.0	+30.6	+ 7.3	+71.9	30,497	B	0.3
G	***New Dimensions**	+34.4	− 4.3	+21.1	+32.1	− 2.3	+53.7	30,896	B	2.1

January 29, 1986

The Outlook

different degrees of risk. When you are bullish, you might put 50% of your money in a growth fund, 30% in a bond fund and the remainder in a money-market fund. If you are less willing to accept risk, some 80% of the money might be invested in a government bond fund and 20% in a growth and income fund, which provides a combination of current income and long-term capital appreciation. If you anticipate a sustained decline in the stock market, you might shift completely to a bond or money-market fund.

Most fund families don't charge for switching privileges; others levy a modest $5 fee each time. Some funds let you switch via a toll-free phone call, although many require a written request.

Most of the large fund families have a dozen or more funds, not all of which are suitable for the average IRA plan. Many of them are more speculative funds that focus on specific market sectors, such as foreign stocks, precious metals or high-technology issues.

About half of the IRA money placed with mutual funds is invested in money-market funds and fixed-income funds. About 25% is in growth funds, with the remainder spread among other types of equity funds.

The table beginning on the preceding page and continuing below shows the performance records of 42 funds belonging to 14 of the largest fund families. Each family is represented by three of its funds— generally a growth fund, an income-oriented stock fund and a bond fund. The funds selected are among the more than 400 funds whose performance is tracked by S&P. Each has at least a five- or six-year history.

The performance figures indicate that, over the past six years, growth funds have fared better than other types of funds on a total-return basis (assuming reinvestment of dividends and capital gains). Income-oriented and bond funds, however, have shown much greater stability, an important consideration for an investor who may be close to retirement.

†Principal Objective	Fund	Performance Record — % Change in Per-Share Assets▲ — Annual Data 1985	1984	1983	1982	1981	1980	‡Value on 12/31/85 of $10,000 Invested 12/31/79	**Rank	Yield %
	Lord Abbett (800) 223-4242 63 Wall Street New York, NY 10005									
GI	***Affiliated Fund**	+25.6	+ 6.2	+25.1	+22.3	+ 0.2	+24.2	$25,396	B	5.0
IS	***Bond-Debenture Fund**	+19.5	+ 4.7	+16.4	+24.9	+ 5.0	+ 8.4	20,703	D	10.2
G	***Developing Growth**	+15.0	−22.2	+24.6	+28.4	+ 6.8	+35.0	20,638	B	0.6
	Merrill Lynch Funds (609) 282-2800 P.O. Box 9011 Princeton, NJ 08540									
GI	***Basic Value**	+30.4	+ 6.1	+29.0	+25.0	+ 1.8	+22.2	27,754	B	4.0
I	***Corp. Bond High Qual.**	+20.1	+13.8	+ 9.1	+26.7	− 5.1	...	...	N.A.	10.2
G	***Pacific Fund**	+35.9	+ 3.4	+37.1	+ 0.3	+18.5	+38.0	31,599	B	0.4
	Oppenheimer (800) 525-7048 2 Broadway New York, NY 10004									
G	***Directors Fund**	+22.8	−16.9	+25.1	+31.6	− 8.2	+44.2	22,240	C	1.6
I	***High Yield Fund**	+17.6	+ 3.1	+14.2	+25.8	− 8.2	−11.1	14,215	E	12.9
GI	***Equity Income**	+29.6	+ 1.9	+32.8	+28.6	+ 5.2	+20.7	28,638	C	5.0
	T. Rowe Price (800) 638-5660 100 E. Pratt Street Baltimore, MD 21202									
G	**New Era**	+21.2	+ 3.2	+25.3	− 0.2	−14.7	+49.5	19,945	D	3.3
G	**New Horizons**	+23.5	− 6.9	+19.0	+17.4	− 7.6	+54.7	22,960	E	1.1
I	**New Income**	+16.6	+11.1	+ 8.3	+22.3	+ 7.1	+ 2.8	18,891	C	10.6
	Putnam Funds (800) 225-1581 One Post Office Sq. Boston, MA 02109									
IG	***Conv. Inc.-Growth**	+26.1	+ 4.0	+13.3	+25.9	+ 6.5	+37.3	27,352	C	5.3
I	***High Yield Trust**	+18.4	+ 6.8	+14.1	+35.2	+ 4.7	+ 6.6	21,773	C	13.2
G	***Voyager**	+36.1	− 5.5	+15.4	+31.5	− 5.5	+38.9	25,618	C	0.8
	United Funds (800) 821-5664 P.O. Box 1343 Kansas City, MO 64141									
G	***Accumulative**	+24.2	+ 4.8	+22.5	+24.9	− 3.8	+33.7	25,616	B	4.2
IS	***Income**	+32.2	+ 5.2	+31.2	+29.0	+ 2.7	+14.3	27,631	B	3.6
G	***Vanguard**	+22.6	− 3.3	+21.3	+42.8	+ 7.1	+57.8	34,704	C	4.4
	Vanguard Group (800) 662-7447 Valley Forge, PA 19482									
GI	**Index Trust**	+30.7	+ 6.0	+21.2	+22.0	− 5.2	+31.1	25,459	E	3.8
I	**Investment Grade Bond**	+20.5	+12.9	+ 6.5	+26.2	+ 7.1	+ 4.3	20,426	C	11.8
G	**Morgan Growth**	+28.1	− 5.0	+26.0	+23.3	− 4.6	+33.8	24,133	B	2.2
	♦S&P 500—Stock Index	**+31.6**	**+ 6.1**	**+22.4**	**+21.4**	**− 5.0**	**+32.3**	**26,067**		

**Load (sales commission). †Principal objective in order of importance: G-Growth; I-Income; S-Stability. ▲Percent change derived by taking net asset value (NAV) at end of period plus capital gains and dividends distributed during the period less NAV at beginning of period divided by NAV at beginning of period. ‡Growth of $10,000 is computed by compounding annual performance since December 31, 1979, assuming all dividends and capital gains were invested at year end. Calculations exclude any sales charges. **Number of periods (the six calendar years 1980-1985) in which the fund outperformed the S&P 500 Index (A—5 out of 6; B—4 out of 6; C—3 out of 6; D—2 out of 6; E—1 out of 6). ♦Dividends included. N.A.—Not available; fund in operation only five years.*

January 29, 1986 **The Outlook**

Standard & Poor's Corp.

hand, since your adviser is paid partly on the results he obtains for you—the capital gains—he is not apt to trade merely for the sake of commissions, as a broker might do.

There are many well-known investment advisory services, such as the Wright Investors Service, Standard & Poor's, Moody's Investors Service, and James Dines' service to name a few. Some of these services offer direct management of accounts for a fee. All publish regular advisory brochures, usually weekly, to which you can subscribe for a nominal amount each year; they can be very helpful for the new investor.

Don't forget that subscriptions to investment advisory services as well as fees for managing accounts can be deducted from your taxable income. Thus if you are in the 30 percent tax bracket about one-third of the money spent is saved.

A final thought is this. It is foolish to expect miracles from any kind of investment management in a short space of time. If you do hire an adviser, turn your money over to a bank, or invest in mutual funds, be patient for at least two years before you judge the results.

You can judge the results of the mutual funds you are interested in by checking *Forbes'* mutual fund issue (usually published in August) or other magazines like *Money* that present a monthly roundup.

11

Togetherness Can Be an Answer

Investment Clubs Are Educational

Investing can be—and should be—fun. It doesn't have to involve a grim, greedy pursuit of dollars. Nor do you have to go it alone.

A much more gratifying approach for women than mutual funds, I think, is to join an investment club. If you cannot find one in your neighborhood needing a new member, then consider forming one with a group of friends, associates in business, or women in your community whom you meet in group projects.

Indeed, intelligent, sophisticated women can obtain the benefits of mutual funds—diversification and experienced handling of money—and yet enjoy the excitement and achievement of investing individually by belonging to an investment club. In a sense, you can have your cake (with icing) and eat it too, because investment clubs entail none of the onerous costs of many mutual funds—the 8 percent loading fees and/or the costs deducted for the fund's high-priced management.

In the last thirty years investment clubs have grown like wildflowers in unusual places, wherever there are a few enterprising people. In 1951, the year of its founding, the National Association of Investment Clubs (NAIC, for short) estimates there were several hundred investment groups in the nation. As far as we know, the first progenitors of today's investment clubs began around 1900; the concept is not new, even though you may not have heard much about these clubs until the last few years. Today the number of clubs totals 6,000, with well over 100,000 members, according to Thomas O'Hara, a founder of NAIC. He said that in addition about 13,000 people join NAIC as individuals. He said that the peak number of the clubs was back in 1970, when there were 14,101. However, some of the stock market breaks since that year led to the breakup of some of the clubs.

As of the end of 1984, Mr. O'Hara said that the then 5,000 clubs held investments of about $400 million. His survey also found that the average portfolio of each club member, not including the club's holdings, totaled $73,000, indicating that most members were quite solid citizens financially and quite sophisticated about investing.

"We are adding about a hundred a month to our membership now," he said. Besides clubs in every state, including several in Alaska, Mr. O'Hara said there are clubs in 14 foreign countries. Each year the organization holds an annual meeting, and in 1985 about 9,000 attended the gathering in Chicago.

As you can imagine, investment clubs vary widely in membership and aims. Some clubs follow the "men only" rule; others consist of married couples, while a few have a mix of single men, single women, and couples. Some have members mainly in the same age bracket; others welcome a variety of age groups from the young careerist to the person approaching retirement. Often clubs attract persons with more or less the same backgrounds, people who mingle socially with each other in clubs, business, or churches. On the other hand, certain clubs take pride in the fact that their membership includes a group of persons with widely varying backgrounds who do not necessarily see or know each other in business or social life, but meet mainly at club meetings.

However, if you are a professional woman or a married woman whose husband cannot spare the time, or does not have the interest, to become associated with an investment club, perhaps the best type would be a women's group.

When a logical woman first thinks in terms of a new interest or an avocation apart from her daily life she considers the drawbacks and the possible deterrents. "My husband would laugh about it," a woman might say when the subject of investment clubs is raised. Some men visualize women's investment groups as a kind of harem of voluble women, parroting their husbands' ideas about investments while they meet to sip coffee and munch cake, in between discussing children or work, with a few interpolated remarks about stocks based on tips from friends or rumors in newspapers. Then, after a quick telephone call to a broker but without research, the group votes to buy such and such shares and then adjourns. To save fuss, such a club keeps bookkeeping to a minimum, trusting to the smartest member of the group to give a financial report from time to time. No doubt such investment clubs do exist, giving the husbands of the club members plenty to smile about.

Successful clubs with women members do not operate this way, and they need not do so these days because good help is available at little cost.

Thomas O'Hara's enthusiasm for investment clubs had a practical basis when he started NAIC, because he was an early member of one of the most prosperous of them all. He joined the club, the Mutual Investment Club of Detroit, in 1941, a few months after it was organized, and contributed $20 a month for a period of years, for a total of $3,820 (he skipped a few years when he had financial problems). By the end of 1959, almost 18 years after its founding, the value of his holdings had reached $23,624. It has continued to prosper at a much faster pace in the years since. The club's assets totaled $1,492,000 in 1985; members withdrew $405,000 earlier. All they put in was a total of $186,000.

The typical club follows these four basic principles:

1. It invests a sum once a month in common stocks regardless of market conditions.
2. It reinvests dividends and capital gains immediately, for faster growth of money. Money begets money, especially when the fast compounding principle is at work.
3. It concentrates on buying growth stocks in companies whose sales appear to be increasing at a rate of at least 10 percent or more compounded yearly. The focus is on companies that could reasonably be expected to be financially stronger five years from the time of investment.
4. It follows the principle of diversification.

All this sounds good, but you might ask another question, "Well, suppose I don't like the women involved in an investment club?" An answer to this is that many clubs are composed of women—or men—not necessarily moving in the same social groups or sharing the same interests. Variety can add a great deal to a club.

A woman can be a skilled athlete—an expert golfer or tennis player much of her life—but that need not prevent or deter her from associating with serious intellectual types, or with social butterflies. After all, if she serves on committees in the local hospital, for charities, or in her church, she rubs shoulders with all types. She may be antisocial and prefer the confines of her own home, but in a businesslike venture such as an investment club she could tolerate gregarious, talkative types with whom she might not feel comfortable socially. She might worry about some domineering types of women—the eager church worker who always heads the altar guild, the PTA president who thrives on running meetings, or the "superstar" career woman or female politician—but a well-organized investment club has rules to restrain the overzealous and stimulate the stragglers.

Most successful investment clubs operate by a strict set of rules providing that the "jobs" in the club are rotated regularly among members and that all must participate. When it comes to deciding on an investment after thorough research, the group votes, using majority rule.

"What about money?" a woman might ask. "Can I afford it?" "Can I trust the other members?" These are good questions. Many investment clubs provide that members can put in as little as $10 a month and usually there are top limits, perhaps a ceiling of $30 a month so that the eager members can be limited and not dominate. Mr. O'Hara said that a recent average was $25 monthly.

As for honesty, very few investment clubs, properly organized, have found defalcations. In the first place the money is put in the hands of a good brokerage firm—a transaction handled by the treasurer, usually with a check—and if cash is to be permitted to accumulate for later investment it usually goes into a savings account, with the usual provisions that only certain members can check it out.

Many clubs have bonded their members at a slight annual cost through insurance companies. Furthermore, membership in the NAIC, which costs $30 a year for the club and $7 for each member, includes a $25,000 bond covering any such difficulties.

"What about taxes?" a woman might ask, and this perhaps is the best question of all. Here again the NAIC has a manual that outlines the ways of organizing an investment club. The usual approach is through a partnership because of simplicity and certain tax advantages, unless the members of the club are in a very high tax bracket.

The law involving taxes on a partnership applies the conduit principle. The profits—whether from dividend or capital gains—flow through the club to the individual member, or "partner." She must report them on her income tax.

Here is the way a leading tax organization expresses the system: "Each member reports her proportionate share of dividend income (as if dividends were received by her) and capital gains or losses (as if they were her own capital gains or losses) after offsetting the club's expenses against such income. Once the club member reports her share of club income she is not taxed on it again.

If it is not distributed by the club that year or in ensuing years she adds the reported gains to her cost basis of club membership.''

Suppose that a member wants to resign from a club after a few years and take out her money. Generally the club has a provision for this, just the way a mutual fund does, based on the valuation of the club's investments at the time. The bylaws would contain a provision as to the actual procedure.

Let's take a look at a typical successful women's investment club called the Mobiles, in Royal Oak, Michigan, that had thirteen members. It included a group of women in various fields: a nurse, a telephone company employee, a beauty shop manager, a substitute school teacher. Some were married and middle-aged while some were young, professional women.

The club operated on the theory that they were not in the market for frivolity but working to attain some practical knowledge of investment while at the same time building up funds for later years. Their contributions amounted to only $10 a month, but in 1969, after about five years of investing a total of $9,160, the club had virtually doubled that amount. In fact, their average rate of return had been much better than many mutual funds—26 percent a year. Later monthly payments were increased.

The aim of the club as outlined in the bylaws was to concentrate on sound growth stocks they might want to hold for several years for price appreciation. Their target was to double their money on stocks every five years.

In researching a stock they considered the company's outlook and its management, not the condition of the stock market at the moment. Thus they used a method called *dollar cost averaging.* By this method the club invested the same amount of money periodically, usually every month, in the same stock it had been accumulating. When market values were high, the same amount of money, say $130 a month, bought fewer shares than a month later when stock prices dropped 5 percent or so. However, over a period of time they believed that the market cost of their shares would average out well below the high point the stock would reach in price during a year.

Sally Janke, one of the members of the Mobiles, discussed this investment theory in an interview: ''Generally what we do is to buy more shares of something we already hold and know is good. We like to accumulate a hundred shares of an issue.'' She was speaking at a time when the stock market had fallen quite sharply and many investors were dismayed. ''It's hard,'' she added, explaining that club members often were assailed by doubts at a period when the stock market was low generally. ''We even tend to lose faith in the stocks we own because they are falling, too.''

However, since dollar cost averaging was the club's basic policy, it stuck to its intention. Individual investors often fared well with dollar cost averaging.

In fact, NAIC advocates such an approach to the market because over the long period it has paid with good results. In any event it urges each investment club to adopt and stick to a specific investment policy, or at least to set basic guidelines as to what it will buy and how it will act during inevitable periods of boom or recession.

Nuts and Bolts of Club Operation

Some pointers follow:

Investment ideas. Most investment clubs wisely eschew hot tips and rumors that periodically make the rounds via friends, business acquaintances, or written materials. Women love to gossip but usually such tidbits should be avoided in the investment thinking of a club. Members on their own can pursue such will-o'-the-wisps, if they wish, but a club is advised to avoid them.

Clubs should regularly keep charts because they can tell a story more effectively than mere figures or conversation about a company. One group of charts should be kept on the stocks already owned, showing the prices of the stock, perhaps on a weekly basis of highs and lows, and indicating annual sales volume and per share earnings. The second group of charts should be kept on stocks being considered by the club. From these charts the members can get a good idea of the past history of each company in terms of sales and profits and price action of the shares, which can be compared with other investments.

Where do investment clubs get ideas for securities? Their broker might turn over to the club recommendations of his firm's research department with the figures they want. Members of the club, who regularly read newspapers, investment letters, and magazines, will suggest ideas. Then there are the inevitable suggestions from friends and other outsiders.

Club size. The NAIC recommends that clubs limit their membership to about ten and no more than fifteen persons and that contributions be a minimum of $20 a month.

If a club allows itself a bigger membership, even on the theory that some new members will drop out after the initial eagerness wanes, it runs into logistics problems. The average living room, in a house or apartment, would be overcrowded with more than fifteen persons, even allowing for an absence or two. And since most club hostesses serve coffee and cake or cookies during the monthly meeting, serving more people than fifteen could become expensive, even though the hostessing of the meetings is rotated each month.

At the same time clubs should remember that they face the prospect of attrition; sooner or later a few members will move from the community, become sick or even die, or lose interest and resign. It's a good idea for the club to anticipate this by asking occasional guests to the meetings with the idea of adding "new blood" to fill out the vacancies as they occur.

Finding a broker. A club might have to do some serious searching—or even selling of itself—to arouse the interest of a good broker (see Chapter 7). Some clubs have tried to do this by inviting a friendly broker, man or woman, to join the club. However, most brokers probably will say they are too busy or already belong to such a group. In fact, I think it is preferable not to have a broker member because then the club might be overly swayed by his superior knowledge of the market. They might lean on him too much for ideas and not do enough of their own research.

A young broker, perhaps a little hungry to build up his roster of customers and contacts, often is a good person for an investment club to seek out. If the club's investments are successful the individual members probably will want to open their own accounts with a brokerage firm—a good source of business for the broker. Furthermore, most women club members have husbands or friends who could also bring business to the broker. This could be stressed by the club's committee assigned to pick out a broker.

Once a broker has been found, then the club should appoint one person (or two at the outside) to deal with him—calling with orders to buy and sell, or asking for research material and recommendations. In other words, the other members of the club should not be permitted to bother the broker with vague questions or a scattering of inquiries.

Some years ago the NAIC reported that some clubs were turned down by brokers who claimed that small groups did not do enough business to merit the expense of opening and handling their accounts. Unfortunately, Wall Street and its member firms had been going through a period of discouraging the small investor. However, some of the big brokerage houses with many branch offices cannot—and dare not—take this attitude because they rely on volume. Try them if your group receives a cool reception.

Organization. Every club, as well as every business, needs a table of organization, detailing the duties of various office holders. For example, one person in an investment club should be assigned the job of contact with the broker. Another might hold the office of treasurer for a year. Another member might have the task of charting the prices of stocks, along with sales and per share earnings of the portfolio investments, reporting each month on how the stocks are performing and if the investment goals are being achieved. A study group might be assigned to make recommendations for new shares to be purchased, backing their proposals with charts.

Other members might be assigned to give reports each month on various factors relating to investments. Often a club will find that it need not change its portfolio, and field reports can keep the group alert and interested when there is little to discuss about current investments. For example, periodic reports could be made on topics like these:

Economic trends.
Emerging industries: the new growth areas that every club should follow.
Overlooked stocks that might recover in price.
Esoteric investments such as puts and calls, commodity futures, commercial paper; probably the club will not invest in these, but it can help educate members as to their role.
Individual industry groups and their trends: banks and financial stocks, public utilities, railroads, steels and other metals, chemicals, autos, etc.

Bookkeeping. The clerical aspects of a club need not be boring, especially if the club follows a simple principle of limiting new investment to units of $10. Thus a member can invest each month in two units worth $20, for instance, with some sort of maximum so that wealthy investors would not be able to dominate the club by having a much larger investment stake than the average member.

Meetings. On the principle that there should be no silent partners in investment clubs, the club probably should adopt a rule that members must attend at least nine monthly meetings a year, or be asked to resign. Exceptions could be made in the case of long sicknesses or accidents, etc.

Portfolio mix. An interesting recommendation of NAIC is that a club's portfolio should be a mixture. About 25 percent of the club's monies should be in stocks of big companies in major industries, which show a pattern of regular growth. Another 25 percent should be allotted to stocks of smaller companies in somewhat riskier fields—the fast-growth-type stocks. The remainder should be put into companies ranging between these extremes.

See Figure 11-1 (pp. 128–129) for a recent analysis of a club portfolio in NAIC's magazine, *Better Investing*. From time to time, *Better Investing* lists the 100 most popular stocks held by its member clubs (Figure 11-2, pp. 130–131).

Consider the words of John Maynard Keynes, quoted by NAIC's *Better Investing* magazine:

> The spectacle of modern investment markets has sometimes moved me towards the conclusion that to make the purchase of an invest-

Table 11-1. $10,000 investment compounded.

Rate of Return	*10 years*	*20 years*	*30 years*
3%	$13,440	$18,060	$ 24,270
5	16,290	26,530	43,220
8	21,590	46,610	100,630
10	25,940	67,280	174,490

ment permanent and indissoluble, like marriage, except by reason of death or other grave cause, might be a useful remedy for our contemporary evils.

Better Investing noted that it knew of at least one club that did not heed Keynes's words. Would you believe that the club has sold 26 issues? Would you also believe that the club's portfolio is now worth only about one-third of what the members have invested? You can believe it.

On the other side of the coin a member of NAIC who has owned Eastman Kodak for a considerable number of years (it's first public offering of stock was in 1884) can give us a beautiful example of the value of compounding and long-term investment. Although the longevity of this particular example is carrying things a little beyond the scope of our usual thinking, even the modern picture is significant.

One share bought at $100 in 1884 would have grown to 24,536.84 shares in 1985.

Reinvestment. The NAIC urges clubs to invest dividends and capital gains so that the fund can grow as fast as possible. However, there will always be members who need to take their dividends or gains out, possibly to help pay for children's college bills, hospital bills, etc. This should be allowed, provided a little advance notice is given so that the club can obtain the cash.

The point about steady reinvestment is that with a large amount of capital the club can take advantage of buying round lots of stock (100 shares) as well as attracting more active interest from the broker.

Remember the importance, too, of compound interest, something the average investor learns back in high school days and promptly forgets. Table 11-1 will remind you of the power of compounding.

The records of many investment clubs show that a 10 percent and more return (dividends and capital gains) can be achieved without miracles over a period of years.

Figure 11-1. A typical investment club analysis.

the repair shop

Ralph L. Seger, Jr., C.F.A.
President,
Seger-Elvekrog, Inc.

Watch the 'Loss' in Stop Loss Selling

"How do we get the most out of our investment dollar," asks the president of the Executive Woman Investment Club of Ashtabula, Ohio. "We would appreciate your ideas for improvement with help in deciding when and what to sell," she continues.

This four-year-old club has been favored by three years of a rising market. All of the stocks in the portfolio were acquired since late 1982. A 23% gain on cost indicates a successful investment strategy. The club uses the NAIC Stock Selection Guide before buying and has spent much effort learning the fundamentals of stock valuation as taught by the NAIC stock study tools.

The club has stop loss orders to sell on all but two issues. The stop loss orders are liable to be executed in the form of market sell orders with any sharp decline in the market. By selling with a stop loss, an investor both loses and gains depending on the severity of the market reaction.

If the price of the stock goes well below the price of the stop loss, the investor avoids turning a profitable situation into a paper loss. However, by selling with a stop loss the investor gives up part of the potential profit. For example, with **National Medical Enterprises** the club's cost is $21.376 a share. At the 9/9/85 price of 24 the club had a profit of $328 or $2.624 a share. If their stop loss at 23 is executed the gain is $1.624 a share or $203. All this is less commission costs of course.

If the stock is considered overvalued at 23, it is overvalued at 24. Neither is correct. National Medical Enterprises is estimated by Standard & Poor's to earn $2.30 a share for the fiscal year ending May 31, 1985. At a price of 24 that's a P/E ratio of 10.4. That is in the lower end of the historical P/E ratio range and certainly not a sale based on overvaluation.

If the stock got up to 37¼, a P/E ratio of 16.2, it could be considered overvalued. A P/E of 16.2 is the average high P/E ratio of the last 5 years. That's the point for a stop loss.

Another way to look at a sell point would be a price of 41¼ which I calculate as an upside/downside ratio of 1 to 1. I think the stock might go as high as 65 if earnings grow at 15%. The downside risk seems to be about 17⅝, the lowest price during market pressures of the last two years.

To find the price that provides an upside/downside ratio of 1 to 1 is simple. The total price range is 47⅜ (65 minus 17⅝). If we divide 47⅜ by 2 and add the result to 17⅝ it will

Executive Woman Investment Club

Company	No. Shares	Cost	9/6/85 Price	Value	Gain/ (Loss)
Nat. Medical Entr.	125	$2,672	24	$3,000	$ 328
Banc One	82	1,739	21¾	1,784	45
Dover Corp.	50	1,401	37	1,850	449
Tucson El. Pwr.	100	2,859	39⅝	3,963	1,104
Alamito	10	728	92½	925	197
Franklin Group Gold Fund	52	653	7.76	404	(249)
Amoco	30	1,496	64½	1,935	439
Cyprus Mining	3	42	14	42	0
Maytag	20	1,036	56¼	1,125	89
RPM	125	1,439	16¾	2,094	655
Telxon	150	886	16⅝	2,494	1,608
TRW	25	1,650	75⅝	1,891	241
Browning Ferris	25	1,000	52⅛	1,303	303
Rockwell Int'l.	50	1,829	41¼	2,063	234
Parker-Hannifin	50	1,602	33¼	1,663	61
Cash		2,672		2,672	0
Total		$23,704		$29,208	$5,504

produce a price which provides an upside/downside ratio of 1 to 1.

$$\frac{47.375}{2} = 23.69$$

Then 23.69 + 17.625 = approximately 41¼.

Let's test it:

$$\frac{(65 - 41.25)}{41.25 - 17.625} = \frac{23.75}{23.625}$$

At an upside/downside ratio of 1 to 1, the odds of gain no longer are greater than the odds of losing.

There are two ways of determining when a stock is overvalued:

(1) Selling at a P/E ratio equal to or greater than the historical average high P/E ratio.

(2) Selling at a price that produces an upside/downside ratio of 1 to 1 or less. Naturally, the computations have to be updated no less frequently than once a year. As earnings advance the estimated 5 year high price will move up and probably the estimated low price will too. This will advance the price that produces an upside/downside ratio of 1 to 1.

As the estimated EPS for the coming year moves ahead, the price that produces a P/E ratio equal to the average high P/E ratio will increase.

These techniques work for a stock that is meeting its estimated growth pattern. If the fundamentals shift and the EPS expectations are not met, the reason needs to be examined. If the reason turns out to be that the profitability of the company seems to be impared for some reason other than a temporary one, the stock may be considered a sell candidate.

Aside from the Franklin Group Gold Fund mutual shares, all of the stocks in the portfolio appear to be good choices. However, 16 issues in a $29,208 portfolio are too many in my belief. I suggest the club cut back to 10 or 12.

The **Cyprus Mining** spin off from **Amoco** is too small a holding.

The club can get the most out of its investment dollar by continuing to employ the NAIC Stock Selection Guide. Paying attention to price-earnings ratios is also important. Try to buy at a P/E ratio, based on the coming year's estimated EPS, that is equal to or less than the historical price-earnings ratio. This sets the stage for the biggest way to get the most out of an investment dollar – a price-earnings ratio expansion.

Figure 11-2. Top 100 favorite stocks.

Company	Rank by # of Clubs Holding	Number of Clubs Holding Stock	Rank by Total Shares Held	Number of Shares Held by NAIC Members	Rank by Total Value of Shares Held	Total Value of Shares Held by NAIC Members on 12-31-84
International Business Machines Corp.	1	1,558	1	681,144	1	$83,865,855
** American Telephone & Telegraph Co.	2	1,320	4	523,728	7	10,212,696
Wendy's International, Inc.	3	1,208	3	527,403	11	8,768,075
American Home Products Corporation	4	920	11	285,240	2	14,404,620
** Sears, Roebuck & Co.	5	912	10	292,559	9	9,288,748
Schlumberger Limited	6	867	9	297,258	5	11,332,961
MCI Communications, Inc.	7	854	12	281,175	64	2,108,813
American Family Corporation	8	761	2	601,207	3	13,978,063
Chesebrough-Pond's Inc.	9	753	6	360,089	4	12,107,993
** Baxter Travenol Laboratories, Inc.	10	727	8	328,386	30	4,310,066
** Hospital Corporation of America	11	705	39	114,756	29	4,332,039
** Pfizer, Inc.	12	673	30	132,571	19	5,601,125
National Medical Enterprises, Inc.	13	620	7	349,115	12	8,160,563
** Humana Inc.	14	521	27	149,777	35	3,519,760
Abbott Laboratories	15	496	25	170,561	15	7,120,922
** Comair, Inc.	16	480	49	95,480	88	1,217,370
** Wal-Mart Stores, Inc.	17	467	58	80,747	47	3,058,293
Johnson & Johnson	18	405	23	174,726	17	6,311,977
PepsiCo, Inc.	19	394	13	223,042	8	9,562,926
* Exxon Corporation	20	380	24	173,069	14	7,788,105
W.R. Grace & Co.	21	361	33	127,185	22	5,055,604
** Kmart Corporation	22	358	28	148,219	21	5,224,720
** The Dow Chemical Company	23	352	14	209,877	18	5,771,618
** Dayton Hudson Corporation	24	346	47	98,145	46	3,091,568
** Tracor, Inc.	25	344	41	110,525	50	2,901,281
** Philip Morris Incorporated	26	339	52	88,316	16	7,120,478
Masco Corporation	27	333	18	194,819	20	5,454,932
General Electric Company	28	327	19	192,734	6	10,913,563
Quanex Corporation	29	326	5	378,212	49	2,931,143
General Motors Corporation	30	320	40	112,808	10	8,841,327
Mobil Corporation	31	318	20	184,762	23	5,011,669
Tandy Corporation	32	316	51	92,345	57	2,239,366
Wang Laboratories, Inc.	33	313	32	127,402	35	3,264,676
** RPM Inc.	34	311	36	116,884	80	1,607,155
Glaxo Holdings	35	302	46	103,387	85	1,305,261
Chi-Chi's, Inc.	36	295	55	85,353	94	1,045,574
** Beatrice Companies, Inc.	37	291	72	62,172	72	1,740,816
* Hewlett-Packard Company	38	286	83	51,259	73	1,736,399
* Chyron Corporation	39	284	15	205,088	65	2,050,880
* Texas Oil & Gas Corporation	40	281	26	167,860	48	3,000,498
Eastman Kodak Company	41	274	42	109,096	13	7,841,275
Apple Computer, Inc.	42	270	68	65,075	69	1,895,309
** Federal-Mogul Corporation	43	263	34	119,780	32	3,713,180
Texaco Inc.	44	259	59	78,005	53	2,661,921
** Ralston Purina Company	45	257	80	56,841	66	2,032,066
Kaneb Services, Inc.	46	241	22	175,238	78	1,602,952
Moog Inc.	47	238	17	204,220	60	2,246,240
American Hospital Supply Corporation	48	236	35	118,939	40	3,419,496
G. Heilman Brewing Co., Inc.	49	233	21	184,290	44	3,155,966
** Kellogg Company	50	232	53	87,404	37	3,496,160

Company	Rank by # of Clubs Holding	Number of Clubs Holding Stock	Rank by Total Shares Held	Number of Shares Held by NAIC Members	Rank by Total Value of Shares Held	Total Value of Shares Held by NAIC Members on 12-31-84
** Chrysler Corporation	51	227	37	116,515	31	$3,728,480
* Fort Howard Paper Company	52	225	98	30,108	71	1,780,136
* Hershey Foods Corporation	53	221	77	59,086	58	2,282,197
* Ford Motor Company	54	217	86	48,364	61	2,206,608
* Hillenbrand Industries, Inc.	55	207	85	50,146	93	1,053,066
Westinghouse Electric Corporation	56	198	44	105,027	51	2,743,830
The Boeing Company	57	197	73	61,335	38	3,473,094
Bob Evans Farms, Inc.	58	195	16	204,510	34	3,681,180
** McDonald's Corporation	59	192	54	85,714	27	4,424,985
Syntex Corporation	60	191	50	93,840	26	4,562,970
** Minnesota Mining & Manufacturing Co.	61	186	69	63,152	24	4,965,326
* Dana Corporation	62	184	62	72,188	67	1,922,006
** John H. Harland Company	63	181	89	44,755	62	2,131,457
** Browning-Ferris Industries, Inc.	64	180	93	34,262	86	1,267,694
* BellSouth Corporation	65	177	100	24,111	96	819,774
* The Limited, Inc.	66	172	94	33,875	95	914,625
** Borg-Warner Corporation	67	170	43	105,360	59	2,252,070
AMETEK, Inc.	68	166	29	141,187	39	3,459,082
* Eli Lilly and Company	69	164	67	66,209	28	4,369,794
American Express Company	70	163	66	66,751	54	2,511,506
** The Quaker Oats Company	71	160	57	83,008	43	3,164,680
* IC Industries, Inc.	72	158	92	40,680	90	1,169,550
Anixter Bros., Inc.	73	157	88	45,473	97	790,093
Worthington Industries, Inc.	74	156	38	116,214	52	2,672,922
* Atlantic Richfield Company	75	150	60	73,466	41	3,241,687
Koppers Company, Inc.	76	147	31	131,604	56	2,368,872
** Van Dorn Company	77	145	48	97,312	68	1,921,912
Dover Corporation	78	142	71	62,190	63	2,130,008
** Longs Drug Stores, Inc.	79	139	56	83,200	33	3,681,600
** Archer-Daniels-Midland Company	80	138	96	31,947	99	610,986
SmithKline Beckman Corporation	81	133	97	31,374	77	1,639,292
* Standard Oil Company (Indiana)	82	131	74	60,663	42	3,207,556
* Burlington Northern Inc.	83	130	45	103,560	25	4,867,320
** Georgia-Pacific Corporation	84	129	87	47,306	89	1,182,650
* ServiceMaster Industries Inc.	85	128	82	52,128	83	1,420,488
* Magic Chef, Inc.	86	127	91	40,989	82	1,449,986
* The Pillsbury Company	87	126	99	24,544	91	1,092,208
** Intel Corporation	88	125	76	59,710	75	1,671,880
Ball Corporation	89	123	65	69,922	45	3,146,490
Cooper Industries, Inc.	90	122	75	60,101	74	1,705,366
Apogee Enterprises Inc.	91	121	61	72,923	98	647,192
United States Steel Corporation	92	120	78	57,408	81	1,499,784
Shoney's, Inc.	93	119	84	50,530	79	1,610,644
Mary Kay Cosmetics, Inc.	94	118	79	57,311	100	522,963
* Parker Hannifin Corporation	95	115	90	42,190	84	1,328,895
* United Technologies	96	114	81	55,318	87	1,230,826
* Alaska Airlines, Inc.	97	112	63	71,682	92	1,084,190
* International Paper Company	98	110	95	33,750	70	1,818,281
Allied Corporation	99	107	64	71,031	55	2,450,570
Community Psychiatric Centers	100	104	70	62,785	76	1,671,651

12

The Stuff of Dreams

Speculation Can Be Heady

Speculation is a heady thing, the stuff of which dreams are made. If you think about it, everyone is a speculator, but the degrees of risk-taking range widely. The word comes from the Latin *speculari,* which can be translated several ways: to spy, explore, reconnoiter, observe, watch for. All meanings indicate that the speculator is a careful, shrewd risk-taker.

Risk belongs inescapably to daily living. For example, the National Safety Council tells us that every time you, a presumably safe driver, climb into a car and drive a few miles to the local supermarket you are putting your life at risk. More car accidents happen within twenty miles of a person's home than on the major highways where speed is dominant.

The point is that putting your money in the stock market can be risky, and for some people more speculation will be involved because they choose to take more risks than other persons. Yet, more than driving a car on dangerous highways, more than picking a husband, stocks can involve predeterminations and knowledgeable speculation. And they can be quickly sold; cars and husbands cannot be changed so readily.

In speaking about the stock market, brokers or news writers often talk this way: "Speculative buying pushed prices up today"; or "The government is worried about too much speculation; margin requirements may be raised." It sounds as if speculation was dangerous and slightly unsavory, or a darkly unrighteous act.

Speculators generally can be defined as large or small. The large ones have plenty of money to move in and out of the market and take risks. Since they have sufficient money and borrowing power they can afford losses. The small speculators operate with much more limited funds, are more apt to be hurt financially if prices drop sharply, are less sophisticated, react too much, even panic their way into losses.

What Is Speculation?

Basically speculation involves one or more of these eight factors:

1. Risk
2. Quick trades
3. Stress on high percentage return
4. Stop orders
5. Borrowed money
6. Leverage
7. New areas, new issues
8. Systems, or determined approaches

Risk

To speculate implies taking a certain amount of risk. An elderly conservative woman would take a risk if she kept virtually all her money in the shares of one company, though she might not realize it was risky.

Years ago my obstetrician, an elderly, brilliant, very successful New York doctor, often chatted with me about the stock market. He told me that he lived through the Depression and since then he had kept most of his money in bonds, corporate and government. In being so conservative he took a risk with his future because bond interest did not keep pace with inflation, until interest rates rose sharply in the 1980s.

The father of a man I know was a professional writer, articulate, pleasant, never drank too much, didn't smoke, never lost jobs, made a good salary writing, didn't go out with other women besides his wife, but he had a glaring weakness—gambling. He spent most of his salary each week betting on horses, football pools, anything. He couldn't resist a bet. As a result he lost his wife, his house, an inheritance, and everything except his job, even though the boss threatened to fire him from time to time because of creditors on his heels. A psychiatrist couldn't help him. He was at the razor edge of risk-taking, where losses cut deeply.

A famous risk-taker and consummate salesman of ideas was real estate tycoon William Zeckendorf. His grandiose dream of building vast real estate complexes always involved a large amount of risk, glamour, and borrowed money. He would have fared all right except he built on some "sand," and when a recession came along a few years ago his creditors forced his firm into a reorganization. Now the company is run profitably by his son.

The point is that many people take risks unconsciously; others cannot resist risk-taking to the point of testing their fate. The wise risk-taker knows how much he can afford to risk (or lose) at a certain time and how much risk might be involved. He builds on realities or good possibilities, not just hopes or fear.

Quick Trades

A speculator pays little attention to dividends and current income. He stresses price appreciation. Of course, in calculating his overall return he does figure dividends plus appreciation. He hopes to turn over his money as many times a year as possible, so he is prepared psychologically to move quickly in and out of the market, without regard to the six months' holding period for establishing capital gains. However, if a situation does require half a year or more to work out, he willingly holds on.

This requires knowing the commission rates and figuring how much of a rise—a point, two points, or more—is needed for a quick, worthwhile profit after commissions and income taxes.

Let's see how a quick trade might work out. There has been a rumor that Photo Corporation (imaginary company) plans to introduce a new type of camera. You buy 100 shares of the stock after investigating the company (you find out it has a good earnings record, etc.). The broker gets you the stock for a price of 10 a share. A round trip commission (the total of the commissions charged when you buy and when you sell) will require about $50, plus state transfer taxes of a few cents a share when you sell. This means that your 100 shares of the stock must move up half a point to cover these costs alone. You are in the 30 percent tax bracket, meaning that Uncle Sam takes that percentage of any profit you make above your cost. If the stock goes up to 11½, you figure you will make about $100 above the commission and you can keep about $70 of this (the remaining $30 goes to Uncle Sam). So you tell your broker to sell at this point—11½—on the theory that you will be content with making $70 for an in-and-out trade. The trade is completed and you are happy at the result even though the stock jumps higher before a reaction sets in.

Stress on High Percentage Return

Speculators want at least a 10 percent return on their money. A smart trader does not wait until the last moment to sell; he is content with a quick, tidy profit. In the Photo Corporation example above, if he makes only one such successful trade per month he has made 12 times $70, or $840 a year on his $1,000, or a very high return after taxes. A good speculator turns his money even faster than that in a favorable market.

Sometimes speculators who trade in and out spend part of the day either watching the board in their broker's office or consulting with him frequently over the telephone. Quite often they are chart traders, which means that when a certain formation appears on the charts they keep of price movement for favorite stocks, they will act. They tell their broker to buy at a certain price and sell at a certain price, with the use of stop orders placed slightly below their purchase price; they will automatically be sold out if prices run counter to their thinking. Speculators classed as successful do not let emotion or ego keep them in a stock whose price is moving against them.

Stop Orders

Typically, a speculator makes more use of stop orders than most investors, resorting to them both as downside protection and upside profit assurance.

The smart speculator doesn't grab for a stock. He approaches it with the caution of a man approaching a cobra—quietly, determinedly, and patiently. This is a ''thing'' the speculator wants but on his own terms.

For example, many speculators will place a buy order—GTC—until they get a stock at their price. The price might be a few points below the level around which the market for the stock has been jumping for a few days or weeks. Speculators know from experience that day-to-day movements usually range widely enough over a period of time so that their orders often can be filled at the price they want.

Once the shares have been bought the speculator keeps in close contact with his stock, a basic difference between him and an investor. The investor relaxes and waits; the speculator watches his stock day by day, jots down price changes, probably charts them for a better view.

He isn't bothered by the day-by-day changes necessarily, but he wants to detect and follow trends. He has set for himself a target price for the stock—not a greedy one, if he is wise. He might expect it to rise 10 percent. Once it has achieved this he would sell. A stop order would be in the market on the upside to automatically take him out at that point.

Naturally, if the market for the shares was booming, perhaps along with the trend in stocks generally, he might raise his upside stop order from time to time. At the same time he would protect himself from downswings by stop orders under the current market price. Thus if he bought a stock at 50 originally he might place a stop below this level at 47, figuring if he was so wrong in his estimate of the stock's potential a $3 loss per share (minus commissions) would at least free him from a bad situation.

If the stock proceeded to move up to 53 he would move up his downside stop order as well, perhaps to 50. At that point his new stop price matches his original price for the shares, meaning if he was sold out at that level there would be no loss except the commission. Suppose the stock rises to 54, and his stop has been upped to 51. Now he has covered the price of the round trip commission, and if he sells above this level he will have a profit. Also, he raises his topside limit to 58.

Let's assume the stock rises to 58, a price about 16 percent above his purchase price. This is the point at which he placed his upside stop order and the stock is sold.

I have a feeling that if a speculator places a stop order at the time he first buys the shares, there is the possibility that it can have a good psychological effect. The order to sell at 58 shows up on the specialist's book on the floor, along with the order to sell around a point or two below the market level. If a specialist has a large amount of sell orders well above the current price for the shares, it might serve to reinforce his own thinking about the stock. The specialist with his feel for the market often judges his own position by what appears in his books.

The problem is that the average investor and broker don't know what the specialist has on his books in the way of buy and sell orders.

Borrowed Money

Many speculators have margin accounts with a brokerage firm. Buying on margin is a method by which one can trade stocks with the use of borrowed money.

First of all, it requires the opening of a margin account with a brokerage firm. A margin account can be dangerous in this respect: the Federal Reserve system, the nation's central banker, sets the so-called margin rate on a percentage basis. When speculation tends to increase sharply, the Fed often raises the margin requirement. On the other hand, when market prices are in the doldrums, the Fed might decrease its margin requirement to encourage more purchases of securities.

Let's suppose the margin rate is 75 percent. That means that you must put up in cash in your margin account or have securities available in the account to provide enough loanable value to be the equivalent of 75 percent of the purchase price of a stock. The broker will lend you the remaining 25 percent, for which he will charge you the current rate of interest. Between 1962 and 1972 the margin rate on such trades ranged from 50 to 80 percent. In recent years it has been 50 percent.

If the margin in your account runs below the requirement because of a decline in the price of your stock your broker will notify you immediately, by telephone or telegram, that you must provide more cash or collateral; this is known as a margin call. Some brokerage firms, in order to give themselves additional protection, require more margin than the basic Federal Reserve regulations.

Remember if a margin call goes out to you one day, it must be answered the next. If not, the broker can sell out the stock, and you have no legal recourse against him even if the stock gains 10 points the next day. The responsibility rests upon you.

The tumbling prices of stock in 1929 when many investors used margin accounts were accelerated by the forced sale of stock owned by people who couldn't raise the cash to save their positions. In those days, before the advent of much government control, speculators often bought stocks for 100 percent margin. They were buying hopes and dreams and mortgaging their souls for them.

The woman speculator who believes that she needs to obtain more money for her ventures can do it by a method a little safer than buying on margin. She can first purchase 100 shares of a sound stock, the kind that ordinarily doesn't show much price volatility, and take these shares to her local bank. There she can ask for and generally easily obtain a collateral loan.

For example, a woman might invest in 300 shares of AT&T selling around 22, for a total of $6,600, on which a bank might lend her 75 percent of the amount, or roughly $4,900 in cash. Then she could use the $4,900 to speculate. Meanwhile the AT&T shares would pay a dividend each year, and if the bank asked her to reduce the loan from time to time she could use the AT&T dividends to help do this. I consider this method much less dangerous than using a margin account; yet at the same time it provides what can be called the leverage of more money.

Naturally she will have to pay the loan off at the bank someday, but if the basic shares are sound the bank probably will let her loan remain on its books for a long time. She will have to pay interest quarterly at whatever the current rates are.

Leverage

Investors often hear the word "leverage" used, just as above it was applied to borrowed money that gives an investor more funds for trading. There are other forms of leverage, too.

Brokers and speculators speak knowingly about "leveraged" situations. These are stocks that for various reasons can show high price swings. They offer speculators good chances for fast profits.

A typical leverage situation might be this, involving a company we will call Super Electronics. Let's say that this is a well-established company in a growth industry, which has a bond issue requiring $100,000 in interest payments yearly, preferred dividends that take another $100,000, plus 100,000 shares of common stock.

In 1983 the company earns $300,000, and to a stockholder its status looks like this:

$100,000	for bond interest
100,000	for preferred dividends
100,000	remaining for stockholders, or $1 a share

Now let's suppose that in 1985 Super Electronics completed a big order for a new product sold to the government, and earnings increased sharply to $500,000.

$100,000	for bond interest
100,000	for preferred dividends
300,000	remaining for stockholders, or $3 a share

In other words, operating earnings (for simplicity's sake we haven't considered taxes) have increased by about 66 percent or $200,000, but for holders of shares of common stock this has resulted in an earnings increase of three times $1, or $3—triple their money.

Naturally, the mere fact that earnings have increased sharply does not mean the company will necessarily pay out the additional net income to stockholders: most growth-type companies, especially small ones, conserve their cash for reinvestment in more plants and equipment. But speculators in a leveraged situation like this count on one or two things happening.

The shares purchased at, say, 25 a share when earnings were $1 might have risen in price to 50 a share in 1985 when they earned $3. Furthermore, even if the company didn't increase its cash dividend it might issue some dividends in the form of more stock. As mentioned before, stock dividends in a growth company tend to reflect the higher price hopes of investors.

Speculators gravitate to situations where leverage like this can occur. Often they can find it when a company has senior securities such as bonds and preferreds ahead of the common.

New Areas, New Issues

When they can buy them, speculators like new issues. As mentioned before, your broker probably will not be able to fill orders from you to buy shares in companies offering their stock publicly for the first time—the so-called new issue market—unless you happen to be a large, important customer (or a relative) or unless the new issue is a large one or has somehow failed to arouse the public appetite. Two uncommonly large new issues were Comsat, offered years ago and touched with the allure of space,* and the "Radio City" securities offering in 1985 made by the Rockefeller family to divest part of their real estate properties.

However, you might be able to pick up new issues at reasonable prices a few days after they have reached the market. Sometimes, a short time after the new issue is sold publicly the speculators who were able to buy shares dump them, and the price of the stock drops sharply in reaction.

Before you buy a new issue your broker is required by law to provide you with a prospectus, a brochure that must be filed first with the Securities and Exchange Commission. It gives you basic, unvarnished facts about the company, and the aim of the SEC is to make sure that the truth is told in an unvarnished way. Naturally, the lawyers who file the prospectus with the SEC try to say as little as possible, but the SEC can insist that they revise it, often half a dozen times. For instance:

A cement company in Oklahoma had to explain that it had no plant in operation at the time of the stock offering and was going to operate in a largely agricultural community. Oddly enough, it turned out to be a very good investment. Its name: Oklahoma Cement Company.

A fried chicken company had to state that its most important asset was the name of the company, which had been "rented" from a leading singer, Minnie Pearl. She would receive a certain amount of money each year for the use of her name. Said the prospectus: "If Mrs. Cannon (whose stage name is Minnie Pearl) should die or become physically disabled the loss to the company of her

*Comsat, formally called Communications Satellite Corporation, operates the commercial communications satellite system. Comsat was formed as a private corporation, with stock outstanding, by an act of Congress in 1963. It is traded on the New York Stock Exchange.

continued promotion could have a materially adverse effect on the success of the company.'' The company did not fare well after a few years.

An ''act of God'' takes on significance in the case of one company—the Real Eight Company, a treasure-hunting salvage business. In its prospectus the lawyers wrote: ''A violent hurricane or other act of God could possibly shift the present sunken valuables where the company is conducting salvage operations . . . or could bury these valuables under a substantial amount of sand.'' Furthermore, the state of Florida must share any of the company's treasure findings, with its take put at 25 percent of the market value. (The reader of the prospectus for this fascinating venture also learns that ''the diving operations do not require professional deep sea divers and it generally employs qualified scuba divers who are frequently college students.'' Obviously, this is not a prospectus that a woman should pass on to her son, if she wants him to settle down after college into a nice, easy desk job.)

Sometimes, as in the case of another company called Monroe Combining Company, which provided laminating service to fabric converters and apparel manufacturers, the prospectus reveals deficits. In this case the prospectus also noted that the underwriter's commission was quite high.

Don't ever consider buying a new stock without reading the prospectus, word by word. Not only do prospectuses make fascinating reading, but they also can change your thinking. As mentioned before, the prospectus is the one time when a company has to ''let down its hair'' and tell the truth, at least in so far as the Securities and Exchange Commission's lawyers can make them mention some of the possible difficulties, drawbacks, or competition the company faces.

Sometimes reading a prospectus is enough to warn an investor away from a certain issue. Then if he buys the stock and it turns out badly he has no one except himself to blame. While the Securities and Exchange Commission makes a company reveal essential negative facts, it does not in any way endorse or not endorse the issue. It is a watchdog, not a judge.

The investor stands alone when he judges a new issue, and even his broker does not have responsibility beyond providing the prospectus and recommending against the stock, if the issue appears to be too far out or speculative. Reputable brokerage firms do not like to underwrite or put their customers into situations that turn sour. As you gain experience you will learn which firms are more reputable than others in the underwritings they handle or stocks they recommend. And even good brokerage firms, with the best of intentions, can make mistakes about new issues, especially during a period of intense speculation.

The speculator, or indeed any smart investor, must be on the alert constantly for new areas of investment or for overlooked ones. Perhaps the overlooked industry of today will produce the growth stocks of tomorrow; it seems to me that the number of actual new industries will be limited by the already fast pace of economic growth.

Few people these growth-conscious days pay much attention to the dear old steel stocks, like Bethlehem Steel and U.S. Steel, corporate bastions both and important to basic industry. True, there has been much talk about competitive steel being imported cheaply from overseas and competing products like aluminum and plastics stealing somc of the traditional market away from steel. However, at low prices the steel industry appears to be out of fashion and often overlooked by investors. This kind of neglect occurs in any typical business cycle when investors are distracted by more glamorous industries. Yet, financially, an underpriced stock can offer the same lure of appreciation as an overpriced growth stock—if not more. Sooner or later certain steel stocks will be desirable again.

Another neglected situation, for example, appeared several years ago when savings and loan association shares were low priced because of a lull in the construction market. A stock like Financial Federation could have been picked up in 1966 for 8 a share; in 1968 it sold as high as 40, a good increase for an investment held about two years. Later the company was acquired.

Who bought Financial Federation at its low point in 1966? Speculators who believed that an upturn in building would soon follow, as it did, and that savings and loan companies would participate, as they did. It was a worthwhile speculation combining the best elements of an industry in a depressed cycle of activity with inherent growth in demand for its product—money to build houses. The nation needs additional housing to meet the needs generated by a rapidly expanding population and by rising aspirations of dwellers in substandard buildings. In fact, the person who reasons out an investment opportunity like this can consider himself more of an astute investor than a hit-and-run speculator.

Naturally new growth situations also capture speculators' attention, and they can be more risky by nature. The interest in them often is cyclical, with a few alert stock traders nibbling at attractive growth stocks, then other "fish" joining them, and finally a rush for the bait by the speculative public. By this time some of the big fish are already moving out of the stock into others, taking their profits. Typically such a speculative boom collapses. Thus the smart speculator tries to get in early, or not at all. Selling out *before* the stock attracts large public support is important.

A list of some important growth areas since World War II provides an interesting chart of speculators' interest:

Group I

Photography	Electronics
Textbook publishing	Savings and loan associations
Boating	Computers
Uranium	Bowling

In the group above each industry mentioned has been the object of a speculative boom followed by a sharp decline after some second thinking by investors. The correction of speculative excess is a fact of life, usually resulting with the "bandwagon" investors getting hurt. Later, some of the industries reasserted themselves, such as textbook publishing, which is now a solid investment field.

Group II includes some more recent speculative industries:*

Group II

Lasers	Nursing homes
Fried chicken	Ski resorts
Oceanography	Auto clinics
Silver refining	or repair shops
Hospital equipment	Motels

Let's take bowling from Group I as a typical example of speculation that proved successful for agile investors and tragic for the less sophisticated ones.

Back in 1960 two major companies, both listed on the New York Stock exchange, spearheaded the growth of popularity of bowling as a sport for the entire family. Many companies, as you may remember, formed employees' bowling teams for weekly exercise and fun. Bowling tournaments were televised, testimony to the widespread interest in the sport. Many former baseball or football stars permitted their names to be linked with bowling alleys. High schools had bowling teams and so did some colleges. It was an "in" sport.

Two companies dominated the field, primarily because modern bowling requires complex "spotters," which have replaced pinboys who used to set up the pins. Their names were American Machine and Foundry Company (now called AMF, Inc.), maker of several lines of complicated equipment such as bread-making machines; and Brunswick Corporation, better known for sports equipment such as billiard tables.

AMF developed its automated pinsetter somewhat ahead of Brunswick. At first AMF rented its equipment, while Brunswick sold its line. To promote the sport both companies spent large sums of money for contests and prizes, and helped finance alleys.

Unfortunately, like so many fads, the business got out of hand. Too many bowling alleys opened in relation to the amount of actual business in some areas; some operators entered business without experience and with too heavy

*To this list should be added some speculative industries expected to grow in the future: biotechnology, ceramics and polymers used in space-age vehicles, health management, prison management, and waste recycling.

borrowings; some parents didn't like the type of people hanging around bowling alleys; and as in all sports fads, public interest eventually turned elsewhere.

As business revenues in the alleys dropped sharply, the two companies found themselves as creditors with some bankrupt bowling properties on their hands and public interest declining. At the same time some smaller bowling companies, not as diversified or as well managed as AMF and Brunswick, went into bankruptcy. And many of these fringe companies had raised capital by selling stock to unwary speculators.

Brunswick, with its earnings badly hurt, decided to diversify further. Today bowling supplies, which once accounted for a major part of company sales, now constitute a very small percentage. Here are the price ranges of Brunswick stock before, during, and after its glamour period.

1958	4–9
1960	21–50
1961 peak price	74
1967	7–17
1972	37–55

Same company in 1958 as in 1972, yes, but earnings and prospects far different. There wasn't much to say, unhappily, to speculators who bought at the price of 74. On the other hand, the speculators who bought at between 4 and 9 a share in 1958 and sold later at a much higher price can well recall Brunswick as a sound investment.

The prices for AMF show much the same pattern in the years 1958–1967. Note the 1972 price range.

1958	8–15
1960	24–46
1961 peak	63
1967	14–25
1972	47–63

Today both Brunswick and AMF continue to be listed on the New York Stock Exchange, and they show little of the drama they did during the exciting days of the bowling boom.

Remember a few years ago when Atari home computers were the rage, and then a few years later the Atari craze was over, as other home computers at relatively low prices became available. Now Atari is having some financial problems.

The interested woman speculator should persistently seek from her broker and elsewhere lists of growth areas. Sometimes she can glean ideas of where growth will occur from her own experience as an observer of fads as well as from her reading. At the same time she should keep in mind those industries that have recently gone through declines—and a shakeout—but yet offer renewed growth possibilities, like textbook publishing, teaching machines, cycle issues like steel shares or building materials suppliers, makers of sports equipment, etc.

She should remember what is here today in this fast-moving world can be jaded and played out tomorrow—at least temporarily. Speculation requires speed, imagination, and lack of sentimentality. Good speculators are willing to change their investments with as little emotion and as quickly as they would change a pair of shoes.

Systems, or Determined Approaches

Speculators in the course of history have adopted some unusual techniques. In fact, often the successful ones will smile and say vaguely, "I have a system."

Probably the most successful speculators are those who buy growth stocks and then trade by using charts (see Chapter 14), buying and selling as their charts indicate. But I have heard, and you will, too, of many unusual approaches.

One elderly retired broker I know once had the greatest admiration for the business acumen of two Texans called the Murchison brothers, who built a fortune investing. For a period of years they bought shares in many small insurance companies. Sometimes they merged the companies. This broker bought shares in the same insurance company every time he read that the Murchisons had made a purchase. By doing so over a period of years, he made a good profit. Perhaps other small speculators can capitalize on following the actions of the big boys, if they can find out who the big boys are and what they're doing.

Another person I know recently has been buying stock in every company that T. Boone Pickens tries to take over, and by so doing he has made quite a bit of money. He usually buys the day after he reads that Mr. Pickens is known to have a position in a company—Unocal and Phillips Petroleum, to name a couple.

An elderly woman I know disapproved of drinking, smoking, and chewing gum, and she frowned on speculation. However, she knew that many other people—the great mass of the public—did these things, so she invested much of her money in liquor, tobacco, and shares of American Chicle Company (now part of Warner-Lambert). Her investments fared well.

There's a rabbi in Chicago who has made money for years trading in pork bellies, a commodity future (see Chapter 17), on the theory that "I can't eat it, but I can try to make money on it.'' Millions of people love bacon, which is the product that results from pork bellies. With prosperity on the rise the bacon market grows continually.

Dancer Nicholas Darva used an odd approach to the market, studying stock quotations and picking stocks that seemed to have unusually large price increases in a rising market. After watching them increase for a while, he would buy shares and then place a stop order a few points below the purchase price. As the stock rose he increased the price of the stop order. Adoption of this method fitted his itinerant life because he gave dance recitals in many unusual parts of the world, often far removed from stock market quotations. Using cables or telegrams he could keep his broker informed; through stop orders he protected his positions.

In Chapter 11 on investment clubs it was mentioned that many clubs use dollar cost averaging, picking a growth stock and buying a certain number of shares at regular intervals. When market prices are up they pay more and thus get fewer shares; when the stock's price is down, the same amount of money buys more shares. They work on the theory that the average price over a period of time will be favorable if they have picked a good, growing company.

Contrarians, led by investment analyst and adviser Humphrey Neill and his associate James L. Frazer, long used a theory called the contrary-opinion theory. They liked to do the opposite of what most people were thinking. When most people are pessimistic and out of the market, the contrarians often take the plunge into the cold water. When the public takes a swim, and especially a long bath, they are sunning on the shores waiting to plunge again. It is a worthwhile attitude and you can read more about it in Mr. Neill's books obtainable in a public library.

As you read more about investing, you will begin to learn which are the growth areas today. In 1985, they were biotechnology stocks, many computer company shares, although some of the companies did not fare so well, and stocks in health management areas. You should keep up with current trends. It's useful to jot down notes on new areas that brokers believe are growing. In 1986, biotechnology, lasers, robotics, and artificial intelligence are growth areas.

13

How to Be a Bear without a Growl

Hope springs eternal, it is said, and nowhere is that more evident than in the stock market.

Americans have always had faith that time would better all things, that stocks would go up and therefore much would be well with the world. Oddly enough, over the last two hundred years or so the bulls in America have been right—the population has grown steadily, industrial production has surged, gross national product (the total of all goods and services in terms of dollars) has increased almost steadily year after year, and the standard of living has improved. Except for occasional setbacks, stock prices have shown a rising tendency.

Yet some interesting facts can be cited to show that there is always room for the pessimist, and especially for the pessimist with a sense of timing.

The National Bureau of Economic Research made a detailed study of recessions for the hundred-year period stretching from 1854 to 1954. From this perspective it found that the one hundred years encompassed 24 business cycles. On the average the economy expanded for 29.9 months in the typical cycle and then it contracted for 19.9 months.

Generally, a booming economy has brought with it a booming stock market, the enthusiasm for one probably inspiring zest for the other. These upswings have then been followed by recessions or depressions, usually causing much lower stock prices.

As you might guess, the longest and sharpest of the contracting periods came following the 1929 stock market crash, and it lasted for forty-three months.

The 1929 crash and ensuing Depression proved so devastating that it brought profound changes in the government's whole attitude toward the economy. Since then the government has played a more active role in the economy, providing Social Security benefits, unemployment compensation, make-work projects, deficit spending to encourage business expansion. Furthermore, the Federal Reserve system has refined and sharpened its techniques of operating in the money market, so that it can encourage economic growth or slow down an overheated economy. It can effectively change interest rates and raise or lower margin requirements on securities trading.

Americans have become imbued with the idea that never again can this country suffer a depression like the Great Depression. They probably are right in this assumption. But that hardly limits the opportunities for an investor to act and think like a bear, if he knows how. The opportunities still remain.

The Standard & Poor's chart in Chapter 3 (Figure 3-1) shows the price trends over a long period of years. Each of the setbacks offered a bear the chance to make money.

Yet the typical investor, always the optimist, did not look at declines as opportunities to conserve profits already made or to take aggressive action to make money by acting like a bear. Instead, he placed more reliance in the growth figures, such as the fact that the Dow Jones industrial average has progressed upward from as low as 161 back in the period after World War II to just below 1,000 in 1966, and it moved above 1,000 late in 1972. In 1986 it exceeded 1565 for the first time.

Since recessions in the economy and the stock market are a fact of life, then why don't more investors, especially intelligent ones, try to learn how to protect themselves?

Books on the stock market by the hundreds tell the investor how to buy common stocks for their growth potential. But very few books, possibly a handful, tell him how to profit from an inevitable bear market. The irony is that back in the early 1960s the growth-stock psychology so gripped the imagination of the investing public, brokers, and writers that books on the stock market did not even mention short selling or the use of "puts" or other methods of protection. Instead, books tried to vindicate the payment of prices astronomical in terms of current earnings, carrying out the thesis of growth, growth, and more growth to carry prices inevitably upward. The 1962 denouement changed opinion somewhat, but still there were few books that told the story of profits from bear operations.

The reasons for so little attention paid to downturns apparently belong to the fuzzy area of psychological trauma in the minds of many stock market writers. No one likes bad news, especially brokers who find it hard to persuade customers to act bearishly. Today few brokers can even remember the Great Depression. The thinking among many brokers is that the activities of bears should be the prerogative of professional traders and speculators. Operating as a bear can be risky, a fact that is all too often pointed out. "Don't sell America short" has become kind of a brokers' fishing line. And in fact it's hard to discourage the investor, who has bought some shares with the idea that they will go up steadily. Hence investors tend to hang on, or if they do sell, they tend to panic and dump shares at the wrong time.

Books that do mention methods of acting like a bear, such as selling short, hasten to warn the reader that many famous bears have died in bankruptcy. Daniel Drew usually heads the list, although the books don't usually add that his once good friend Jay Gould tricked him into his downfall. Jacob Little is another bear cited as dying a poor man.

Some books even go to the extent of quoting that elder statesman Bernard Baruch as saying, "Bears don't live on Park Avenue." Yet Mr. Baruch made a large amount of money as a very young man taking a bear position in a famous so-called growth stock of the early 1900s—Amalgamated Copper. But more about that later.

In fact, the American psychology of eternal optimism runs counter to bearish thinking to such an extent that a stock market iconoclast can suffer in his personal relations if he is unwise enough to discuss his pessimism. For example, it's pleasant enough to say to a friend who works for AT&T something like this: "You're with a great company. I have some of the stock and have owned it for years. I'm sure it will keep going up. It's the kind of stock people ought not to sell—ever." For this the speaker will receive, no doubt, an appreciative smile and nodding acquiescence. Most employees tend to be faithful to their company's stock.

On the contrary there's nothing simple or even socially acceptable about saying to the same man, "Your stock is going up too fast. It's headed for a fall. Suppose the government investigates rates. You ought to sell." The result: a cold look and instant argument, possibly even the end of a friendship.

By nature, the bear must be a lonely person, able and willing to keep her pessimism to herself unless she can find a few others thinking along similar lines. Even if she proves temporarily right and makes money, or at least preserves her money, she remains suspect.

Even the soundest stock, like AT&T before its 1984 divestment and stock dividend, will be hurt in a bear stock market. Declining prices won't leave it untouched any more than they will some fly-by-night stock in which speculators have had a run for their money. True, the drop may not be as sharp as in more volatile stocks, but there will be one.

Even such dominant companies as AT&T can be hurt by the prospect of a government investigation—an influence that will be translated into lower stock prices. What other impacts can hurt a big company? Copper companies lost some of their market when a sharp price increase in the metal led consumers to use substitutes. The poor showing made by General Motors during Ralph Nader's first big auto safety investigation undoubtedly hurt the company's image and the price of its stock. More recently, Japanese car imports hurt GM. A major lawsuit against a company can have a devastating effect on stock prices; so can a sudden unexpected upheaval in management. A new development, such as a dental group's endorsement of Crest toothpaste, can help one manufacturer at the expense of others.

Perhaps what today's investor sorely needs is a better sense of history. For this there are several good sources. In *Extraordinary Popular Delusions and the Madness of Crowds,* Charles Mackay explores one of the momentous stock price breaks in history—the "South Sea bubble," which occurred in the eighteenth century. His book was written about a hundred years ago but it still remains pertinent for today's investor. Anyone who reads it will never look at the stock market with rose-tinted glasses again. For the 1929 break, economist John K. Galbraith has written a fine study called *The Great Crash, 1929.*

History is with the bull; economic growth is with the bull; psychology is with the bull; and books on the stock market cater to the bull. Where does that leave a bear? In a very comfortable position *if* she has the right approach. She must be a loner and an individualist and coolly analytical, willing to act contrary to the crowd or the herd of bulls. If she is right more times than wrong she can achieve the satisfaction of knowing she stands out among the group.

How then can the investor know when a market nears its peak and when she should act like a bear? No one can pick the top exactly, but as the market reaches new heights there are some guideposts. A few stock market analysts become restive. There are certain well-known ones who tend to act more bearish than others. Subtle warnings will be sounded. Perhaps these will be limited at first to suggestions that the outlook is hazy and that the investor should begin to build up some cash to take advantage of opportunities later, coupled with a warning to eliminate weak sisters in a portfolio.

There may be talk of large investors taking money out of the market and putting it in the bank, or in bonds, or in hedge stocks like utilities. The term "large investors" includes not only wealthy individuals but the mutual funds, pension funds, insurance companies, and other such organizations. Analysts have a sense of the market, a closeness that other investors often lack. They soon learn when some of their firm's large institutional customers are moving out of stocks and building up cash.

Then, too, there are basic economic questions the investor hoping to be an active bear will ask. Is unemployment rising? Are industrial orders falling? Are machine tool orders falling? What about corporate profits? Are they falling or are profit margins narrowing? What about sales of autos, a key industry? What about inflation? Is consumer income dropping or being cut by taxes or higher living costs? Are stocks priced too far in the future in relation to current earnings? In the 1980s there have been worries about the country's growing trade deficits.

If the bear is concentrating on a certain stock, rather than the market, she will focus on its special weakness. Often a bear can find a deteriorating situation in a single stock at a time when she has no particular worries about the stock market as a whole. In this case she will be asking such questions as: Is management poor? Is the company losing its share of the market? Has it been outpointed in technology by another company? Have its growth prospects slowed? The steel industry is an example of a business that seems to have a cloudy future.

Both types of bears—the one watching the market as a whole and the one following a single stock—should keep their eyes on the *short interest* figures, published each month by the New York Stock Exchange (the American Stock Exchange also issues short interest figures). A copy of this release can be obtained from the exchanges, but an easier method is to read the major New York newspapers, such as *The New York Times* or *The Wall Street Journal,* which usually carry a story and data each month on the short interest figures for leading companies.

A short interest situation arises when a person sells stock he does not own, by borrowing stock temporarily with the idea of returning the stock later, on the assumption he can buy it back then at a lower price. A large short interest position in a stock indicates that a great many people believe the price may drop.

However, a point to remember is that every short position must ultimately be covered. So if shares drop in price the shorts—the speculators who sold short—must enter the market and buy an amount of stock equivalent to the amount sold short. Some of the short sales, of course, could be against stock already owned that could be delivered.

Some analysts follow these figures with interest, but their interpretations vary. However, the short interest amounts to a relatively small part of total sales of stock, never more than 5 percent even in 1931.

How to Act Like a Bear

There are four basic ways of translating a bearish outlook into action:

1. Selling out and putting the cash into savings accounts. When stock prices are at unusually high levels and the market is dominated by speculative activity, the government is likely to take corrective measures, such as increasing margin rates and raising the discount rate. An increase in the discount rate—the charge banks must pay when they borrow from the Federal Reserve system—tends to raise interest rates along the line: the prime rate banks charge their good customers, the rates on personal loans, the interest on mortgages. As interest rates rise, deposits in savings banks, savings and loan organizations, and such institutions look more attractive. Thus investors are assured of a good return on the money they take out of the stock market, probably higher than the dividend yield on many common stocks.

Bonds, too, offer an inviting haven for money taken out of equities. In a period of high interest rates, outstanding bonds sell at depressed prices, and therefore offer not only a good yield but some capital gains possibilities. When the business cycle has turned upward again and the Federal Reserve system has once again lowered the discount rate, the prices of bonds rise again.

2. Selling short. There is little real difference between selling a stock short and buying it long as a process; but most investors, though they may be perfectly willing to risk their money buying expensive stocks of speculative appeal, can't think in terms of selling short.

A short sale arises when a customer asks her broker to sell, say, 100 shares short for her; and to do this the broker "borrows" the stock, from another customer who leaves the shares in the broker's hands, or from shares that the firm owns, or from another brokerage firm. Then the broker sells the shares as he would handle any other selling order. The money received from the sale goes into an account held by the broker in the short seller's name.

The short seller must eventually buy back from the market the borrowed shares and close out the position. (If the price should happen to move against her—go up instead of down—she will be required to put up cash to meet margin requirements.) When she closes out the position, if she buys at a price lower than she "sold," her profit will be the difference between the sum in the brokerage account received from the sale of the borrowed stock and the amount it costs to buy back the 100 shares of stock to be returned to the lender. The profit will be minus commissions, taxes, etc.

Short selling has long been popular among professionals and sophisticated individuals. However, it must be pointed out that there is an upside risk. A stock owned can go down sharply in price but it can go no lower than zero—the point at which no one will pay a cent for it. But in the case of a short position the upside price is theoretically unlimited. A stock could zoom from 5, to 50, to 500, and even higher. But while the warning is worth considering, the rules of the stock exchanges these days prevent squeezes. Also, most short sellers help protect their positions on the upside with a judicious use of stop orders, so that if a sudden rise should send up the price too high, too fast, they will automatically close their position by purchasing shares. This cuts the risk.

3. Selling against the box. Many investors are understandably reluctant—possibly for tax reasons, possibly for sentimental reasons—to sell stocks they have bought or inherited at a very much lower price. Or, perhaps they are unwilling to sell because they own shares of the company in which they work. To protect themselves and yet avoid liquidating their positions (and avoid stiff capital gains taxes) they can sell short, against the box, a variation on the short sale.

Visualize, for example, an investor who owns 100 shares of General Motors priced around 100 as the market begins to make highs. She becomes worried about the outlook, expecting a decline in prices. So she asks her broker to sell 100 shares of GM short. If, as she expects, the market falls, dragging GM to 85, she can buy 100 shares in the market and make delivery to close her short position.

She still owns her 100 original shares, and though they are down to 85 at current market levels, she has made a 15-point profit on her short sale (minus the brokerage expenses involved). In essence, she has protected her investment at around the $100 level. If, contrary to her judgment, the market moves up, she would have a profit on her own original shares, but a loss on her short position. Either way, she has an "insurance policy" fixing her price at the $100 point, minus expenses.

4. Buying options named "puts." (See also Chapter 17.) While this has been less widely used, the system appeals to some bears because it gives them leverage—a large position relative to the money put up—and a known exact amount of dollar risk at a given time.

Briefly, a put is an option to sell 100 shares of a stock, generally a stock listed on the New York Stock Exchange, at a prearranged price within a certain time. A buyer of a put believes that the price of the stock will go down.

A call is just the opposite, namely an option to buy 100 shares of a stock for an agreed price within a fixed period. In this case, the buyer of a call expects the price of the stock to move up.

For the privilege of buying an option—either a put or a call—the buyer pays a premium, a fee in other words.

What are the advantages? Why, if you think that AT&T will rise in six months, would you buy a call rather than buying the 100 shares of stock? Leverage, for one thing.

For a small amount of money—the premium—the buyer of a put (or a call) has the right to sell (or to buy, as the case may be), a substantial amount of stock in terms of money.

For example, a call might be offered on a stock priced at 57 to expire January 13, or in about five and a half months. At the time the price of that stock was about 53 a share.

Suppose that you thought that the price of the stock was cheap at 53 and would rise well above 57 by the end of the year or early in January. Yet, at the time you didn't want to sell more than $5,000 in stocks to pay for this purchase. So you decide to buy the call. You risk only the premium and any commissions you might have to pay. You figure that after these costs you could break even if the stock rises to 59½ a share, which becomes your target price. Suppose that the stock, under the influence of good earnings, a rising stock market, and good investor interest, rises to 62 a share. You can take delivery of the shares at $57 for each or let your broker give you the profits. You have realized $2.50 a share, or $250 on the 100 shares.

If you were wrong about the stock the most you could lose would be the premium cost. You choose whether you want to exercise the option.

Puts and calls are traded regularly on several exchanges. Thus the underlying shares bought or sold to fulfill the contracts, when exercised, are handled by brokerage firms. Anyone can buy a put through her own brokerage firm. Large New York newspapers regularly carry quotations indicating what stocks are being offered as either puts or calls and the premiums involved. Ask your broker for a brochure.

In one sense, the use of puts involves more technical knowledge than short selling. Furthermore, many account executives of brokerage firms, long accustomed to short sales, do not have quite as much experience with puts as they do with calls. For example: she owns United Airlines, in which she has a good profit. Believing the stock still shows a rising tendency, but satisfied with her own capital gain, she decides to write a call on her stock. This obligates her to deliver 100 shares of United to someone who has bought her call. For writing the option she receives the premium of several hundred dollars, minus the broker's fee. When the call is exercised, as she expected it would be, she delivers her own 100 shares of stock. She has closed out her position and earned a few dollars while doing so.

A variation on this idea is the writing of options covering both sides—a put and a call. In the trade this is called a *straddle.* Generally only one side would be exercised. However, the option writer would have received two premiums—one for writing the call and one for writing the put.*

Successful Bears

One of the most impressive bears of all time was none other than Bernard Baruch, who tells the story of his own winning venture selling short Amalgamated Copper many years ago.

Without putting up a penny of their own money, a group of businessmen decided to launch a company called Amalgamated Copper Company, which acquired Anaconda Copper and some other properties in exchange for a bank check made out for $39 million, not to be cashed for a while.

Then the organizers sold $75 million of securities in the new company at $100 a share, with plenty of fanfare. Once this money was in hand, the owner of Anaconda who had agreed to sell the properties was told he could cash the $39 million check.

Then the fun began. Men with prestigious names became directors or sponsors of Amalgamated. Their aim was to form a trust that would control much of the world's copper supply and thus keep prices of the metal high. Those were the days when industrial trusts were popular and the government had as yet made few attempts to break them up.

The price of Amalgamated moved up quite steadily to 130, within a few months of the offering date of the shares.

Bernard Baruch had watched the formation of the company, including its obvious overcapitalization, and he was convinced that the price of the share was much too high. More than that, he reasoned that the current high prices of copper would eventually curtail demand and then the market would become glutted with unsold supplies of the metal.

At this point he sold Amalgamated short. As it does in Wall Street, the news got around that Baruch was selling short, and some important business friends warned him not to antagonize "the big fellows."

"I was also being told how wicked it was to be short of the market, and to tear down a constructive enterprise. All this is nonsense, of course. If the Amalgamated organizers had not overcapitalized and then blown the stock up, it would never have risen to such heights or descended to the depths it afterwards did. What was dropping the copper shares was the irresistible

*A person with a good-size portfolio could earn possibly 15 percent a year by writing straddles on her shares.

force of economic gravitation seeking its proper level,'' he recalled in his memoirs.

Amalgamated soon cut its dividends from $8 to $6 a share, and the news of that forced the stock's price further downward. Eventually it dropped to 60. Mr. Baruch, who was only 31 at the time, reported that his profits on his short transaction in Amalgamated amounted to $700,000.

In the spring of 1962 a modern bear named Jeb Wofford made a small fortune in the stock market while many people were losing large fortunes. A Midwesterner best known as a member of the 1952 Olympic equestrian team, Jeb Wofford (unlike Mr. Baruch) had no experience on Wall Street. In fact, aside from the rigorous discipline required to train for championship riding, he had few qualifications for any kind of business.

Late in 1961 he had become seriously worried about the handling of his family's money, much of which was held in trust by a large Midwestern bank. The bank officers refused to sell out the common stock holdings, pointing out that the investments were in high-quality companies like American Telephone and Telegraph and International Business Machines. Where could they find sounder investments? And what about the capital gains taxes that would have to be paid? Such stocks, they insisted, would ride out any economic downturn. Besides, they doubted that any drastic market break would occur.

Mr. Wofford, believing that the market was heading toward serious trouble, disputed this kind of thinking. He reasoned there must be effective ways to operate as a bear—that is, one who expects stocks to decline—and thus protect one's capital in a market downturn. He began to read everything he could find about business cycles, and he subscribed to numerous market letters and advisory services. Having carefully studied the basic ways of operating as a bear and the costs involved, he began to try his luck in the market around the beginning of 1962.

By April, Jeb Wofford had begun to make substantial sums of money. A stockbroker brought Wofford to the attention of *The New York Times,* and an article about him appeared in June. By then there was no doubt about it: Mr. Wofford had profited greatly from his operations as a bear prior to and during the second biggest stock market break in history, during which the Dow Jones industrial average dropped about 26 percent. His profits were estimated at several hundred thousands of dollars by his broker.

There was no skulduggery involved. Jeb Wofford, thanks to his own determination, disciplined judgment, and shrewdness, succeeded as a novice where many more experienced men had failed.

What he did any other investor can, and possibly should, do, at least to some extent, if she believes that a market has moved up so far that it stands in danger of a sharp reversal. He devoted himself and a limited amount of capital—$30,000—to buying puts. He centered much attention on IBM puts, owning more than 20 of them at one time. On each he made a profit. The prices of IBM the first six months of 1962 show that he could not lose:

January 2	572
February 1	554
March 1	543
April 2	525
May 1	462
May 28*	361
June 1	385
June 14	300

Do bears follow fundamentals or do they use the technical approach? Among professional traders, there are many (perhaps a majority) who follow a strictly technical approach, selling short when their charts, usually kept daily, indicate that price levels have been broken on the downside. If they are faithful chart followers then they must sell.

However, many individual bears tend to watch the fundamentals. For example, Bernard Baruch took the short position in Amalgamated Copper because of his faith in facts—namely that the metal had become overpriced and that sales must decline. A chart in this instance probably would have indicated a bullish outlook because of the artificial support given the stock by promoters. The promoters attracted unwary investors who through lack of information about the copper price situation and the overcapitalization of the company bought the stock at high prices on hopes.

Jeb Wofford also followed the fundamentals, believing that overspeculation in the stock market would correct itself. However, he applied a technical approach in keeping with his own interest in statistics. He kept voluminous price records of the companies in which he held puts.

It can be argued with irrefutable logic that a bear *in the long run* must surely lose because of the steady growth of the economy of this country and of the world. Bears like Bernard Baruch and Jeb Wofford knew this as well any bull, but they believed that quick short-term profits could be made with a bear approach, and they were right.

Thus the important idea for every sophisticated investor to grasp is that it pays to be a bear at times, but not all the time. However, as indicated before, there are times when it pays an investor to be bearish in a specific stock even though you are not pessimistic about the trend in the market as a whole.

In the case of a technological breakthrough, one classic example is the introduction of Crest toothpaste and its endorsement by the American Dental

*Day of big break; a drop of 37 points from previous day.

Association. The ADA endorsement ''bulled'' the shares of Crest's maker, Procter & Gamble, and hurt the prospects of rival toothpaste makers, such as Colgate-Palmolive.

Summary

To summarize, the smart woman investor can—and should—act like a bear at times, even when her old reliable stocks are involved. She can do it in three ways, depending on her acumen.

1. She can sell her shares and sit out a recession with cash or short-term government securities, or enter the bond market.

2. She can sell short, stocks that she thinks will be hurt by either a recession or a setback in its own industry. She can, of course, sell short against her own holdings, the device known as ''selling against the box.'' By doing this she ''nails down'' the paper profits she has in her position.

3. She can, if she wants to be an active bear, purchase puts. This way she knows the exact cost of the risk if she happens to guess wrong about the trend of the stocks.

14

The Proper Perspective on Tops and Bottoms

How to Use Charts

Your broker, speaking for the investment analysts from whom he gets his information, may talk impressively sometimes of ''fundamentals'' versus ''technicalities'' influencing your stocks (they were described briefly in Chapter 13). To put it differently, he might speak of fundamental research as contrasted to technical research, or the fundamentalists versus the technicians. Don't let the high-flown language ruffle your poise.

It's not so difficult to understand. In Chapter 8 on the work of the analyst, the stress was on some of the practical methods he uses to arrive at his conclusions, such as sales and earnings trends, competitive factors, price earning trends, economic cycles. In applying these your broker uses what he calls fundamental research. He remains largely disinterested in the so-called technical factors ever present in the market.

Generally speaking, most of the research that reaches you—the investor—is of the fundamental variety: advice to buy or sell based on basic information plus some educated judgments of managerial skills and competitive factors.

However, most analysts also keep some sort of charts that give them a picture of the way a stock's price is acting—in relation to earnings, in relation to general stock movements, and in relation to changes in the economy. In the same way, the analyst watches the charts of price trends of the so-called stock market averages. These are a tool to help his thinking just as a computer is.

Some analysts go further than this and live or work almost wholly by charts. They plot the course of stocks on their charts just as a navigator charts a ship's course, jotting down price changes sometimes hour by hour, day by day, week by week. Often they use complex interpretations. They call themselves technicians.

These technical analysts take themselves very seriously and sometimes to the average investor their talk sounds like riddles. They approach the market with a dramatic flair. From my observation they usually are the type of person who thrives on modern art because they can weave their own messages into it, and use technical jargon to interpret what they mean. True technicians ignore fundamentals: they trade stocks strictly by their charts. Their followers tend to be the more sophisticated type of in-and-out traders.

The formations made by their charts in relation to the volume of shares traded at the same time tell them a story. They can give an opinion, for example, as to when a stock is under accumulation and thus is rising in price because of the impact of large buy orders. On the other hand, they can "read" from their charts when a stock is being sold in volume, forcing down the price. At a time when institutional buyers, namely the mutual funds, pension funds, college endowment funds, and big trusts, account for about fifty percent of the trading volume, such information is important.

The charts can tell them when a stock rises to the point where resistance sets in and enough sales can be expected to come into the picture to force it down. Or, conversely, they can figure when a stock sells at a low enough price to attract enough orders on the buy side to firm its price once more.

It stands to reason if every investor, and hence all investment analysts, bought or sold only on the basis of similar interpretations of what charts say, there would be a rush to buy (or sell) the same stock at the same time. Like a hopeless traffic jam, traffic in the shares would have to stop or slow down.

Luckily it doesn't work out that way. There are so many investors, individual and institutional, in the market at any time that some may be buying and some selling the same stock at the same time, and all for very logical reasons.

Obviously, if hundreds of thousands of investors are watching a stock for technical indicators to either buy or sell, it is valuable for an investor to be aware of how much charting is done.

As you become more skilled in investing you may want to keep charts yourself. Furthermore, you probably will be curious about the technical aspects.

Perhaps the best books on the subject have been written by John Magee—a doubleheader, boxed together, called *Semantics of Wall Street* and *Technical*

Analysis of Stock Trends, in which he covers the various important formations that can be seen on charts. Public libraries would have them.

In a sense, a chartist can be described as a person who wants to follow the crowd—of fellow sophisticates, that is. As you remember from Chapter 5 on how the stock market operates, there are specialists who "run the books" for particular stocks on the floor of the exchange. They keep little books in which they write down orders to buy and sell shares that cannot be exercised currently because the prices are "away" from the orders. Obviously when quite suddenly a large number of the orders on their books are exercised, then the spate of orders for such stocks will show up on the tape and will have an effect on the market. Charted, these price swings under the impact of buy and sell orders at various levels constitute the "food" the chartists digest hungrily.

This information might come to you in capsuled form like this from your broker, "Well, Polaroid has just made a triple bottom. It looks like a buy."

What would this mean in terms of a chart? It means that over a period of time the stock has dropped, say to a price of 50; then buying, perhaps from a batch of orders listed in the specialist's book, has suddenly been activated and pushed the price ahead. Perhaps the price continues up again for a while and then drops once more to about 50, with the result that another group of orders enters. Once again the price moves up quite sharply. After a further decline to the 50 level, the price might once again take off for an even higher level than the two upswings before. To a technician the triple bottom might indicate a stock ready to take a sustained flight, if not into the wild blue yonder at least up high enough to satisfy some traders' desire for capital gains.

Perhaps at such a point you should buy, too. Your broker, if he has faith in the technical analysis done by his firm, might suggest that you do so.

A triple top, on the other hand, acts like a red flag for some analysts. It can indicate that a stock is having trouble rising above a certain level. Let's say in this instance the price of the stock moves up to 70, at which time selling enters and slaps it down smartly like a naughty child. Once again it dares rise to the same level and once again it gets put down by a large number of selling orders. Perhaps quite a few owners of the shares have good profits and want out at 70. Once again after the decline the stock thrusts it head upward to the 70 point, then declines. About that time a technician might advise that the stock should be sold, or at least not bought, because it has been unable to move above the 70 level.

No wonder that brokers and analysts are excessively interested in tops and bottoms during the working day. A top means the point or level at which the stock apparently cannot move higher—a time to be cautious and possibly sell. A bottom indicates a point or level at which a stock's price probably cannot go lower but which could indicate a recovery.

Since brokers are much more savvy about bottoms than tops—about urging you to go into a market rather than to get out of it—they will talk to you more often about bottoms.

When a stock is falling fast and steadily no one can tell the prices at which a turn will come. Perhaps the person with the best idea, if he's alert, is the specialist on the floor of the stock exchange. He can take a look at his book and know how many buy orders he has at various prices. True, the stock buyer can change his mind overnight or a few hours after he has placed an order, but still the weight of orders must give the specialist a good idea of the market. The trouble is that only the specialist is supposed to know what is on his books.

However, chartists, by keeping their noses close to their charts (many of them are serious, bespectacled types) and their computers handy, think they can figure the turn about the time it comes, if not the exact price.

One of their most useful configurations is called "the head and shoulders formation" (see Figure 14-1). It looks very much like just that; with a little imagination you see the left shoulder, then the price rise and decline that form the "head," followed by another little rise that takes the right shoulder no higher than the left, and then drops even more sharply as if to form an arm.

A technician following the chart in Figure 14-1 might advise a sale around the time (and price) that the right shoulder fails to go much higher than the left—that is, around October 23. Of course, a little shrug might alter his opinion.

On the chart, from October 16 to November 27 you see the almost exact reverse involving the shoulders and the head. The technician would note that the left shoulder (facing you) droops, steadies, then droops to a much lower head, followed by an upswing and a leveling that evens the process.

All this signals to the avid chartist a bullish outlook for the stock. Its declines apparently brought in enough buying orders at such lower levels to bring an upswing. Hence the technician might be writing reports urging the firm's customers to buy, buy. With this he would include a few fundamental facts such as prices, dividends, and perhaps targets to which he thinks the price might rise based on the earnings outlook. In this case there was an upswing.

Generally, even the most technical of the chartists, who maintains that he lives by charts alone, does include a few fundamentals in his analysis, though he probably won't admit it. By the same token, the fundamentalist who claims he hates charts uses them at least to give him a picture of the movement of a stock he is discussing.

Should you keep a chart of your pet stocks, those you already own and those in which you are interested enough to consider buying? Yes. It can be a very rewarding experience to follow the course of your stocks on paper, especially if you plan to hold them for a relatively long period of time, such as long enough to establish capital gains.

Suppose that you have acquired a portfolio of half a dozen stocks, includ-

Figure 14-1. A "head and shoulders" chart.

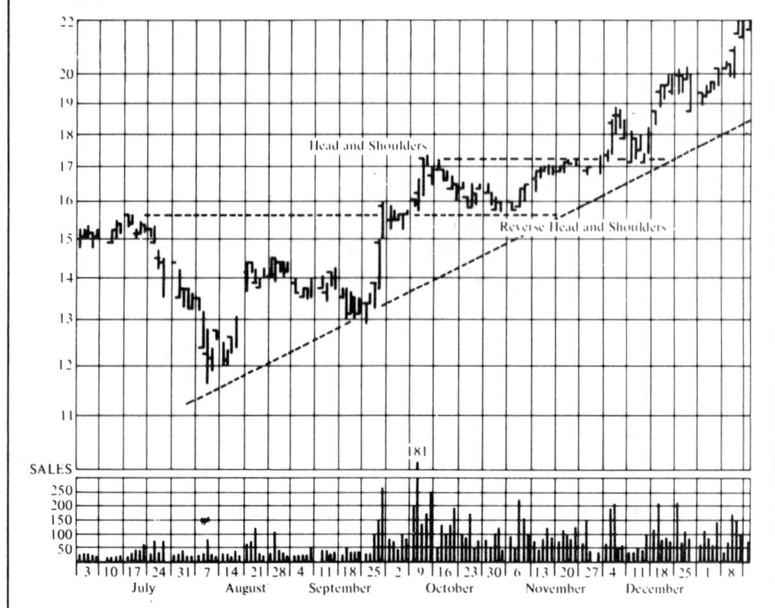

Broker's Comment: SYS 1,680,000 Shares Common. There would be those who would say that "SYS" has "broken the up trend" and is therefore weak. We don't exactly agree. We see no real weakness here at this time. We see a stock that has moved generally up in a steady trend. We would not split hairs about the failure of "SYS" to "bounce" off the long-term trendline. We would be considering also the volume action; and the various support levels. Notice that every time this stock has reacted it has retreated only to a previous support level; a previous top or series of tops. We see nothing wrong here.

Recommended: To buy SYS at the market. Closing Limit 20.

This is a typical comment made by a broker who likes to follow charts of a company. If you are interested in technical analysis you will run into charts like these very often.

ing some pivotal ones and a couple of fast-growth types, with the idea that you will hang on to all of them until they have given you a 15 percent increase in price, in each case.

Of course, not being a completely blind or a foolhardy investor you will sell before you reach these targets if your broker advises you to get out of a stock for a specific reason such as a change in the company's earnings outlook, or if your own research gives you a solid reason for selling. A belief that the economy is headed into a recession or that the stock market will reel backward under the impact of credit restrictions because of the government's fight against inflation could be a good reason—a sound reason for getting out of the market altogether.

You decide that you will chart your stocks regularly, picking a weekly schedule. For simplicity's sake let's say that you decide to take the range for the week and the final price each Friday. You need six pieces of graph paper, quite large, a pencil, and a Sunday newspaper that carries the high-low range for the week and the closing price in its stock quotations.

Most every school student can provide a parent with graph paper, and it's a good way to induce your child subtly to take an interest in the stock market, too. Mark out a long horizontal line near the bottom of one piece of this paper and a long vertical one (near the left edge) that meets it at right angles. The horizontal, or base, line should be notched into 52 parts, with the printed lines of the graph paper giving you a vertical sweep. In this way your chart can cover a full year.

On the vertical lines you pencil in the price levels for your stock. In essence your chart consists of simple little vertical lines with two or three "ticks" on each:

Obviously, the week's high price is the top tick made with your pencil, and the low is the bottom one. The middle tick, in this case, is the closing quote. It might, of course, be the same price as the high or low. Ignore the fractional prices, raising them to the nearest full price if more than half a cent, and cutting them to the next lower price if less than half a cent, unless you are a stickler for more accuracy. Whichever way you approach your charts, at least be consistent.

A second important part of your charting (and now you become a fundamentalist) is to note major news events on your chart, such as a report by your company of much higher quarterly earnings. You have to use your sense of logic. For example, a worsening of the Mideast crisis often alarms politicians and makes front-page headlines, but particular stocks may be insulated against such reports. A cosmetics stock probably would not react, unless of course the whole market swings up or down. If there is a definite market movement on news, then you should note this on your chart.

In making your charts you might find that prices also drop when the company pays a stock dividend. The date and the amount of the stock payment should be noted on your chart. Generally, you will notice that the stock dividend is soon absorbed and the stock moves on without much change.

However, if the dividend happens to be of the size called a stock split then you will have to revise your chart accordingly. For example, if a stock selling for 100 is split two for one, the price probably drops to the 50 level for a while and then, hopefully, edges upward in price. The reason is that often stocks that are split belong to companies that have rising earnings, the kind attractive to eager buyers like you.

If the stock split is two for one or three for one your charting doesn't become that much harder because you can think in terms of halves, or thirds. You can rechart the year's prices, or you can simply double (or triple) the prices in the newspaper after the split becomes effective and continue your chart through the year.

Now for the neat, clean Grecian touch of bar graphs at the bottom of your price charts:

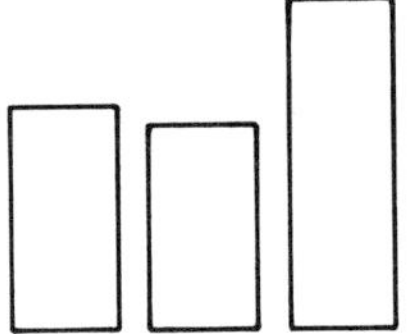

They will tell you the trading volume in your stock each week. For a chartist this volume is important because by means of it she notes, for example, that when the price falls to a certain level a large amount of volume enters, apparently pushing the price upward again.

Another helpful addition to your chart keeping (it need not take you more than a few minutes now and then) is a series of sales and earnings graphs for your company. These could be bar graphs:

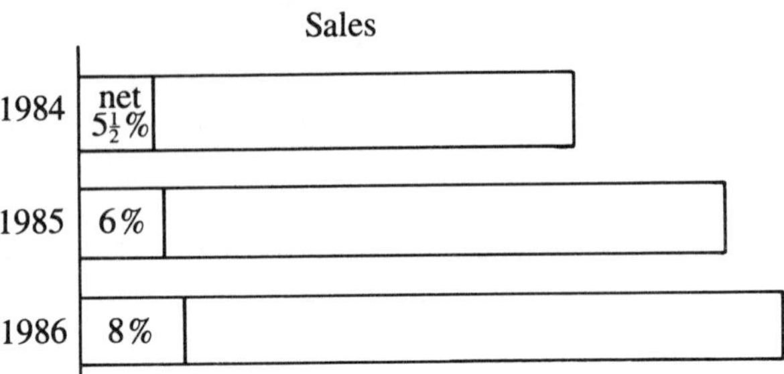

If your company is growing it should be increasing sales each year and earnings, too. If it can increase the percentage of net income to sales, so much the better.

As a stockholder, you need to follow these important relationships because if sales falter you want to know why. It might be a time to sell. Also, if earnings do not rise as fast as sales, that also gives you something to ponder about.

Once you have become accustomed to—and enthusiastic about—keeping charts, then you might want to add more sophisticated variations. Frankly, I prefer the simple approach to charting outlined in this chapter.

15

The Care and Feeding of Securities

Technicalities of Ownership

Your stocks deserve personal attention much the same as your children. You should be enthusiastic, determined, persistent, analytical, and the more objective the better. You cannot sit back relaxed, saying, "They can take care of themselves." Even if you have held a stock 21 happy years or more, it still needs watching.

Items to Watch

In handling your investments, it is crucial that you use your best judgment to advantage. The most important aspect of a stock, like a child, is how it turns out. Its behavior takes close watching.

Dividends

The first thing to know about your company, once you have become a stockholder, is its dividend policy, which often can be figured from prior years.

When you bought the stock your broker probably said something like this during the discussion, "The stock pays four dollars a year." Perhaps you had obtained some data on the company from reference manuals or from brokerage firms' analysis.

From his remarks you might assume that every three months you could expect $1 a share, but you could be wrong. Some companies do have a "regular" common dividend rate, which they would not miss despite earthquakes, wars, or other catastrophes.* Others might lower their dividends or skip them if earnings become bad, but otherwise stick to a regular schedule.

Suppose you are entitled to a dividend and it fails to arrive. Wait about ten days after the payment date and then check with the company. Remember mails are slow and inefficient these days. In writing the company write directly to the secretary, at the head office. However, if you have been a stockholder for a while you probably have noticed the name of the bank on which the dividend check is drawn. For faster service you can write directly to the bank. The name of the bank or "transfer agent" handling dividends should be written in your notebook.

Most companies report that very few dividend checks are lost. On notification, the bank will stop payment of the check and issue you a new one, after confirming your mailing address—an incorrect address is the reason for some lost checks. There will be no charge to you, but don't confound the problem by cashing the same dividend checks twice, or you will cause much trouble.

Losing a stock certificate is a much more serious matter, and it can be costly to you in money and trouble, not to mention worry.

Since stock certificates can become lost, especially when they are owned by absentminded or much-traveled investors, the better part of wisdom is to have the shares registered in your name (meaning the dividends and annual reports will come to your home) but held by your broker. Then the certificates themselves are his responsibility. Regularly you will receive a statement from the brokerage firm indicating what shares it holds in your account. If you happen to be in Pakistan or Alaska and suddenly decide to sell you can notify your broker, and he has the shares on hand.

*The Pennsylvania Railroad (which became the Penn Central) regularly paid dividends every year from 1848 to 1969, even in years when it had losses. Then in 1970 it was derailed into bankruptcy. The Singer Company is a well-known persistent dividend payer, starting with 1863; it is still going strong.

Stock Dividends

Many companies pay dividends in the form of shares of stock, or a mixture of cash and stock, especially in the case of growth-type companies that want to conserve cash and funnel it back into the company.

Stockholders often relish stock dividends on the theory that they generally receive something worth money. In truth, they don't. If you pause to think for a moment, you can liken a stock dividend situation to a pie that is sliced a little thinner. Suppose a company has 1,000,000 shares outstanding, and you own 100 shares or $\frac{1}{10,000}$ of the company. Now let's assume that the company suddenly announced a stock split of two for one. It now has 2,000,000 shares outstanding, and it sends you a certificate for 100 additional shares, giving you a total of 200 shares. Now figure out your proportionate interest—still $\frac{1}{10,000}$ part of the company. Your slice of the company is just the same, although it really is two slices of the pie. It has been cut into smaller pieces just as you might do if you suddenly expected more guests for dinner.

However, a shareholder in a growth company likes these splits because generally they are issued only by companies whose earnings are growing, and thus when the stock is split two for one, the price doesn't quite drop to one-half the former price. If it does, it soon moves proportionately higher.

Stock splits are mentioned ahead of dividends in stock because they are easier to understand, and easier to follow in terms of price trends. Actually, splits and stock dividends are close relatives, both indicating that the same company is cutting the pie—the same pie. The rule of thumb of the New York Stock Exchange is that a split is anything amounting to more than 20 percent, while anything less, such as a 5 percent payment in stock, would be called a dividend. A 20 percent payment could be dubbed a one-for-five stock split—namely one new share for each five owned.

Suppose that a company declares a 15 percent stock dividend, and you own 100 shares. You would receive a certificate for 15 additional shares. If you owned only 10 shares, a 15 percent stock dividend would mean $1\frac{1}{2}$ shares. The company might mail you one new share and the cash equivalent of the fractional shares. The cash amount would be based on the average price of the stock at a certain date, such as the date the declaration of a dividend was made.

IBM has been mentioned endlessly by financial writers as the classic example of a company that has grown fast and done well for its stockholders by conserving cash and paying stock dividends and stock splits. IBM's progress illustrates the case of a company whose stockholders share a pie that grows more valuable with persistent regularity. However, there may be other reasons for a company to split its shares. If the stock over a period of time has risen to a high price level—for example, 100 or 150 or more—the company might split the shares two for one, three for one, or even five for one, to lower the price and hence make it more accessible to small stockholders.

Still another reason is that a company might want its shares lower priced so that it could help ward off a takeover by having the shares more widely held by a large number of stockholders, assuming that more investors would buy the stock. Naturally, it would cost more for an outside group interested in taking over a company if it had to reach many thousands of stockholders, compared with just a thousand or so.

Often when the stock is split, the company raises its dividend rate. Thus a $50 stock (current market value) that paid a $2-a-share dividend might be split into two shares, worth $25 each after the split, but paying a $1.10 dividend each.

A company quite often splits its shares and raises its dividend at a time when it fears a proxy fight, a psychological move to please stockholders with the possibility that the split shares might eventually rise in value proportionately higher than before the split, nudged upward by the higher dividend in cash.

Proxy Fights

A proxy fight is a battle usually waged by an outside group to get control of or otherwise change the management of a company by an outside group. Of course, in some closely owned companies proxy fights have been waged by unhappy members of the family owning control of the company. At the other extreme, occasionally a proxy battle is begun by one small stockholder in a large corporation.

In any event, the dissident group appeals to other stockholders for approval, asking them to vote in favor of a new slate or a few new members to the board of directors. Directors play a key role in a company because a corporation is ostensibly run by its directors.

However, there are boards and boards. In some companies the board is nothing more than a rubber stamp group that smiles at the chairman and/or president and votes whatever they suggest.* Other boards work hard, argue hard, and voice opinions.

For years the nation's big oil companies generally had "inside" boards, composed almost entirely of company officials and the companies' legal counsel. The oil companies used positions on the boards to reward retired or elderly officers and as a training ground for executives who hadn't yet reached the top of the ladder but might soon. The theory was that the oil business needed, not

*In 1984 the government demanded the resignation of most of the board members of Chicago's Continental Bank by the time of the 1985 annual meeting. The reason was that the board had failed to prevent the bank from making some bad loans.

outside blood, but an infusion of executive talents within the company because of the specialized nature of the business. This attitude has changed somewhat.

The theory for outside boards, especially in consumer-type industries, is that a group of business leaders from many fields can contribute new and varied ideas.

In either case, since the board of directors at least nominally runs the company, it remains the focus of interest in proxy fights.

Preemptive Rights

One of the valuable rights made available to you as a stockholder in some companies, American Telephone and Telegraph and Consolidated Edison, for example, is called preemptive rights. It means the right of the stockholder to buy shares, usually at a favorable discount, ahead of the public. Sometimes the rights offering involves an offer of debentures or preferred stock.

The company will mail you a letter outlining the rights offering and giving you a chance to exercise the rights. Don't ever throw away the letter containing the rights in the offering because most always it has some money value for you. In Chapter 18 you can find more details about rights offerings and how to figure by a formula what the rights should be worth in cash.

The Annual Report

Once you become a stockholder you will begin to receive quarterly reports. Not all companies mail them to stockholders, because they are expensive, but the typical large listed company does. Some are quite elaborate, such as the quarterly reports of General Motors, picturing a new model car on the cover. Others are a simple sheet of paper or a two-page folder. The quarterly statements usually include sales, earnings, net income per share, and a simplified balance sheet for the recent quarter.

Sometime after the end of the company's fiscal year but some weeks before the annual meeting, the shareholder receives the annual report. These too range widely from fifty-page booklets in full color to a two-page folder. Some have a short message from the president or chairman; some a lengthy one that discusses not only the company's operations and the industries in which it operates, but also comments about the state of the economy (and occasionally even the world).

Reports, especially some of the British corporate statements, have a fascination all their own. Large companies with worldwide operations must have a grip on local events in various parts of the world. An annual report can provide some interesting insights. I have often thought that a good historian should read annual reports of major industrial corporations over a period of years to get an interesting new course of study.

You cannot gain a full impression of a company just by reading the annual report. For real insights, try to attend the annual meeting.

Be an Involved Stockholder

Be sure that before you go to your company's annual meeting you read the proxy statement. It will tell you about any proposals that will come before the meeting. Such proposals can run an unusual gamut. I remember one in which it was mentioned that the company intended to buy the president's house for $200,000, certainly a subject that could be bitterly debated at the annual meeting. Still others contain proposals on changing the bylaws to make it harder for outsiders to take over the company by merger.

The proxy statement will also contain the names of directors to be voted at the meeting, or by mail. Be sure to mail in your signed proxy, voting for directors and the proposals, or against them as you see fit. Better yet, go to the annual meeting in person. It will be worth the effort in broadening your investment IQ.

The annual meeting is conducted according to an agenda. At some efficiently run meetings, the stockholders receive a copy of the agenda, carefully indicating at what points they can speak. Other times the chairman or president, whichever one presides, will announce the procedures, indicating when stockholders can make motions or ask questions, and when the voting for directors will begin.

Obviously, it is much fairer for the questions by stockholders to be raised before the voting of directors, so don't sit idly if a management pushes through the voting, walking over such an obvious right.

What are some of the questions that a stockholder might want to raise?

Mergers. These days many companies have become merger-minded. Some mergers work out well for a company; others cost too much in terms of the stock or cash that must be paid for the company acquired.

Managements differ widely in their attitude about mergers, and it is a subject that should be aired with the stockholders. For example, some companies acquire only those firms that make sense, that fit into their corporate structure neatly. Warner Lambert, a pharmaceuticals company, acquired American Optical, a maker of scientific instruments. The two scientifically oriented companies seemed to fit together, although a few years later Warner Lambert indicated it might sell the optical unit. Gulf+Western Industries is a conglomerate that doesn't make much "sense," since it has spread itself over fields as widely varied as motion pictures, cigars, agricultural products, auto parts, and zinc. How a stockholder can analyze the prospects of a company like that, I cannot understand. Perhaps they didn't either. G+W is currently selling off several unrelated parts of its holdings.

Products—successful and not so successful—should be a subject for discussion. Sometimes stockholders can give management hints or ideas about products. Every company, sooner or later, has a product failure, and stockholders have a right to know why.

Management turnover. Sometimes if many top people in a company's management are leaving, it can spell trouble ahead.

There's usually a reason. For example, vice presidents came and went at Revlon some years ago like people going through a revolving door. The president was hard to deal with. It took a while for the situation to be smoothed over; meanwhile, the stock jittered in price. At the time Revlon and its "musical chair" vice presidents provided plenty of laughs for onlookers. It became almost a badge of honor to have been a Revlon vice president for a few months.

Now the practice of wholesale firings, one after the other, has become less of a joke and more of a typical scenario. For example, Beatrice, the big food maker, fired or forced the resignation of more than two dozen top officers in the years 1979–1985, under the whiplash rule of James D. Dutt. In 1985 Dutt was eased out as chairman and chief executive officer.

Labor costs, ever rising, are a point of discussion at many meetings. Does the management expect a long strike in a particular year? How can increasing wages be offset by more automation?

The annual meeting is the one time of year when a stockholder can ask questions freely—and expect answers. Furthermore, other stockholders listening to the answers or in some cases the lack of answers from management can get ideas about the investment quality of the stock. Often at the meeting the chairman or president will volunteer a prediction about the outlook for the year, or look even further into the future. This is not necessarily information that he puts into the annual or interim reports. It may come in reply to searching stockholder questions.

Unfortunately, I have attended some annual meetings as a financial reporter during which no stockholder asked about future earnings, and the president offered no prediction. I cannot imagine a stockholder not wanting to know this information, and yet the opportunity slipped by.

Don't be shy. Get on your feet and ask what the outlook is. The head of your company has the job of ordering his experts to plan ahead, budgeting both costs and reinvestment of capital, along with scheduling new products. He knows what the company plans to spend on plants and machinery; he knows how sales are now going and he has, possibly in his pocket, projections made by his sales managers for the ensuing months. He knows also the level of expenses; his labor relations director probably has alerted him to the higher cost of wages, especially if a new contract is about to be negotiated. A strike or other crisis can always occur and change the best-laid plans; but often a company president even has a pretty good idea whether this will happen. In the company's laboratories, there are often unpublicized new products ready for the production line, and the president has a pretty good idea of their potential too. Naturally a large number of new products, more than the investor realizes, fail each year for lack of enough advertising, inability to get consumer acceptance, or other reasons. Still, a company president has a good idea of what new products can do to help earnings and their chances of success.

If he doesn't know all this then he might not be a good president. As a stockholder you have a right to ask questions along these lines. In some cases you will receive straightforward answers; sometimes the replies will be devious. The more stockholders ask, generally the better the meeting is and the better answers they receive.

Naturally, stockholders also want information about dividends, and a president has some good ideas about this, too. He will often field the question by saying that only the directors can declare dividends—an obvious remark. However, a persistent stockholder might point out that directors usually act on dividends in accordance with the suggestions of the company's president. Many presidents are quite willing to tell the annual meeting what they plan to recommend.

Companies vary widely in their thinking about dividends. Growth-type companies like to pay little or nothing, relying on stock dividends or the fast price growth in the shares to keep stockholders happy. Other companies regularly allot about 50 percent of earnings to dividends; still others pay out up to 90 percent.

At many annual meetings you will see in action some of the so-called gadfly stockholders—a group epitomized by people like Lewis Gilbert, his brother John, and Mrs. Wilma Soss, all of whom are quite old now. Unfortunately a new generation of colorful gadflies has not arisen. You may not like them, either their personalities or their persistent questioning of management at meetings, but they have been crusaders, making major gains for the small taxpayers, just as Ralph Nader has won safety features in cars from a recalcitrant auto industry.

In the 1930s, as a young man, Lewis Gilbert went to the Bethlehem Steel Corporation annual meeting. He stood up and demanded to know why the management was paying a retired corporate official, Charles Schwab, then in his eighties, a pension of $250,000 a year. True, the official in question had helped develop the company, and there was no doubt that Bethlehem Steel was a wealthy organization. But Mr. Gilbert challenged the right of management to pay what even nowadays would be regarded as a huge pension and bonus.

It is unfortunate that many successful business leaders develop an ego complex so advanced that they think it should be measured in terms of millions of dollars payable to them by their companies. In this case the pension would have been the highest ever paid to a corporate official, at least as far as anyone could find out at the time. Remember, those were Depression years.

Mr. Gilbert, a bustling, determined man who can be sarcastic when necessary, astounded the meeting with his protest. How much is a man worth?

In those days it never occurred to the stouthearted, dignified, high-handed leaders of major companies that the high pensions and salaries they voted officials—usually a rubber-stamp vote—would be questioned by humble stockholders, especially ones that owned only a few shares.

In the case of Bethlehem, Mr. Gilbert won the battle ultimately and the company cut the pension to $180,000.*

Often even today corporate officials deride Mr. Gilbert, his brother, and Mrs. Soss for their persistent questions. Fellow stockholders sometimes shout, *Sit down, shut up,* and worse. Still their various crusades have highlighted one significant point—an owner of one share has just as many rights as the owner of a million shares. He can question, criticize, suggest at the annual meeting. The so-called gadfly stockholders have stung many managements into improvements that might not have occurred otherwise.

The awful truth is that most stockholders are not willing to fight for their inherent rights and they tend to sit quietly, or limply sell their shares if the management fails to move in the right directions. Sometimes they are so limp that they watch the company go slowly down the drain, without even plugging their own losses on the shares by selling.

It takes a feisty, determined, vociferous, embarrassment-proof stockholder to stand up year after year and demand improvements in the midst of arrogant corporate officials and antagonistic stockholders.

To their credit the Gilberts and Mrs. Soss have scored some advances:

1. Companies like Bethlehem Steel have become more sensitive about paying huge pensions and bonuses.
2. Companies now provide more data in annual reports and also (in many cases) issue interim reports and post-annual meeting reports.
3. Reports break down more items like sales and earnings by divisions and foreign operations.

*Mr. Gilbert commented: "I was satisfied at the reduction, especially since Schwab told me he was hard up."

4. Meetings are being rotated to other cities from the company's corporate headquarters, so that wider groups of stockholders can attend.
5. Some companies have adopted cumulative voting for shareholders, permitting stockholders to lump their votes for directors; the effect is that minority directors have more chance of getting elected.

The gadflies have insisted on company auditors being present at meetings for questioning by stockholders—a good idea at a time when some companies have had accounting problems.

For example, some years ago there was the Billie Sol Estes case, which involved several large finance companies holding, the gadflies thought, collateral in the form of fertilizer that did not exist. Or the famous "salad oil" swindle involving a subsidiary of American Express Company and vegetable oil that did not exist. In this case some major banks holding warehouse receipts for the oil were caught without any oil to back the receipts; a brokerage firm failed as a result of the swindle and another was forced into a merger. The swindlers went to jail.

Such cases were not by any means uncovered by small investors, but the fact that the Gilberts and Sosses and their younger counterparts stand ready to ask questions does keep management more alert, even running scared sometimes.

Stockholders' own worst enemies these days are themselves. If a few more would rise and ask questions at annual meetings they would get more answers and be treated better.

For example, some years ago a small woman stockholder (owner of a few shares) rose at the Engelhard Industries annual meeting in Newark and asked why the company had so many vice presidents, all obviously highly paid officials. One logical answer to the question could have been that the company had gone through a merger and thus acquired quite a few officers who were vice presidents. A second reply could have been that the company, which deals in precious metals, is basically a selling business that requires skilled experts to head each of its many types of selling operations. But management, apparently surprised by the question, did not have a good answer and floundered quite badly. Those of us who attended the meeting got the feeling that the management would think a long time before it created new vice presidents.

Brokerage firms, especially the large, well-known ones, have a lot of respect for the power of small stockholders. That became evident when Baldwin-United went into bankruptcy. One by one the firms told the small investors who had been sold the Baldwin annuities by their aggressive salespeople that their losses would be made up, at least partially. Of course, the firms had the Securities and Exchange Commission prodding them into action.

Women stockholders too often appear to be unsure of themselves or shy at annual meetings. This is a shame, especially since they often have the time and energy to attend meetings. And one stockholder voice crying in the corporate wilderness can bring—and in fact has brought—worthwhile changes.

Many years ago there was a famous engineer-inventor working for General Motors named Charles Kettering, who became fascinated by the prospects of a new kind of engine invented by a German named Diesel. For some years Kettering tinkered with a diesel engine in a boat he owned; then he convinced the GM management that diesel engines could be used successfully in railroad locomotives. The nation's two leading builders of steam locomotives scoffed at the idea, convinced that the diesel could never perform as well as the modern steam engine. While Kettering tried desperately to find a railroad president adventurous enough to buy and try one of his diesels, the two engine manufacturers, American Locomotive and Baldwin Locomotive Works, apparently ignored his efforts.

Finally, Kettering found a man named Budd, the president of the former Chicago, Burlington & Quincy Railroad, who took a chance and tried out the first GM passenger locomotive diesel. It succeeded so well that gradually other railroads began to buy diesels, but still the two old-line steam engine builders lagged behind.

The result was amazing for U.S. industry. GM, the large automobile builder, won the market for diesel locomotives. Baldwin went into bankruptcy; American Locomotive experienced some lean years.

Stockholders of those days, if they had been alert, could have predicted the outcome—and sold their stock in the steam engine builders who lost a multimillion-dollar market.

Probably much the same action—to sell out—would have been taken by truly attentive stockholders present at Merritt, Chapman and Scott annual meetings in recent years. The management was led by Louis Wolfson, who often failed to attend the meetings; or if he did come, he sat quietly ignoring most stockholder questions.

Mr. Wolfson was a "raider." In the 1950s and 1960s there were any number of fast-moving men like him, empire builders, raiders, organizers of conglomerates, who took control of various Big Board companies. When names of men who are known as raiders appear on the board of directors of your company, make sure you go to the annual meeting. It can be revealing. It can be a warning signal for you to consider selling your shares. Is the raider interested in building up the company? Or did he obtain control to sell it out, dissolve it, or just put his relatives into lucrative jobs? These are questions you might consider.

While you're at the meeting, take a good look at the directors and principal officers. Are they the kind of people you would trust with your cash? Recently I went to an annual meeting during which a stockholder asked a good question:

Why had the president put his son on the payroll as the advertising manager? The president, on the defensive, immediately justified the appointment by claiming the son was the person best suited for the job. Perhaps, but I wouldn't buy a share in that company. Nepotism is an ugly word in a company trying to build up good relations with stockholders. Naturally, if it's a small, family-dominated company, that is another matter. There the stockholder usually goes into the investment with his eyes open.

Let me put it more bluntly. As a newspaper reporter, I have covered hundreds of annual meetings. If I look at the board of directors of a company and say to myself, "I wouldn't want to marry any of them or have my daughters marry them either," then you can be sure that I would never invest a cent in that company, even if it was the fastest-growing one I could find. Such a company comes to mind, not because of the annual meeting, but because the president told me once he spent a large amount of the corporate money on art. As a stockholder I wouldn't like that, although I enjoy good art.

Just reaching conclusions about the character and attitude of the company's officers and directors on various occasions has saved me more money than I have lost, by not putting it into such a company's stock. It is an application, I suppose, of that characteristic called woman's intuition—something that most men would deride but that for some reason works much of the time.

The role of the small stockholder, I think, will widen dramatically in coming years, especially in the light of recent narrowing of profit margins and real slowing of corporate growth, which has eliminated some of the phony growth that comes from inflation.

Don't forget that small stockholders have waged some long and dramatic—and successful—corporate battles. Perhaps the most colorful in modern history involved a man named Walter Meyer, a lawyer in New York. He was a common stockholder for years in a railroad called the St. Louis Southwestern, more familiarly called the Cotton Belt, since it operated in the large cotton-growing area of Texas.

The Cotton Belt was a "bridge" line that stretched from St. Louis south to cities like Houston, Texas, and Little Rock, Arkansas. It carried a large amount of agricultural produce such as cotton and rice from the Southwest. Southern Pacific (SP), a much bigger railroad that owned large amounts of Cotton Belt's bonds, took more than a paternal interest in the smaller railroad because it linked SP lines with others in the area.

During the Depression the Cotton Belt, like other Southern carriers, flopped into bankruptcy. As the creditor (owner of all those bonds), the Southern Pacific was only too happy to have the Cotton Belt go through the bankruptcy wringer, because in the process the stockholders would be eliminated. And as the major bondholder SP would end up as virtual owner of a railroad with a new, streamlined capitalization.

However, SP's lawyers reckoned without Mr. Meyer, who proved a very formidable small stockholder. He jockeyed the case through the courts for a very simple reason: he had the foresight to believe that the Cotton Belt, formerly a good, sound earner, was only temporarily embarrassed financially. He also guessed that the South would grow industrially (which it did, especially after World War II), owing to new businesses in the area. He also believed it was unfair for the SP to eliminate any chance for the common shareholders to participate in what could be a bright future.

He turned out to be right. The railroad soon began operating at a profit because of World War II; and after the war it continued to fare well. Yet still SP insisted on its rights as bondholder to take over the railroad. The case moved slowly and ponderously, as most lawsuits do, through the courts up to the Supreme Court.

By the time it reached the apex—the Supreme Court—the truth had become embarrassingly obvious to SP, to the government, and to the public: the Cotton Belt had not only recovered from the effects of the Depression but had become one of the most prosperous railroads in the nation. Yet still it was technically in bankruptcy. Finally, Mr. Meyer won his case.

The Cotton Belt emerged from bankruptcy, probably the only railroad in history that could make such a claim. Its stockholders fared well, all because of Mr. Meyer's bitter, tedious fight.

Another outstanding corporate battle won with the help of small stockholders involved the late Robert R. Young. In those days I worked as a financial writer for the brokerage firm Merrill Lynch. One day my editor said, "I noticed a little item in *The New York Times* about Alleghany Corporation receiving about ten million in cash from sale of an investment. Go interview Robert R. Young and find out what he is planning to do with the cash."

I made an appointment to see Mr. Young, head of Alleghany, who greeted me with Southern gallantry, leaping up from his chair and sitting me down near his desk. He said, "I can spare only fifteen minutes." An hour later I left in a slightly dazed condition.

After some preliminary questions I had thought out ahead of time, I posed the ten-dollar—or ten-million dollar—one. He thought for a moment and then said with a little smile, "Oh, I might use it to take over the New York Central." I could hear a gasp from his public relations director, Thomas Deegan, sitting nearby on a couch.

Back at the office, no one believed my report that Mr. Young had made such a statement about the New York Central. For one thing, the railroad was dominated by the Vanderbilt and Morgan interests. Furthermore, it had vast assets compared with Alleghany Corporation. It sounded like a very small corporate flea trying to irritate a very large dog.

Disbelief prevailed to such an extent that I had to telephone Newport,

Rhode Island, with a Merrill Lynch vice president listening, to have Mr. Young repeat from his summer home his plan about the New York Central. The brokerage firm had a scoop, which it sent over its wires and gave to the news services such as Associated and United Press.

Mr. Young was a brilliant man, and in the back of his mind he knew that he needed small investors to help him win control of the New York Central. So he gave the scoop to my brokerage firm, the largest one in the country, and one that had long positioned itself as the small investor's friend. His proxy fight, with the help of small investors, proved successful: he did take over the New York Central in one of the most colorful fights in history.

Proxy fights can be profitable for the small investor. As the battle approaches a climax, she will find herself approached by both sides wanting votes. In such a case, the small investor should consult her broker. As the battle reaches a climax, the price of the shares probably will rise. Whether she should keep them and what side she should favor are the questions she must decide.

In conclusion, as a stockholder don't underestimate your power. Don't overestimate the quality of the management of your company. You have a right to view them critically, without rose-colored glasses.

Don't ever get caught, as many small stockholders did some years ago, in a company such as U.S. Hoffman Machinery. It was badly hurt financially by its chairman, Harold Roth, later sentenced to jail. For years he had borrowed money from the company, at the same time he received a salary of about $50,000 a year. As a result of his financial downfall from overspeculation, Mr. Roth established an unusual claim to corporate fame. As far as I know, he was the only chairman who ever appeared on a corporate balance sheet as a liability because of the money he owed the company. Each year for a long period the company deducted a certain sum from his salary to pay off the loan. He shouldn't have been kept on the payroll, but he was—despite shareholders' objections.

And what about the shareholders? At one time the shares sold as high as 22⅛; today the company is out of business.

16

Your Demanding Uncle

The Impact of Taxes

Uncle Sam is a rather benevolent fellow who has given women lots of opportunities to make money in the form of capital gains. Unfortunately, he has a very shrewish mistress, Taxes, who intimidates some conservative investors. At present, like Madame Pompadour of centuries ago, she seems to have the upper hand in government.

However, 1985 will be remembered as the year when Congress began to make efforts to change the requirements, through simplifcation, elimination of some popular shelters, and a general lowering of rates. From all indications such reform would help lower-income people a little, hurt upper-middle-income persons, and soak the very rich. The total government intake from income taxes probably will not change much.

Government officials and federal and state legislators say weakly, "We can't do much about stopping the rise in taxes." They can, of course, by cutting back spending and waste; but consumers don't make their wishes known forcefully, at least not as loudly as the government spenders do. At local levels, however, voters have been rejecting more and more bond proposals for new schools and other public endeavors. Like inflation, taxes are something the investor has to learn to live with and understand.

Sometimes men and women say rather grandly, "I have such a large capital gain in that stock that I can't afford to sell it.'' What they are saying—foolishly, I believe—is that they are scared to take their profits and pay taxes on the gains. But in reality there's *no* gain, no profit, until it is nailed down in cash, especially these days when stocks move up and down quickly in price and fashions in investments change. The point to digest is: take your capital gains at appropriate times. Don't be scared about the high tax you might have to pay.

How do taxes work? In the first place, in terms of your personal income, the federal government applies two types of taxation: regular income tax depending on your income level after exemptions and deductions, and a second form called capital gains taxation levied on profits you have made in property like stocks, your house, paintings, etc. This applies only when the specific property is sold.

Generally speaking, your family fares better if you can file a joint income tax return, a method available to married couples. A widow or single person with dependents can file as head of household, which is more favorable usually than filing as a single person.

As you know, there are certain exemptions allowed such as $1,000 a person for 1984 taxes and a similar amount for any dependents, which, indexed for inflation, rose in 1985.

Dividends that you receive from any company in which you have stock are included as regular income. However, a small amount of dividends can be excluded by taxpayers. Interest you receive from bonds, or that is credited to your account in savings banks or comes to you from a credit union (this is often called a dividend but is classed as interest payment for tax purposes) must be listed as income. Interest is not deductible as dividends from stocks are.

If you buy a security such as a bond or stock and sell it within six months, then you have what is called a *short-term capital gain.* You must add any profit you made on the transaction to your regular income to be taxed at the rate applicable to your tax bracket. Naturally you can deduct the cost of commissions, transfer tax, etc., before you arrive at the figure for the profit. The simplest way to figure this is to take the purchase price and add to it the fees paid when you bought and when you sold it, and subtract this total from the price at which you sold the shares.

However, if you have kept the bond or stock more than six months, the profit becomes subject to a much more favorable rate. You have what is called a *long-term capital gain,* and this is subject to a lower tax rate: you add only 40 percent of the gain to your taxable income.

In case you have a potpourri of short-term and long-term gains, here are the general rules that apply:

1. All long-term gains and all long-term losses should be added up separately. The difference between them will be either a net long-term gain or a net long-term loss.
2. In the same way, the taxpayer should add up short-term gains and losses, to determine whether she has either a net short-term gain or a net short-term loss.
3. If the taxpayer finds that she has a net short-term loss, the total can be used to offset up to a certain amount of ordinary income. Furthermore, the Internal Revenue Service permits individuals to carry over unused losses for additional years. When carried over they retain their "character" as either short- or long-term losses.
4. If the taxpayer has more net long-term gain than net short-term loss, she offsets and treats the result as net long-term gain.
5. If the net short-term gain runs larger than the net long-term loss, the difference can be handled as net short-term gain.

Be wary of something the IRS frowns upon: "wash sales." It is a trap into which a sentimental shareholder might easily fall. Often unwitting investors think they will sell a stock to take a loss on it, but then they want to buy it back. An example might be a dear old favorite like AT&T, which falls quite sharply sometimes and then attracts more interest again.

However, the IRS will not permit the taxpayer the loss if she buys back substantially identical stock within 30 days before or after the sale of the original holding. The advice, if you want to buy back such a stock, is to wait at least 31 days, or invest your money in a company in a similar industry. But note that the "wash sale" rule applies only to losses and not to gains. Thus you can sell a stock and nail down the profit and buy shares in the same company shortly afterward.

A good question is when you should sell as a calendar year is about to end. You should think about it shortly after Labor Day, because sophisticated investors are doing just that—pondering their portfolios. Some brokers believe that the well-heeled, well-schooled investors sell well before the year-end to establish either capital gains or losses because they have no psychological block about clinging to stocks, especially those in which they might have losses. They want to make a clean sweep and be ready for a new year of trading.

The smaller, less sophisticated investor tends to wait to take his gains or losses until almost the last moment. Often prices of stocks in November and December move lower under the impact of such selling. This last-minute gain- or loss-taker often gets lower prices late in December and then finds it might cost him more to invest again after the new year begins. With the help of your broker—and his tax brochures—plan your strategy.

The tax break for long-term capital gains explains why so many investors speak of them favorably, especially if they are in high income tax brackets. Suppose that you and your husband are in the 33 percent tax bracket (meaning an income after exemptions and deductions of about $35,200), and you have a gain of $1,000 that year on stock. You will pay about $330 of it to Uncle Sam if you sell before six months, but wait that one day after six months and your tax liability drops to less than half. Worth waiting?

Remember the actual day you buy a security and the day you sell are important. The Internal Revenue Service measures the six months' holding period this way:

The holding period must be six months, plus one day, for a gain to qualify as long-term. The holding period does not begin until the day after the purchase date, *but* it does include the day of sale. Example: stock bought January 15 would qualify if sold on or after July 16. Or property bought April 30 would become long term if sold November 1 or after.

Taxes have various complexities, as you probably know. Since some women do not fill out their own tax forms, relying instead on their husbands, accountants, or lawyers, they generally know little about some important and helpful gimmicks. In fact, once they digest the fact that capital gains are tastier than straight income, they neglect the rest of the menu served up by Uncle Sam.

Using that small, ever-present stock notebook, it's a good idea to keep track as you buy and sell shares of your profits and losses, whether they are long-term or short. You can get the facts easily each month when the broker sends you a statement about your account. As the year-end approaches you will have an idea of your tax position. Then you can consult your broker about what you should do.

Your comment might be like this: "I have fifteen hundred dollars in long-term gains, and about a hundred and fifty in short-term gains, on paper. What shall I do? Is it a good time to sell?"

Before each year-end there comes a period, usually in October and lasting partly into November, when brokers begin to talk about tax selling. The firm will probably bombard you with written material about tax selling and switches for tax purposes. Read carefully even if you don't understand at first. At this time you can be sure the sophisticated investors are busy selling to establish losses or gains, as they want, in relation to their own tax position. It is as if brokers come alive in the fall, suddenly remembering your existence and hoping they can persuade you to make some trades, too.

Is it better for you to spread gains over two years, gains you have on paper? It might be wiser not to sell all your stocks and take profits if you expect your income to be the same next year as it is this year. In other words, by selling only half you can balance your tax liability better between the two years. Remember the whole point is to keep your tax bracket as low as possible. If this is the case, your approach might be to sell part of your investments toward the end of the year and sell the others that have gains early the following year. Remember your tax year, although you file an income tax every April 15, runs from January through December 31 of the prior year. In other words taxes for the year 1984 were paid, or the final return filed, by April 15, 1985.*

Does it appear that next year your income might fall sharply? Perhaps you plan to retire and live on your pension, or there may be other reasons. Then you might want to postpone selling any stocks until next year. Do you or your husband expect a large increase in salary next year, or will you inherit some money? Then take the gains this year if it is more favorable.

Unfortunately, many small investors overlook this idea of scheduling, because they don't realize they can save taxes or they think saving a few dollars is not worthwhile. A few dollars saved each year over a period of years adds up. Even $50 saved in taxes can be worthwhile, if it can be achieved by a little forethought in planning when you will take your gains.

In summary, remember three things about taxes:

1. If possible keep stocks six months and more to achieve the more favorable capital gains rates. But keep in mind that it would be foolish to hang on to stock for six months if the market is going against you, just to achieve such gains.
2. Don't hang on to a stock forever just because you are afraid to pay capital gains. That's being penny wise, pound foolish. Or as one broker I know says, "It's penny-ante thinking."
3. Try to think in terms of relating your income in a particular year to potential gains (or losses), so that you can schedule in your mind the best time to take such gains—or losses.

Remember, Congress is expected to revise tax laws sharply in 1986, and you will have to learn how the changes affect you.

Getting Off Tax Free

For years, as I mentioned in Chapter 2, there has been one form of security exempt from federal income taxation: municipal bonds. Unfortunately it is now

*Naturally, most people who work pay a large part of their taxes each year through withholding by their employer. Also, many people file quarterly and pay taxes on income not subject to withholding.

being eyed by legislators and government officials as a form that must yield to their needs for higher taxes. Municipal bonds have been excluded from federal income taxation, and sometimes taxation by the state in which they are issued, because of a man only remembered by his name, Hugh McCulloch. Ironically, he was a government official.

It seems that the state of Maryland much preferred its own banks to the bank called the Bank of the United States, which had been organized by the federal government; a brainchild, in fact, of that capable financial planner Alexander Hamilton. Banks in those days (the early 1800s) had a fondness for issuing money; sometimes it could be described as printing-press money, because there were few assets behind it. As long as the banks kept it busily circulating it couldn't come home to roost for redemption into gold, of which there was a great shortage.

The federal government wanted a more solid basis for the banking system, an organization that would issue money and control the amount in circulation. Hamilton's thinking about a sound currency proved too advanced for his time. In Maryland, a clique in the legislature passed a law taxing the money issued by the branch of the Bank of the United States in Baltimore, with the idea of hurting the bank's business. A government official named Hugh McCulloch sued the state of Maryland on behalf of the government to prevent the severe penalty tax.

The case, called *McCulloch v. Maryland,* went to the Supreme Court, which rendered a decision that has stood through this day. Mentioning the theory that the power to tax is the power to destroy, the judges ruled that Maryland could not tax the issues of the federal bank; and therefore by implication that the federal government could not tax the issues of the states.

Ordinarily this case would not be important for the average investor, but it sometimes makes headlines because of charges that many wealthy persons can escape a large amount of federal taxation by investing in municipal bonds.

Municipalities, states, counties, school districts, sewer authorities, and such have financed billions of dollars in improvements by issuing the securities called municipals because they can be issued at relatively low rates of interest to entice investors interested in the sweetener—tax exemption.

Naturally taxpayers in the municipalities like it because otherwise their taxes would rise to cover the interest on higher-interest-bearing issues. Investors like it, especially those in the 30 percent tax bracket and above.

Many observers do not believe that Congress can hurdle the protective fence around municipals erected by the old Supreme Court decision in *McCulloch v. Maryland* and some subsequent decisions. Also, it is doubtful whether the municipalities will give up without a fight. The nontax feature enables any community to offer such bonds and find ready buyers in the highly competitive bond market.

However, the government is whittling away at the fence. A minimum tax has been imposed on wealthy investors who receive income from preference sources such as municipal bonds. Another approach has been to have the government underwrite some municipal issues when a city or town has been willing to give up the tax-exempt feature.

For the moderate- and high-income investor the subject of tax-free municipal income remains worthwhile to pursue, especially since each year with the rise in the cost of living taxpayers tend to move into higher tax brackets through compensatory salary and wage increases.

Individual Retirement Accounts

Women, especially these who work, should take a look at IRAs—Individual Retirement Accounts. Individuals who work can contribute up to $2,000 each year to an IRA and deduct that from gross income. It comes off the top, so to speak, reducing the amount subject to taxation. There is also a spousal IRA—a certain amount put into an IRA by a working spouse for a nonworking spouse. If a husband and wife both work, then each can have an IRA, contributing up to $2,000 each a year.

In addition, there are rollover IRAs; money that is received when a person leaves a company or retires can be put into an IRA account and continue to collect dividends or interest tax free.

IRS rules say that money cannot be taken from an IRA without penalty before the age of 59½, and that it must be taken by age 70½. When it is taken out, it becomes taxable that year at whatever the individual's income bracket is at that time.

Since there are strict rules about setting up IRAs, especially the rollover ones, it is wise to consult the IRS, a tax expert, or an accountant. Have all the information you need before making a decision.

In summary, the beauty of an IRA is that it encourages savings for retirement, cuts taxable income, and allows dividends or interest to accumulate tax free.

Similar to an IRA, a salary reduction plan under so-called Section 401(k) can be set up, allowing an individual a tax break. The plan differs from an IRA in that it must be sponsored by an employer, who may or may not contribute to it. The employee agrees to have salary reduced by a certain percentage. This amount accumulates tax free until withdrawn. Early withdrawals (usually before age 59½) may not be made without penalty. The moment it is withdrawn, the money becomes subject to income tax.

Gifts and Taxes

If you are a mother (or a grandmother) there is one aspect of investment planning you should consider. You can reduce your own taxes by giving stock or the money to buy the stock to children under 21.

For example, at present the government permits you to turn over up to $10,000 a year to as many individuals of any age as you want. You do not pay a gift tax on this and they do not pay any income tax upon receiving it. If you had a hundred grandchildren, cousins, or friends you could give them $10,000 each, or a total of $1,000,000 that year. You can do the same every year.

If you join with your husband in the gift giving, together you can turn over a total of $20,000 a year per recipient to as many individuals as you want, cousins, friends, parents. It's a valuable aspect of taxation to consider even if you are in a moderate income tax bracket.

For example, suppose you have saved up $40,000 for your son's college education; you could turn it over to him at the rate of $10,000 each year. Then if the money were invested in stocks he would receive the dividends to be used for his expenses. You would save because your income would be reduced by the amount of dividends on which otherwise you would be paying taxes. A short-term trust could also be used to do a similar job for you—getting income away from you in your high tax bracket to a child who is in a low or no-tax bracket. Naturally, you need help from a trust officer, lawyer, or accountant in setting up such a plan.

To summarize: It may be beneficial for you to give away money annually to one or more people throughout your life, thus reducing your tax liability.

One exception to the rule is that a gift made in contemplation of death can be challenged by the Internal Revenue Service. In such an instance the government applies a three-year rule. If the donor lives three years after the gift is made, all is well. If he dies within the three-year period the government might try to tax the amount involved at estate tax rates, which are higher than gift tax rates. The IRS will claim the gifts were made in contemplation of death, often hard to disprove. The giving habits of the donor would be a factor. Did he make gifts regularly? Or did he wait until after he had a heart attack or was very old?

A classic case was decided in 1972 involving Mrs. Hilda Beecher Stowe (related by marriage to Harriet Beecher Stowe).

Mrs. Stowe gave her sons large gifts of money and stock, but died within the three-year period. The IRS claimed the gifts should be part of the estate, thus taxable at higher rates. No, said the court. In its decision the court stressed the fact that Mrs. Stowe had danced at the St. Regis Hotel, in New York, until

3 A.M. one night at her birthday party, an indication of her liveliness despite her old age. She was in her eighties when she died.

There is a lesson to be learned. The moral for families with elderly relatives is twofold:

1. Keep them dancing (enjoying life, playing golf, swimming, traveling, etc.).
2. Fight the IRS in court, where judges are looking sympathetically these days at elderly people who make gifts and then die within the three-year period.

Gifts of Stock

Gifts of stock offer another advantage besides getting income away from the donor. There may be capital gains involved and thus the giver avoids paying the gains. At the time of the transfer the market price of the stock becomes the price the child, or whoever receives the gift, will use as a basis.

Most all investors face charitable demands each year. Some charities, like the Red Cross, Salvation Army, Community Chest, Girl Scout cookie sales, usually are given amounts of money in cash. Investors might well consider giving their church (to which they make an annual pledge) or their college (for annual giving) a gift in the form of stock. The reason is a simple one with two facets:

1. A gift to charity can, to a large extent, be deducted from regular income in reporting taxes.
2. A gift of stock in which there are taxable gains means that the giver escapes the gains tax and yet gets much of the market value of the gift as a reduction.

The new law is complex. Suppose you own Union Carbide stock bought at 40 and now selling for 50. You want to give your church $500. You can take cash out of the bank in the amount. You could sell ten shares of the stock and turn the resulting $500 over to the church, but you would have to pay capital gains on it, as well as your brokerage commission. The third way is merely to give ten shares of the stock to the church.

It may sound complicated to you now, but when you are thinking of making a large contribution to a church or college, think in terms of giving stocks to save on taxes.

Gifts to Children

The New York Stock Exchange campaigned for years to make it easier to give gifts of stock to children—and finally succeeded. Uniform rules now apply in most all states, replacing a hodgepodge of laws that made such giving difficult.

In buying shares for children you must tell your broker to have them registered with you (or anyone you choose) as custodian. The face of the stock certificate might read like this: "Elizabeth Jones custodian for Robert Jones a minor under Uniform Gifts to Minors Act New York." It is wiser to have a third person—not the donor—act as custodian because of the three-year contemplation of death rule.

In such a case the stock probably should be invested in growth-type securities. The parents of the child can still take the exemption for the child on their income tax no matter how much income the child receives from dividends, as long as the child is under 18 or in college and receives more than half of his support from the parents.

If you are interested in gifts of securities for children, your broker can supply a booklet describing the general rules that apply. One significant feature is that the law requires that you hand over the securities to the child when he or she reaches 21 and you have to make an accounting if he or she requires it, so it behooves a donor to keep good records and invest the money wisely.

Furthermore, many states require that the securities be turned over at age 18 in the case of new custody accounts.

17

Investments with Different Personalities

New and Unusual Types of Securities

Like people, securities have varying characteristics. Some rather little-known ones can exert a very powerful influence on your thinking; or if not that, they can affect your life indirectly.

Some of these more esoteric forms of investment will remain on the periphery of your life. You may never own them but as a knowledgeable investor you should know what they are and what kind of help or investment function they perform. For example, there are bonds called "flower bonds" that could be useful for any woman with a dying husband or father. If you don't have cash on hand now there is still a way of buying cheaply 100 shares of that stock you are convinced will double in a year. If you believe that the price of silver is going to rise sharply, there's a method of buying the metal and keeping it stashed safely in some New York banks. Each involves a different type of investment.

Remember that wherever a few business leaders or government officials gather together with the idea of raising money for various ventures, they will think in terms of issuing some type of security to help finance or provide working capital for the operation.

Here are some of the securities or types of investment that you should know a little about:

1. Municipal bonds
2. U.S. government issues
   Savings bonds
   Treasury bills
   Certificates
   Treasury notes
   Long-term bonds
   Fannie Maes
   Ginnie Maes
3. Commercial paper
4. Federal funds
5. Equipment trusts
6. Zero coupon bonds
7. Puts and calls
8. Commodity futures

Let's look at each in turn.

Municipal Bonds

With their traditional tax-exempt feature, municipals have long been called the "rich man's investment." Yet ironically they can help those of us in much lower income tax brackets today. The reason is that over the last decade salaries have risen sharply, pushing many people into higher tax brackets, although perhaps they don't feel much wealthier because inflation has taken such a toll.

The point to remember is that today, even persons in the 30 percent tax bracket might find municipals advantageous. Information about them, and the changes that might come in this investment area, were covered in Chapter 16. Then ask your broker about municipals, especially requesting that he supply you with a brochure about them. In fact, even if you are not interested in them, ask anyway. He probably will be impressed at the question, all of which can be part of your ploy to rouse his interest in your investment future.

U.S. Government Issues

To finance this multi-billion-dollar government of ours takes continuing amounts of money. Sometimes, of course, the Treasury does not need as much money as at other times—around income tax payment dates, for example, when large sums of money flow out of our bank accounts into the government's hands. Almost every week, however, the Treasury is in "the market"—meaning the money market—to raise money. Naturally, like any shrewd business, the Treasury would like to "sell" its securities at the lowest possible cost in terms of interest.

Look at it this way. If the government has to raise $1 billion to pay salaries, feed troops abroad, pay its light, heat, and other bills for a while, it would like to do it as cheaply as possible. The cost of $1 billion at 2 percent interest (and years ago during World War II the government did pay such a low rate for money) would run only $20,000,000; at 4 percent interest the cost would be $40,000,000. In mid-1985 the government was paying 10.84 percent for 30-year treasury bonds. When you think in terms of billions of dollars you can see the difference.

Generally the government offers two basic types of securities: the marketable and the nonmarketable.

The nonmarketable are the types that in all probability you know best—the *savings bonds* of various issues. During World War II they were called war bonds, and later defense bonds, and now they are advertised as savings bonds. As a safe place for money, they are all right; most Americans probably own some. Children often receive them from doting godmothers or grandparents to be put away for ten years or so and collect interest until maturity (the date at which the bond comes due).

They are called nonmarketable because you can't go out and sell them to someone else, but you can turn them in at any time to the government. Your bank will do the work for you, and you will receive a certain amount, usually listed on the bond's indenture (the back of the crinkly certificate), plus the accrued interest to date.

Don't buy savings bonds if you are interested in investing for good return and growth. Such bonds usually carry a low rate of interest, less sometimes than the amount you would receive from a savings bank account. They are a safe storage place for money, but *not* a sound investment in a period of rapid inflation. Occasionally the government tries to encourage additional sales of the .savings bonds by raising the interest rate. But again, stay away from them as an investor.

The marketable types of government securities are much more interesting for investors these days because they can be sold readily to other investors, and

Table 17-1. Treasury bill prices, 1985.

Date of Maturity	*Bid*	*Ask*	*Yield*
6/27	6.94	6.86	7.34
12/26	7.42	7.38	8.19

they respond to changes in interest rate—to changes, in other words, in the cost of money.

Among the marketable types of bonds there are the so-called short-term, medium-term, and long-term issues. As mentioned before, the Treasury tries to operate in the money market shrewdly. If the cost of money is high or rising, the Treasury tends to concentrate on selling short-term issues, in the hopes that later it can "borrow" its money more cheaply after interest rates fall. In a period when interest rates are low the Treasury might stress the sale of long-term bonds, as it did in the 1940s, keeping its costs of borrowing low.

Treasury bills. Virtually every week the Treasury sells bills, securities that are offered on a discount basis. This means that when you turn to the financial page of a newspaper you will find the Treasury bills quoted in terms of the percentage they yield if kept for a year (unlike bonds, which are quoted in terms of 100, 98, 87, meaning $1,000, $980, or $870).

Table 17-1 gives some selected quotations for Treasury bills that appeared in *The New York Times* on May 22, 1985.

Translated into written English this means if you want to buy $1,000 in Treasury bills (they come in denominations ranging from that small to $1,000,000) you would receive interest equivalent to 7.34 percent, if held to maturity, which is June 27, 1985. Remember that your return on a $1,000 bill wouldn't be a full $73.40 because interest is calculated on an annual basis; you will own the bill only from May 23, if you buy it that day, through June. For convenience's sake the bills are quoted on this discount basis. This means that you would pay somewhat less than $1,000 for the bill when you bought it and if you keep it until maturity the Treasury will send you $1,000. Your interest lies in the difference between the price you pay and the $1,000.

Remember back in school, your mathematics teacher stressed the importance of figuring interest on a discount basis. Just in case you don't remember, Figure 17-1 shows you the formula, based on the traditional use of 360 days to the year. The actual investment yield, down to the penny, on a Treasury bill is generally at a slightly higher rate than the discount basis. These are technicalities and needn't bother you unless you plan to do a great deal of investing in bills. The important thing is to realize that such short-term investments exist and might be useful, especially during periods of high interest rates. In some

Figure 17-1. Calculating bond interest.

Formula

$$F = \frac{E}{360} \times A$$

where A = days to maturity
E = discount basis
F = full discount

Example: Let's say you will be holding a bill for two months or 60 days; that's "A" in the formula. Assume it sells at a discount basis of 6.86; that's "E." To calculate the dollar amount of the interest, then:

$$F = \frac{6.86}{360} \times 60$$

$$F = 1.143$$

Which means that each $100 "earns" $1.143, or $11.43 on $1,000.

Working backward, the discounted dollar price of the bond is $1,000 minus $11.43, or $988.57.

years you could obtain a much better rate of return on such bills than from savings accounts—8 percent, 10 percent, and more.

Until recently Treasury bills, like many other government securities, were in bearer form, meaning your name did not appear on the certificate. Thus they could be transferred easily; on the other hand, they could also be stolen easily. The IRS is tightening rules on identifying owners.

Naturally, if you don't want to hold a bill to maturity you can sell it any time in the market; Table 17-1 shows typical market prices.

Treasury bills generally are issued for ninety days, six months, or even a year, but the big buyers of bills, such as banks, big trust funds, corporations, etc., often hold them only a few days or weeks, depending on their needs for cash. In other words they are readily marketable, with buyers always ready to purchase them.

One point to remember is that the IRS considers the difference between the purchase price and the maturity value ($1,000) or the sales price an ordinary gain or loss, not the more favorable (to you) capital gain or loss, even if you keep them longer than six months.

Another significant aspect to Treasury bills is the role of the Federal Reserve system. As mentioned earlier, the Fed can influence the trends in interest

Table 17-2. Typical treasury note prices.

Rate	*Maturity*	*Bid*	*Ask*	*Yield*
$9\frac{3}{8}$	May 86	100.31	101.3	8.19

rates by buying and selling government securities. Every working day it is in the market, somehow. One of its most useful methods of influencing the cost of money is through buying and selling Treasury bills. If it sells millions of dollars' worth of Treasury bills, the interest rates obtainable on them will tend to go down, under the force of the law of supply and demand. If it buys them by the millions they can become scarce and the interest (or cost of them) will rise.

Certificates. In recent years the Treasury has lengthened the maturities of its bills so that nowadays some bills are as long in duration as some certificates used to be. Generally, certificates have been considered a longer-term investment, maturing in about one year from date of issue. They haven't been used much in recent years.

Treasury notes come next on the list. They offer a medium length for investment—generally one year to five years' maturity. Banks and other institutions like them to help space out their portfolios; and conceivably they might be useful to large investors for such reasons, especially at times when they offer a chance to obtain high interest rates, as they did in 1984, if the investors expect that interest rates might drop.

As for the Treasury, it often likes to lengthen its debt when it can favorably do so, in order not to be under much pressure to raise tremendous new sums of money when big issues of its securities come due. This middle-type security called notes permits the government to operate over longer spaces of time than by means of bills, and yet not tie up its credit on long-term bonds at unfavorable periods, such as very high interest-rate years like 1984.

Notes can be obtained in denominations ranging from $1,000 on up to $5,000,000. In newspapers you will find them quoted in terms of $100 like bonds, with a bid and ask price. Next to this price range you will usually find a yield mentioned, which indicates the yield you would receive on your money if held to maturity, a date also mentioned. Besides this is the amount of actual interest the coupon bears. See Table 17-2 for the way *The New York Times* quoted such notes as of May 1985.

In other words, if you buy a $1,000 note, you would pay 10 times 101.31, or $1,013.10, for the security, a premium above the face value of $1,000. You would receive $1,000 at maturity, plus interest earned, in this instance $9\frac{3}{8}$ percent.

Long-term bonds. Generally, Treasury bonds have been issued with a maturity of more than five years. They are available in both bearer and registered form, which makes them useful for various portfolio reasons. Like other marketable government issues they can be easily sold. Like the Treasury notes they are quoted in the newspapers with bid, ask, yield, interest rate, and maturity date.

Perhaps the aspect of them that might puzzle you at first glance is why, if the credit of the United States government is considered A-1, do some of its bonds (and notes) sell well below 100 (or $1,000). You know the answer if you think for a moment.

Since interest rates are so high nowadays for borrowing money from banks and taking out mortgages (15 percent and 13 percent), then prices of bonds issued years ago when interest rates were much lower must reflect this, or no one in her right mind would buy a bond.

Fannie Maes. Perhaps you will hear brokers or other knowledgeable people talk of Fannie Maes. It's a nickname (Wall Streeters love nicknames for securities) for a very popular type of government bond issued by an agency called the Federal National Mortgage Association. The FNMA helps finance home buildings by buying and selling mortgages from and to banks, savings and loan companies, real estate groups, etc., who handle mortgages. When a bank wants more money to lend to you and other people interested in buying houses, it can sell mortgages from its portfolio to FNMA, and thus receive cash.

In turn, FNMA raises money to handle its operations by selling obligations, usually called notes or debentures, to the public. These come in bearer form with denominations ranging from $1,000 to $100,000 and in various maturities.

A similar product is known as the *Ginnie Mae,* issued by the Government National Mortgage Association (GNMA). Many brokerage firms package Ginnie Maes and sell you units of the package, not unlike a mutual fund. With Ginnie Maes, you can receive monthly income representing not only mortgage payments on the underlying mortgages but also a return on capital.

Other government agency issues are also available from such issuers as the Federal Land Banks, the Federal Home Loan Banks, and many others. (See Figure 17-2 for sample price quotations.)

Commercial Paper

This is the term used for another type of security that you will hear mentioned often, in newspaper articles and perhaps by brokers. You might sometime in

Figure 17-2. Sample price quotations, government agency bonds.

THE NEW YORK TIMES, WEDNESDAY, MAY 22, 1985

Government Agency Bonds

(Prices in 32d of a point. Composite bill yields in percentage points)

Date		Rate	Bid	Ask	Chg	Yield
FEDERAL NATIONAL MTGS						
Jun	85	8.60	99.29	100.1		7.68
Jun	85	9.95	100	100.4		7.12
Jul	85	7¼	99.25	99.29		7.75
Jul	85	15.65	101.1	101.5		6.53
Aug	85	14.10	101.8	101.12		7.51
Sep	85	15	102	102.4		7.53
Oct	85	7.90	99.31	100.3	+ .1	7.58
Oct	85	8.80	100.10	100.14	+ .1	7.55
Oct	85	10.15	100.26	100.30	+ .1	7.54
Nov	85	13	102.11	102.15	+ .1	7.56
Dec	85	9¾	100.26	100.30	+ .2	7.96
Dec	85	14.90	103.18	103.22		7.89
Jan	86	13	102.27	102.31	+ .2	8.06
Feb	86	11.70	102.6	102.10		8.27
Mar	86	8.20	99.26	99.30		8.26
Mar	86	9½	100.26	100.30		8.23
Mar	86	9.95	101.4	101.8		8.27
Apr	86	10.95	102.3	102.7		8.27
Apr	86	9.20	100.20	100.24		8.28
May	86	11	102.11	102.15		8.30
Jun	86	14⅝	105.23	105.31	+ .1	8.55
Jul	86	7.95	99.2	99.14	+ .1	8.47
Jul	86	14.30	105.24	106	+ .1	8.60
Aug	86	13.90	105.14	105.22	+ .1	8.84
Sep	86	7.90	98.23	98.31	+ .1	8.74
Sep	86	13¼	104.30	105.6	+ .1	8.91
Oct	86	10.10	101.7	101.15	+ .1	8.93
Oct	86	12.90	104.25	105.1	+ .1	8.93
Nov	86	10.95	102.15	102.23	+ .1	8.93
Nov	86	13.05	105.4	105.12	+ .1	9.05
Dec	86	7.30	97.18	97.30	+ .1	8.75
Dec	86	10⅛	101.9	101.17	+ .1	9.04
Dec	86	14.05	102.20	102.28	+ .1	9.01
Jan	87	10.70	102	102.12	+ .1	9.09
Jan	87	11.15	102.20	103	+ .11	9.12
Feb	87	9.90	100.25	101.5	+ .4	9.14
Feb	87	11.05	102.17	102.29	+ .2	9.16
Mar	87	7¾	97.18	97.30		9.00
Mar	87	11¼	103.3	103.15		9.10
Mar	87	11.55	103.18	103.30		9.11
Apr	87	14.30	108.8	108.20		9.19
Apr	87	12¼	104.25	105.5		9.19
May	87	11.15	103.3	103.15		9.18
Jun	87	7.65	97	97.16		9.01
Jun	87	11.20	103.8	103.20		9.21
Jul	87	9.10	99.11	99.23		9.24
Jul	87	15¼	110.21	111.1		9.40
Aug	87	13.65	107.30	108.10		9.39
Aug	87	14.45	109.16	109.28		9.39
Sep	87	9.85	100.15	100.27		9.42
Oct	87	7½	96.6	96.22		9.06
Oct	87	12⅛	105.9	105.21		9.42
Oct	87	12.55	106.4	106.18		9.41
Nov	87	10.85	102.19	102.31	— .2	9.47
Nov	87	11.55	104.5	104.13	— .2	9.50
Dec	87	10.90	102.21	103.1	— .2	9.53
Jan	88	10.45	101.23	102.3	— .2	9.52
Jan	88	11.55	104.5	104.17	— .2	9.55
Feb	88	10.30	101.11	101.23	— .2	9.55
Feb	88	10¾	102.12	102.24	— .2	9.56
Feb	88	14.40	110.22	111.6		9.61
Mar	88	10.40	101.19	102.3	+ .2	9.52
Apr	88	10.45	101.26	102.6		9.56
May	88	10½	102.5	102.9	— .3	9.59
Jun	88	10½	102.1	102.13		9.57
Aug	88	16⅛	117.10	117.26		9.77
Oct	88	12¾	107.22	108.2		9.88
Sep	88	8.55	96.30	97.14		9.46
Sep	88	13.20	108.26	109.6		9.86
Nov	88	11	102.30	103.14		9.80
Nov	88	11.70	104.27	105.7		9.88
Dec	88	11¼	103.18	104	— .2	9.88
Dec	88	11¾	105.3	105.15	— .2	9.88
Jan	89	11.10	102.30	103.10	— .4	9.98
Feb	89	11.60	104.20	105.4		9.91
Mar	89	12.10	106.5	106.16		9.99
Jun	89	9.30	97.26	98.10		9.81
Aug	89	13⅛	109.4	109.20		10.24
Oct	89	12.10	106.8	106.24		10.15
Oct	89	12¾	108.4	108.20		10.25
Nov	89	11.80	105.6	105.18		10.22
Dec	89	11.30	103.16	104		10.18
Jan	90	11.45	104.2	104.10		10.25
Feb	90	11.05	102.18	102.30		10.24
May	90	10.30	99.28	100.12		10.20
May	90	11.15	103.14	103.18	+ .4	10.21
Nov	90	10.90	102.12	102.28	+ .8	10.20
Dec	90	11.80	105.28	106.12	+ .8	10.26
Mar	91	12	107	107.16	+ .4	10.25
Mar	91	12½	106.12	107.4	+ .4	10.81
Oct	91	7.80	88.4	88.20	+ .4	10.27
Dec	91	11¾	104.20	105.4		10.64
Mar	92	7	83.20	84.4	+ .12	10.30
Apr	92	12	105.28	106.4	— .10	10.71
Jun	92	7.05	82.24	83.16		10.41
Jan	93	10.90	100.20	101.4	— .8	10.68
Mar	93	10.95	100.24	101.8	— .12	10.70
Apr	93	10⅞	100.16	101	— .4	10.68
May	93	10¾	99.28	100.12	— .8	10.68
Jan	95	11.95	106.6	106.18	+ .2	10.83
Feb	95	11½	103.16	103.28		10.84
May	95	11.70	104.20	105	+ .2	10.86
Jun	85	11.15	101.12	101.16	— .8	10.90
FEDERAL NATIONAL MTGS						
Dec	97	7.10	74.28	76.4		10.58
Dec	13	12.35	105.28	106.28	+ .4	11.52
Mar	14	12.65	108.4	109.4	+ 16	11.55
FEDERAL FARM CREDIT						
Jun	85	9.05	99.30	100.2		6.72
Jun	85	9.20	99.30	100.2		6.85
Jun	85	11.85	100.2	100.6		5.26
Jul	85	8.40	99.31	100.3		7.29
Jul	85	11.45	100.9	100.13		7.15
Jul	85	11.60	100.17	100.21		7.33
Jul	85	10	100.8	100.12		7.47
Aug	85	8.45	100	100.4	+ .1	7.59
Aug	85	10.20	100.9	100.13	+ .1	7.62
Sep	85	9	100.6	100.10	+ .2	7.71
Sep	85	9.30	100.7	100.11	+ .2	7.71
Sep	85	12¾	101.7	101.11	+ .2	7.64
Sep	85	14.90	101.26	101.30		7.60
Oct	85	8.80	100.7	100.11	+ .1	7.55
Oct	85	9¼	100.14	100.18		7.54
Nov	85	8.45	100.8	100.10	+ .1	7.68
Nov	85	8.65	100.7	100.11	+ .1	7.64
Dec	85	9¼	100.23	100.27	+ .1	7.44
Dec	85	14.30	103.6	103.10	— .1	7.76
Dec	85	17	104.16	104.20		7.87
Jan	86	9.55	100.22	100.26	+ .2	8.05
Jan	86	10.90	101.20	101.24	+ .2	8.09
Jan	86	15.80	104.25	104.29		7.98
Feb	86	8.70	100.8	100.10	+ .2	8.19
Mar	86	13.95	104.1	104.5	+ .1	8.29
Apr	86	10.85	102.3	102.7		8.26
Apr	86	14	104.27	104.31		8.22
Jun	86	13⅛	104.7	104.15	+ .3	8.49
Jun	86	15.10	106.4	106.12	+ .3	8.48
Jul	86	15.15	106.27	107.3	+ .1	8.58
Jul	86	11⅝	103.1	103.9	+ .1	8.58
Sep	86	13.35	105	105.8	+ .1	8.88
Sep	86	14½	106.11	106.19	+ .1	8.89
Oct	86	9.95	101.2	101.10	+ .1	8.93
Oct	86	10¾	102.3	102.11	+ .1	8.93
Oct	86	12	103.20	103.28	+ .1	9.00
Dec	86	9⅞	101.8	101.16	+ .1	8.84
Dec	86	10	101.7	101.15	+ .1	8.94
Jan	87	9.90	100.31	101.7	+ .1	9.08
Jan	87	13.20	105.26	106.6	+ .1	9.08
Jan	87	14⅝	108	108.12	+ .1	9.06
Mar	87	11.45	103.10	103.22		9.14
Mar	87	12.40	104.27	105.7		9.13
Apr	87	14⅜	108.15	108.27		9.21
Apr	87	14.40	108.16	108.28		9.22
Jul	87	10⅝	102.9	102.21		9.23
Jun	87	10.55	102.2	102.18		9.13
Sep	87	10⅛	101.6	101.18		9.33
Oct	87	10.45	101.31	102.9	— .2	9.36
Oct	87	10.55	102.10	102.16	— .2	9.36
Dec	87	10.30	101.20	102		9.39
Dec	87	10.65	102.10	102.22		9.43
Mar	88	10.90	103.4	103.10		9.50
Mar	88	11.35	103.30	104.10		9.53
Apr	88	12.65	107.12	107.24		9.53
Jul	88	11½	104.24	105.8		9.53
Jul	88	11.70	105.2	105.18		9.61
Sep	88	12⅞	108.12	108.24		9.68
Oct	88	11½	104.18	104.30	— .2	9.76
Jan	89	11.65	104.29	105.9		9.89
Jan	89	13.05	109.1	109.13	— .2	9.92
Apr	89	12½	107.23	108.3		9.94
Jul	89	13.70	111.8	111.24		10.16
Sep	89	7¾	92.20	93.4		9.74
Oct	89	10.60	101.20	101.28		9.78
Oct	89	15.65	118.20	119.4		10.16
Oct	89	12.45	107.20	108.4		10.12
Jan	90	10.95	102.8	102.24		10.19
Jan	90	11.15	103	103.12		10.21
Feb	90	10.85	102	102.16		10.16
Apr	90	11.35	104.11	104.17	+ .4	10.15
Jun	90	14.10	114.8	114.24	+ .16	10.27
Jul	90	10.40	100.12	100.28		10.17
Sep	90	12½	108.16	109	+ .16	10.24
Oct	90	10.60	101.8	101.24	+ .8	10.17
Apr	91	14.10	114.16	115	+ .4	10.62
Jul	91	9.10	94.8	94.24	+ .4	10.26
Jul	91	14.70	117.12	117.28		10.66
Oct	91	10.60	100.28	101.12	+ .4	10.30
Oct	91	12¼	108.4	108.12		10.42
Dec	91	13.65	113.4	113.20		10.69
Jan	92	11½	104.10	104.18	— .4	10.52
Jan	92	15.20	120.16	121		10.70
Apr	92	12	105.28	106.4	— .10	10.71
Jul	92	13¾	114.8	114.24		10.74
Jan	93	10⅝	99.24	99.28	— .4	10.60
Oct	93	11.80	105.20	106.4		10.67
Mar	94	12.35	108.20	109.4		10.71
Apr	94	14¼	118.28	119.12		10.80
Sep	94	13	112.8	112.24		10.78
Dec	94	11.45	104.12	104.20	— .2	10.66
May	95	11.40	99.20	100.4		11.38
Oct	97	11.90	107.20	108.12		10.66
FEDERAL HOME LOAN						
May	85	8⅛	99.29	100.1		6.01
May	85	12	99.31	100.3	— 4	6.02
Jun	85	12.20	100.10	100.14		7.05
Jun	85	15	100.20	100.24		6.38
Jul	85	12.80	100.24	100.28	— .1	7.42
Jul	85	13.90	100.30	101.2	— .1	7.41
Aug	85	9.35	100.7	100.11		7.83
Aug	85	11.95	100.29	101.1		7.70
Sep	85	11.70	101.2	101.6		7.98
Sep	85	14.15	101.29	102.1		7.87
Oct	85	11.20	101.10	101.14	+ .1	7.64
Nov	85	8.10	100.1	100.5	+ .1	7.78
Nov	85	10⅛	101.1	101.5	+ .1	7.76
Dec	85	14.70	103.22	103.26		7.97
Jan	86	9.20	100.17	100.21	+ .3	8.16
Jan	86	8.95	100.5	100.9	+ .2	8.48
Jan	86	12¾	102.27	102.31	+ .2	8.17
Jan	86	13.85	103.18	103.22		8.12
Feb	86	9.55	100.27	100.29	+ .2	8.26
Feb	86	15.30	104.28	105	+ .1	8.31
Mar	86	10.20	101.13	101.17		8.25
Mar	86	15¾	105.30	106.2		8.11
Apr	86	9.15	100.20	100.22		8.35
Apr	86	10¼	101.18	101.22		8.30
Apr	86	11.70	102.28	103		8.25
May	86	8¾	100.10	100.12	+ .1	8.35
May	86	15½	106.19	106.27		8.32
Jul	86	15.35	107.4	107.12	+ .1	8.58
Aug	86	14.60	106.13	106.21	+ .1	8.86
Sep	86	16.40	108.31	109.7	+ .1	8.93
Sep	86	12¼	103.28	104.4	+ .1	8.90
Oct	86	10.80	102.5	102.13	+ .1	8.96
Nov	86	11	102.20	102.26	+ .1	8.96
Nov	86	11.30	102.30	103.6	+ .1	8.99
Dec	86	9⅞	101	101.8	+ .1	9.01
Dec	86	13¼	105.28	106.4	+ .1	9.04
Feb	87	10.10	101.3	101.15	+ .2	9.16
Feb	87	10.45	101.20	102	+ .2	9.17
Feb	87	11.05	102.19	102.31	+ .2	9.16
Mar	87	11.05	102.26	103.4		9.15
Mar	87	11.10	102.27	103.7		9.15
Mar	87	11¼	103.4	103.16		9.13
May	87	7.65	97.2	97.18		9.00
May	87	9⅝	100.22	100.24		9.21
May	87	13	106.17	106.29		9.16
Jun	87	10.30	101.25	102.5	+ .4	9.13
Jul	87	11.35	103.15	103.27		9.35
Jul	87	13.30	107.6	107.18		9.37
Aug	87	7.60	96.23	97.3		9.04
Aug	87	12⅝	106.4	106.16		9.35
Oct	87	12.05	105.8	105.20	— .2	9.40
Oct	87	12.15	105.15	105.27	— .2	9.39
Nov	87	10.65	102.12	102.24		9.39
Nov	87	11.30	103.26	104.6		9.39
Jan	88	10⅝	102.8	102.18		9.51
Mar	88	10.20	101.14	101.30		9.40
Mar	88	11.90	105.13	105.25		9.52
Apr	88	10.15	101.11	101.23	+ .4	9.46
Apr	88	10⅜	101.28	102.4	— .2	9.52
May	88	10.15	101.13	101.25	+ .4	9.46
Jun	88	10.80	103	103.12		9.51
Aug	88	11⅝	105	105.16		9.61
Oct	88	11.40	104.12	104.24	+ .2	9.73
Nov	88	14.20	112.9	112.21	— .2	9.85
Dec	88	10.70	102.9	102.21	— .2	9.80
Jan	89	11⅜	104.5	104.21	— .2	9.82
Feb	89	10.80	102.18	103.2		9.80
Feb	89	15.10	115.10	115.26		9.95
Apr	89	14¼	113.7	113.19		9.97
May	89	10.20	100.28	101		9.89
Jul	89	14⅛	112.20	113.4		10.18
Sep	89	12½	107.12	107.28		10.20
Sep	89	14.55	114.16	115		10.18
Nov	89	11.55	105.4	105.28		9.90
Jan	90	11.20	103.10	103.18		10.21
Feb	90	11.05	102.18	102.30		10.24
Mar	90	11.90	106.6	106.14	+ .4	10.18
Sep	90	12½	108.16	109	+ .16	10.26
Nov	90	13.70	113.16	114	+ .8	10.31
Dec	90	10.90	102.16	103		10.18
Feb	91	11⅞	106.8	106.24	+ .4	10.28
Aug	91	11.10	102.28	103.12	+ .4	10.35
Sep	91	11¾	105.20	106.4	+ .8	10.40
Dec	91	11.40	103.24	104.8		10.49
Feb	92	11.45	103.30	104.6	— .12	10.56
Apr	92	11.70	105	105.16	— .4	10.67
Oct	92	10.85	101	101.16	+ .4	10.55
Nov	92	11.10	102.16	103	— .4	10.51
Jan	93	10.70	100	100.16	— .4	10.60
May	93	10¾	100.12	100.28	+ .4	10.58
Jul	93	11.70	105	105.16		10.67
Aug	93	11.95	106.8	106.24		10.69
Nov	93	7⅜	82.16	83		10.44
Dec	93	12.15	107.20	108.4		10.68
Feb	94	12	106.20	107.12		10.68
Feb	97	7⅞	81.4	81.28		10.60
FEDERAL INTERMED CREDIT						
Apr	86	7.95	99.19	99.27		8.12
Jan	87	6.95	96.30	97.10	+ 1	8.76
STUDENT LOAN MKTG						
Oct	87	11¼	103.8	103.20		9.49
Jan	88	10.10	100.28	101.8	— 4	9.54
Jul	88	11.70	104.28	105.8		9.70
Sep	89	12.85	108.4	108.20		10.29
Feb	90	10.90	101.24	102.8		10.28
Apr	93	10½	98.12	98.28	— 4	10.71
WORLD BANK BONDS						
Jul	85	8.60	99.18	100.2		8.00
Sep	85	11.26	100.12	100.28		8.25
Dec	85	8.85	99.10	99.26		9.06
Mar	86	11.26	101.9	101.25		8.90
Jul	86	8⅜	98.14	98.30		9.40
Sep	86	12.76	103.13	103.29		9.50
Nov	86	16⅜	108.9	108.25		9.90
Dec	86	7.80	96.26	97.10		9.75
Dec	86	14⅝	106.1	106.17		10.00
May	87	7.65	95.17	96.1		9.95
Aug	87	7¾	95.8	95.24		9.95
Aug	87	14⅝	107.24	108.8		10.30
Sep	87	13.45	105.26	106.10		10.25
Mar	88	10⅜	99.13	99.29		10.40
May	88	10	97.24	99.8		10.30
Dec	88	15	112	112.16		10.69
Oct	89	11	99.16	100		10.70
Feb	90	4½	79.20	80.4		9.90
Jul	91	5⅜	78.11	78.27		10.10
Nov	91	16⅝	123.4	123.20		11.35
Dec	91	15⅛	116.20	117.4		11.35
Apr	92	5⅜	74.22	75.6		10.55
Jun	92	14¾	115.21	116.5		11.35
Sep	92	13⅝	110.16	111		11.35
Mar	93	10.90	97.22	98.6		11.25
May	93	10⅜	94.31	95.15		11.25
Sep	93	5⅞	73.6	73.22		11.75
Mar	94	6½	75.14	75.30		10.80
Oct	94	6⅜	73.11	73.27		10.90
Dec	94	11⅝	101.16	102		11.28
Aug	95	8⅜	85.4	85.20		11.00
Aug	96	8⅛	81.7	81.23		11.00
Dec	00	9.35	83.24	84.8		11.55
Jul	01	8.85	79.20	80.4		11.60
Dec	01	8⅜	76	76.16		11.60
May	02	8¼	74.28	75.12		11.60
Aug	02	8.35	75.16	76		11.60
Oct	02	12⅜	104.2	104.18		11.75
GNMA ISSUES						
Rate			Bid	Ask	Chg	Yield
8.00			81.27	82.3	+ 11	10.78
9.00			86.7	86.15	+ 11	11.10
9.50			88.30	89.6	+ 12	11.17
10.00			91.7	91.15	— 5	11.27
11.00			96.26	97.2	— 4	11.43
11.50			98.29	99.5	— .4	11.60
12.00			100.30	101.6	— .5	11.78
12.50			103.1	103.9	— .5	11.93
13.00			105.4	105.12	— 6	12.08
13.50			106.31	107.7	— .3	12.28
14.00			108.26	109.2		0.00
15.00			110.20	110.28	— .6	13.02
16.00			113.11	113.19	— .6	0.00
FEDERAL LAND BANK						
Jul	85	8.10	99.31	100.3	+ .2	7.66
Oct	85	7.95	99.30	100.2		7.74
Oct	85	8.80	100.11	100.15	+ .1	7.57
Apr	87	7.60	97.7	97.19		8.99
Jul	87	7¼	96.9	96.21		8.98
Jan	88	7.85	96.11	96.23	— .2	9.26
Jan	90	8.20	93.8	93.24		9.90
Apr	91	7.95	90	90.16	+ .12	10.12
Oct	96	7.95	81.28	82.20		10.61
Jan	97	7.35	77.28	78.20		10.58
INTER-AMERICAN BANK						
Feb	86	8⅜	98.29	99.13		9.25
Dec	86	14	105	105.16		10.00
Aug	87	10¾	100.17	101.1		10.20
Apr	89	15	112.19	113.3		10.75
Jan	92	5.20	80.5	80.21		9.15
Aug	92	14⅝	115.8	115.24		11.35
Nov	92	6½	81.26	82.10		9.90
Nov	93	6⅜	81.2	81.18		9.90
Aug	94	13¼	109.8	109.24		11.50
Oct	95	8⅜	91.1	91.17		9.95
Feb	01	9	81.6	81.22		11.55
Jul	01	8¾	79.6	79.22		11.55
Jun	02	8⅜	76.2	76.18		11.55
Jan	04	9⅝	84.27	85.11		11.55
ASIAN DEVELOPMENT						
Aug	86	8⅝	98.11	98.27		9.65
Jul	92	0	44.15	44.31		11.50
Apr	96	7¾	78.2	78.18		11.20
May	98	11⅛	98.10	98.26		11.30
BANK FOR COOPERATIVE						
Jan	86	7¾	99.24	99.28	+ .16	7.94

your career have reason to invest in such "paper." Like short-term government bills mentioned earlier in the chapter, commercial paper is an investment for a relatively short period.

Commercial paper, however, is issued by corporations, usually well-known ones with prestigious names. These might include at any particular time General Electric, General Motors Acceptance Corporation, and other important firms.

If you don't recognize the name General Motors Acceptance Corporation, you can probably at least guess (correctly) that it is a part of General Motors Corporation. As a matter of fact, you may have done business with it if you have ever bought a General Motors car. GMAC is the part of General Motors that finances car purchases, not only for dealers who need money to carry all those cars in their showrooms but also for individual car buyers who borrow to finance their cars. To handle the huge business it does with thousands of car owners, GMAC must constantly borrow money, often on a short-term basis, and to do this it issues this type of security called commercial paper—a promise to pay the stated amount at a certain date.

While some wealthy individuals do buy commercial paper, much of it is bought by financial institutions needing short-term investments.

Since the market tends to be a rather technical one in which the appeal is to a small group of investors, you will not find quotations for commercial paper easily available in newspapers.

Federal Funds

This is one security that you should know about but that you will never be able to buy. Yet the interest rates these securities carry play an important part directly in the life of your local banker and thus indirectly in your own. A bank has to keep a certain amount of money as reserves, but from day to day its excess reserves will rise and fall above the required level, depending on the flow of money into it from its depositors.

Suppose that you are a small depositor in a medium-size bank, and your Aunt Minnie's executor suddenly alerts you that she has left you $1 million, which will be deposited on a certain day in your bank account. Your first reaction might be to open a bottle of champagne; your second probably would be to wonder how to invest that money quickly after it arrives. For this you might select Treasury bills, those short-term securities mentioned earlier; or you might ask your banker to put the money in certificates of deposits, much like putting it in a savings account. Many banks issue their own certificates of deposit on which a good rate of interest is paid.

However, it could be that the bank might have the money on hand for a day before you make up your mind how to invest it and therefore might find itself with some excess reserves that day. The bank can sell the use of these reserves in the market to other banks that temporarily lack reserves because of a sudden outflow of money.

Every day banks figure out their reserves and then they "buy or sell" the federal funds. In other words, federal funds arise out of the excess reserves of banks. Every day some banks will need additional reserves while other banks will have too much money. It's usually a temporary situation on both sides.

But it underscores the point a good investor must remember, namely that money always has a price in the market and that money should be kept busy for that reason. The wise investor does not keep more than necessary in a regular checking account, because it bears no interest. She starts by funneling her money into short-term obligations or into savings accounts, both of which give her a return on her money, whether it is to accumulate for a few days or weeks or months. Then when it has accumulated, the idea is to put it into favorable long-term investments.

Just as a bank keeps its excess reserves constantly in the market earning interest, the individual should learn to act with as much agility on a short-term basis, if she wants to permit her money to make as much as possible. Don't let money lie fallow, untended, uncultivated.

Equipment Trusts

These are yet another form of investment with which the public does not usually come into direct contact. Equipment trusts can be bought by anyone, but are not used by individual investors very often.

Next time you take a ride on a train look at the side of the diesel locomotive or the shiny new passenger car; you might see a plaque indicating who owns the equipment, usually a bank.

Railroads and other forms of transportation need constant additions of new rolling stock—engines, passenger cars, etc. They finance these through equipment trusts. Here's how it works: A railroad, for example, will order some equipment; a bank will lend the railroad a certain amount of money with which to pay for the equipment, the bank then owns the equipment in trust until the railroad finally pays for it on an installment basis. In turn, the bank issues equipment trust certificates, which can be bought publicly. While the bank as trustee stands technically as the owner, the actual owners are the buyers of the trust certificates.

Despite the long years of ups and downs, including many bankruptcies, equipment trust certificates have proved one of the safest forms of investment, for an obvious reason. A railroad cannot operate without equipment. Even if it goes into bankruptcy and its first mortgage bonds are worth very little, it still cannot stay in business without engines and cars. If the railroad did renege on paying the interest on equipment trusts, then the bank as trustee would repossess the equipment and would be able to sell or lease it elsewhere. Furthermore, equipment trusts occupy a position ahead of first-mortgage bondholders because of their claim on this moving equipment.

In the financial history of the United States, it is believed that only one issue of equipment trusts ever failed to pay off at face value, and that involved Florida East Coast Railway equipment trusts, which ultimately did return their holders about 90 cents or more on each dollar of investment. In other words, the record of equipment trusts through depressions, wars, and the competitive downfall of railroads in their fight with planes and trucks and buses has been exemplary.

Zero Coupon Bonds

A few years ago some creative underwriting firms* began to issue zero coupon bonds for their client companies. The idea is that the company can delay paying current interest on the bond and pay it all in a lump sum, in effect, at maturity. Depending on how long they will be outstanding, you might be able to buy for $350 a bond that at maturity would pay the face value of $1,000. Many financial organizations offer the bonds, calling them by a variety of names or acronyms such as CATS or TIGRS.

Figure 17-3 shows an advertisement from Chemical Bank, one of the big New York City banks describing its bonds, called STRIPS; the ad includes a table showing yields and value at maturity. Such zero coupon bonds are very useful not only to build up a college fund for children but also for Individual Retirement Accounts, which every working person should have. Be sure that you understand the tax impact of zero coupon bonds before you buy them. Your broker will know.

The latter part of this chapter is devoted to two much more speculative types of "places" (they don't even deserve the name of securities) in which your money can be put.

*Underwriting firms, which may or may not be brokerage firms, handle new securities issues for companies.

Figure 17-3. A sample zero coupon bond offering.

INTRODUCING STRIPS FOR YOUR CHILD'S EDUCATION. A NEW ZERO COUPON INSTRUMENT.

In the next ten to twenty years, a college education will cost more than most people can afford.

Fortunately, Chemical Bank has a plan that can prepare you for those costs. STRIPS for your child's education.

STRIPS were introduced by the United States Treasury in February, 1985. Not only are they government guaranteed, but they offer a guaranteed fixed yield based on a compounded rate of return. So you're assured of receiving a specific sum of money for the time you have invested. What's more, if you need to liquidate your STRIPS for any reason, you can sell them at any time.

Under the Uniform Gift-to-Minors Act, you can purchase STRIPS in your child's name. The income earned on STRIPS will be taxed at your child's rate, rather than at your higher rate. Assuming your child has no other income, over $1,000 of income from STRIPS would be sheltered by his or her personal exemption. And STRIPS are always state and local tax-exempt.

And unlike CATS, TIGRS and other zero coupon instruments created by brokerage houses, STRIPS are a *direct* obligation of the U.S. Government. Which means they're government guaranteed.

WIDE RANGE OF MATURITIES SO YOU CAN PLAN AHEAD.

STRIPS offer a wide range of maturities, anywhere from six months to thirty years, and a high rate of return. So you'll have the funds you need for long-term goals. Such as your child's diploma.

IT'S YOUR CALL.

For more information on STRIPS, call us Monday through Friday from 9-5 at (212) 310-4165. Or if you're outside of the 212 area, call 1-800-227-2033. You'll find you can pay for your child's education today and avoid tomorrow's higher costs.

SEE WHAT AN APPROXIMATE $5,000 INVESTMENT WILL BE WORTH WHEN YOUR CHILD IS 18.

IF YOUR CHILD IS:	YIELD % TO MATURITY	VALUE AT MATURITY
BORN TODAY	11.45	$39,000 IN 18 YEARS
3 YEARS OLD	11.40	28,000 IN 15 YEAR
5 YEARS OLD	11.35	22,000 IN 13 YEAR
7 YEARS OLD	11.15	17,000 IN 11 YEARS
9 YEARS OLD	11.10	14,000 IN 9 YEARS
11 YEARS OLD	11.00	11,000 IN 7 YEAR

YIELDS AS OF 5/6/85. YIELDS ARE SUBJECT TO CHANGE. MINIMUM INVESTMENT OF $1,000 REQUIRED.

CHEMICALBANK

For sophisticated investors these places for money need not be purely speculative, and both types can provide you with fancy profits if they are well handled. The two esoterics that many investors do utilize are called *puts and calls* and *commodity futures.*

Puts and Calls

Puts and calls were discussed in Chapter 13. Most brokerage firms avoid enlightening their customers about puts and calls because they are considered speculative. Another reason, quite frankly, is that many brokers know little about them. However, it is my belief that in the future more information will be made available about them, partly because brokerage firms and put and call dealer firms have been offering courses to the public for some years, and partly because this form of speculation has attracted the interest of the Chicago Board of Trade. Though the Board has primarily been a center for trading in wheat, corn, soybeans, and such commodities, it trades in puts and calls as well. Trading in financial options is gaining prominence.

Naturally, buying puts and calls tends to be speculative, but it gives the advantage of leverage and a fixed, known, prepaid cost via the premium.

There is an advantage that can take puts, for example, out of the realm of speculation: using them as a hedge against your portfolio holdings in a time of declining markets. (This tactic was discussed in Chapter 13.)

Commodity Futures

These offer still another way for a person to speculate. What is a commodity futures contract?

It is a little like buying (or selling) a claim on tomorrow in terms of a basic, useful product. Commodity futures cover essentials like wheat, corn, soybeans, cocoa, sugar, copper, silver, pork bellies (the raw material for breakfast bacon).

For years, commodity futures have existed in the shadow of brokers' doubts. Brokers feared their customers, especially unsophisticated ones, might lose money in commodities and hence their interest in investing altogether. No one likes to lose a customer as a result of a string of losses. It's bad business.

A principal lure of commodity futures trading is the leverage, not unlike the leverage in puts and calls. A person can speculate with a relatively small sum of money, making big profits if she happens to be right.

For example, a speculator who buys one contract of potatoes (50,000 pounds) need ante only about $200–$500, plus about $50 in commissions and a few dollars clearing-house fees. Some brokerage firms require a little more than this, depending on the price of the underlying commodity.

Other futures contracts are more expensive than potatoes, requiring 10 or 20 percent of the total value of the contract. Nonetheless, for a modest amount the speculator controls a large amount of the commodity, fraught though it is with doubts.

She can for example take delivery of the contract when it comes due, or she can sell it before the delivery date, thus getting out of her position.

Suppose, like many people, she thinks that the price of silver will rise sharply and buys a futures contract in August of 1985 that calls for delivery in March of 1986. When the March delivery date comes around she could take delivery of the silver and store it in an approved depository for a small fee each month. If she had speculated in platinum, she could fit the delivery in her pocket, because platinum is such an expensive metal, sold by the ounce, that the contract covers a relatively small number of ounces. Taking delivery of 50,000 pounds of potatoes, however, or 5,000 bushels of wheat is another matter. Hence most speculators sell out their positions before they take delivery.

Who are the speculators? A wide variety of individuals, according to a study made some years ago by the Commodity Exchange Authority. It found that they come from many areas of life, and included housewives, students, retired persons, lawyers, doctors, dentists, manufacturers, and salespeople.

Perhaps the most striking category in the above list is "housewives," because some brokerage firms discriminate a little against women, discouraging them from opening commodity accounts on the theory that they are more emotional than men and lack the necessary practical knowledge.

In New York I knew an elderly housewife who traded daily from her wheelchair. In Chicago, I interviewed and wrote a story about a middle-aged woman who spent six hours a day following the market for egg, pork belly, and live cattle futures—and her brokers told me she made a good living out of it. In Washington there is a general's wife who quite consistently makes money trading futures, mostly grains.

Enthusiasts of futures trading point out that there are fewer commodities to watch and analyze at any time than is true for stocks. Only about three dozen commodities are actively traded, compared with those 2,300 stocks on the Big Board, and hundreds more on the American Stock Exchange, plus unlimited thousands over the counter. Furthermore only about a dozen commodities appear to be really active at any particular time.

Styles change fast in commodity trading, a factor that adds zest and opportunity. Speculators rush to put their money where the action is, and usually on the long side of the market. In recent years financial futures have been introduced, enabling people to speculate on interest rates and other rates. More on this later.

What makes a commodity futures market complex is that the two sides to a contract (the person who has bought and the one who has sold) consist not only of bulls and bears (optimists and pessimists) but also of a group called hedgers. Hedgers generally are not apparent in the stock market.

In commodities hedgers are professionals in a trade who use commodity futures as price insurance. Without them there couldn't be effective commodity markets. In fact, futures markets arose mostly because of the need for such hedging as protection.

What is a hedger? It might be a meatpacker worried about his future supplies of pork bellies, to be sliced into bacon. He can buy future contracts now that call for future delivery of bellies. Then when delivery time comes he can take delivery on the contract, or he can buy his bellies in the open market and sell his contract. He has fixed his price at the moment he bought the contract. Suppose he buys a contract for bellies in May 1985 at 73 cents a pound for delivery in February 1986. Meanwhile let us assume that the price rises to about 90 cents a pound in February. When that date arrives he can take delivery of them and pay the equivalent of 73 cents a pound (minus of course the margin he has put up to buy the contract), or he can sell the contract, and buy the bellies in the open market for 90. In this case the contract has also risen to about 90 cents a pound. Thus he makes a profit on the contract if he sells it, but must pay 90 cents for the bellies. He has protected himself because the 17 cents gained on the contract offsets the higher price in the open market. Or a businessman who imports copper might find himself with too much copper on hand, and he could sell a contract at current prices, if he liked the price.

In this way one can always protect both his money and his inventory position, at a cost of only the small commission involved in the buying and possibly selling of the contract. Thus professional hedgers take both the buy and sell sides of the future markets, depending on their needs. But there must also be speculators, members of the public, willing to take the opposite side. For every buyer there must be a seller and vice versa.

Remember that it is unlike buying or selling a stock, because when you buy a stock you take delivery and are credited with the shares five days later, during which time you must pay the full price to your broker (or arrange for margin trading).

When you buy a futures contract (or sell one) you put up a small amount of money at the time and then you don't have to take delivery until some later date. If you sell a commodity contract, you also put up a small amount of money as kind of a margin payment and then you need not make delivery until the contract date arrives. At any time you get out of your position by doing the opposite. If you own a September delivery sugar contract you can sell it; if you have sold a contract for September delivery you can buy one. In each case you have evened out your position.

In recent years, as mentioned earlier, commodity trading has moved away from the basics like copper and corn, cattle and orange juice, to new types of commodities. Read the financial pages of *The New York Times* or *The Wall Street Journal* and you will see new commodity trading vehicles listed—foreign currencies, Treasury bonds, stock indexes, and others often called financial options.

How should a novice proceed to learn about the futures market? She can ask her broker to give her some basic brochures on commodity trading and on specific commodities. Next she should obtain a good book, usually available at public libraries, on commodity trading.

Then, armed with basic knowledge, she can ask her broker for some current analyses published by his firm on various commodities. Each day she can read the brief and sometimes useful commodity futures columns in newspapers like *The New York Times* and *The Wall Street Journal.*

Now she is ready to begin trading—on paper. She ought to pick some commodities in which she has noticed good trading volume and in which she has an interest. For example, a woman who winters in Florida might be more than a little interested and alert about frozen juice futures. If she has a family member in the food business she might feel comfortable with world sugar, potatoes, or pork bellies. A Midwesterner with some knowledge of farming might like to try her hand at grains.

Once she has selected a commodity or two (but not more than that), the novice should chart its prices on paper and follow closely the news that apparently affects it. Most commodity traders use the fundamental and the technical approaches, so she might also have to study some charting techniques more intensively.

18

The Magic of 72 and Other Helps

Compound Interest, Rights, and Warrants

The Rule of 72

Chanel has number 5, but for the sweet smell of success investors can use number 72. It's a magic number that might be called a "handy double," though it does not apply to horse racing or even bridge playing.

Number 72 works differently. Suppose you want to double your money in the stock market (or elsewhere) in five years and you want to know what rate of return is needed. Divide the number 72 by five, and the answer works out to 14.4, which is the percentage return needed yearly.

Or suppose you have an investment that appreciates in value each year and pays a small dividend. Together, they give you a 12 percent return. How long will it take to double your money if the dividends are reinvested and the stock continues to appreciate? Again, divide the 72 by the 12 percent, and you have an answer of 6—the number of years required to double your money.

Obviously the number 72 has a real place in your investment thinking. It works fairly well even in cases where compound interest is involved. There are, of course, more accurate and complex mathematical tables to do the same job (see Figure 18-1), but number 72 has the advantage of being mentally portable. Jot it down in your stock notebook as a handy method of calculating the expected return from comparable investments.

Suppose, for example, that your broker has recommended a stock that he says is growing at the rate of 10 percent a year but it pays a mere 1 percent dividend and probably will not pay more. You will be getting roughly an 11 percent return. Would you be better off with a stock growing at an expected rate of only 6 percent a year but which pays about 5 percent a year in dividends?

Each adds up to about 11 percent return, which means that the investment at such a rate could be expected to double in a little more than six years. However, the high cash dividends on the stock in the second example are subject to income tax at regular rates. The stock in the first example—the stock that appreciates in value the most quickly—offers a greater amount of capital gain ultimately, subject to the lower taxation on long-term capital gains.

Return of Capital

When is a dividend not a dividend? One answer to that puzzler is when the payment represents a return of capital.

Sophisticated investors have long been taking note of the tax advantage involved in such investments, particularly at times when the stock market is in the doldrums, inflation continues to nip the dollar income in terms of value, and taxes are high.

Blue chip companies, conservative and yet offering some future growth plus dividends that are partly tax free, have an appeal to moderate- and high-income investors.

Some such possibilities can be found among public utility shares. A while back Standard & Poor's, the investment advisory service, recommended Consolidated Edison Company despite what it called the company's "mediocre" earnings. The reason was that a large portion of the yearly dividend was non-taxable. Another suggestion was Orange & Rockland Utilities, serving a heavily populated suburban area of New York City, and another was Puget Sound Power & Light, which operates in a fast-growth area in the Pacific Northwest.

The reason for the tax-free status of certain dividends usually involves

Figure 18-1. Compound rates: $100 principal compounded annually.

Time Period	*5%*	*6%*	*7%*	*8%*	*9%*	*10%*	*12%*	*14%*	*16%*
6 mos.	2.50	3.00	3.50	4.00	4.50	5.00	6.00	7.00	8.00
1 year	5.00	6.00	7.00	8.00	9.00	10.00	12.00	14.00	16.00
2 years	10.25	12.36	14.49	16.64	18.81	21.00	25.44	29.96	34.56
3 years	15.76	19.10	22.50	25.97	29.50	33.10	40.49	48.15	56.09
4 years	21.55	26.25	31.08	36.05	41.16	46.41	57.35	68.90	81.06
5 years	27.63	33.82	40.26	46.93	53.86	61.05	76.23	92.54	110.03
6 years	34.01	41.85	50.07	58.69	67.71	77.16	97.38	119.50	143.64
7 years	40.71	50.36	60.58	71.38	82.80	94.87	121.07	150.23	182.62
8 years	47.75	59.38	71.82	85.09	99.26	114.36	147.60	185.26	227.84
9 years	55.13	68.95	83.85	99.90	117.19	135.79	177.31	225.19	280.30
10 years	62.89	79.08	96.72	115.89	136.74	159.37	210.58	270.72	341.14
20 years	165.33	220.71	286.97	366.10	460.44	572.75	864.63	1,274.35	1,846.08

some complicated accounting procedures relating to accelerated amortization and depreciation charges. Utilities have been the chief beneficiaries of this status from time to time because they spend huge sums continuously on capital equipment like turbines, generators, power lines, even dams for hydroelectric power.

Congress in some recent legislation eliminated or limited the possibilities of such tax-free distributions, which became effective late in 1972.

However, brokers perhaps can offer some recommendations. Other companies that have been able to return tax-free capital include railroads, real estate firms, and some industrial operations. Companies that have racked up large losses or are going through partial liquidation also offer the potential of tax-free return of capital.

For example, some years ago a company called Mill Factors Corporation discovered huge losses suddenly in one of its divisions, large enough to exceed the stockholders' equity. Not realizing the company's condition, the directors had declared a 60 cent cash dividend on the common shares in 1968 and a 15 cent quarterly payment mailed out early in January 1969. But in fact, because of the heavy losses, that dividend and the payments of dividends made for quite a few years past represented return on capital. The point is that although the stockholders in reporting their dividends in such a case paid a regular income tax on them, they were really getting a return on capital and apparently need not have paid this tax.

Under IRS rules, such taxpayers can claim refunds for as many as three years back from the date they make their claim. Thus they should file for a refund within the statutory time limit, usually three years from the date of the filing of a tax return.

Two points to remember about investments that yield a return of capital:

1. Return of capital is not taxable at regular rates, and thus offers, in a sense, tax-free income.
2. The amount received is applied to reduce the cost basis of the shares.

In cases where the stockholders receive a return of capital, the company usually takes the trouble to spell it out for the stockholder, either with a letter of explanation or a notice accompanying a dividend check. If you fail to understand a payment designated as return of capital, consult your broker, or write the company's secretary directly.

Sometimes there is a serious dispute about what is capital and what is income. A recent complex but interesting situation involved the AT&T divestment of seven regional companies. The Internal Revenue Service claimed that all AT&T stockholders receiving shares should report 39 cents a share income on their 1984 return, filed on April 15, 1985. Company lawyers disagreed and wrote AT&T stockholders to that effect, but the IRS insisted that it would search out all AT&T stockholders who did not report the 39 cents a share, which related to Pacific Telesis, one of the divested companies.

It is important for all stockholders to differentiate in their minds straight income and capital gains.

Arbitration

What many small investors do not realize is that there exists an inexpensive way of seeking redress if they think they have a reasonable complaint about their broker.

The method is called arbitration. When an investor becomes a customer of a brokerage firm she may sign a margin agreement—a form with quite a bit of technical language printed on it. In the small print of these agreements there is a statement that goes something like this: "Any controversy between the customer and the firm originating or relating to this contract or the breach thereof shall be settled by arbitration."

The New York Stock Exchange* has been using arbitration to settle securities disputes for more than 150 years. Ordinarily about 85 percent of the cases involve disputes between customers and their brokers; the rest concern fights between the brokerage houses and their employees. The rules of the New York Stock Exchange say that its member brokerage firms must submit to arbitration if a customer wants it, *even where no formal agreement to arbitrate has been signed.*

Arbitration is a formal procedure, recognized by the courts, in which a panel of disinterested experts reach a decision that is binding on both parties who have stated their cases before the panel.

The stock exchange provides a panel of arbitrators. However, if a customer of a brokerage firm is worried about possible bias of the experts she can insist that the case be handled instead by the American Arbitration Association. This is a nonprofit organization that handles thousands of cases a year in many fields, involving building-contract disputes, labor relations, customer complaints against dry cleaners, interpretation of business contracts, and the like. (In fact, a wife shouldn't sign—or permit her husband to sign—a building contract without insisting that the builder insert the usual arbitration clause to handle any difficulties or failures, such as water in the cellar, crooked windows or door frames, cracks in the ceiling.)

The association's panel of arbitrators for a securities case might consist of

*The American Stock Exchange also provides arbitration procedures.

such people as lawyers, retired bank officers, and accountants. The procedure followed in arbitration is much more informal than that of a courtroom. In arbitration you can present your case without a lawyer. This, of course, keeps costs down. Often you will run up against a lawyer representing the brokerage firm, however, so you should have command of your facts and should be able to talk plainly and to the point.

Naturally, the arbitrators try to keep generalizations and the hurling of insults to a minimum, so leave your emotions home. If you think you might become emotional bring along a lawyer or an accountant who can help you keep calm.

The charge for the usual brief arbitration over a simple dispute might be no more than $100 or so, but it could run to more for each day the sessions continue.

Besides the relative cheapness of arbitration another advantage is speed. Most cases can be heard in about four months from the date the dispute is filed with the stock exchange. In one case where time was essential, the exchange was able to handle the arbitration in four days from filing to award. This contrasts with the months and even years it takes for a case to go to court. The delays can cause forgetfulness in witnesses or difficulty in obtaining evidence. Who knows, some of the contestants could die in the interim.

At the Big Board (the American Stock Exchange follows similar procedures) a transcript is taken of the hearing. But if the customer wants one, she has to pay for it.

Generally, the finding by arbitrators comes quickly after the hearing and is presented as a decision, with no explanation of how it was reached. There is no appeal from the arbitrators' ruling except for a few very unusual reasons, rarely available, such as prejudice in the panel members or technical errors of fact in the award.

Recently, a woman customer of a brokerage firm who had filed a claim for $14,000 against a broker was disappointed by an arbitration award of only $1,500, so she went to court. But the court ruled that the award was final, mainly on the basis that she had gone into arbitration willingly. In other words she was trying not to play the game. She wanted to win in court if she couldn't get enough consolation from the arbitrators.

Sometimes this question arises: What if a customer, after having signed an arbitration agreement, wants to skip arbitration and go to court instead? Generally, the answer is that she cannot, unless the case involves a possible violation of securities law by the broker. In 1953 the Supreme Court upheld (in a case called *Wilko v. Swan*) the right of a customer to seek court redress because the broker had violated laws of the securities business.

Another source of help sometimes for an unhappy investor could be the Securities and Exchange Commission or the attorney general of the state in which the investor lives. Both could tell her whether any fraud has been involved or whether other laws have been abused by the broker.

However, keep the idea of arbitration in mind because it offers quick, presumably fair, and inexpensive redress. Furthermore, the fact that you file a complaint with the New York Stock Exchange or American Stock Exchange (and send a copy to the SEC, attorney general, etc.) might induce a brokerage firm to settle the dispute quietly, without even letting the matter go to arbitration.

Preemptive Rights

A preemptive right gives the stockholder a chance to buy a security in her company ahead of the public at large, and usually at a more favorable price.

The theory is that a stockholder, by buying her prorated portion of the additional stock being offered, can maintain her same percentage of ownership in the company. Thus, if a stockholder owns 1,000 shares of a company with 1,000,000 shares outstanding, she owns $\frac{1}{10}$ of 1 percent of the company. If she received—and exercised—the right to buy one new share for every 100 shares owned, she would have a total of 1,010 shares.

The number of shares outstanding on the company's books would increase to 1,010,000 shares when the rights offering was completed. With her new shares the stockholder would still own the same $\frac{1}{10}$ of 1 percent of the total. However, she would have had to spend money to keep her proportion. If higher earnings resulted from the inflow of the new capital, fine. On the other hand, not to exercise the rights would mean that the stockholder's relative slice of the company would be thinner.

When you, a stockholder, open the mail and find a notice from a company that it plans to offer the opportunity to exercise rights to buy additional shares (often a computer card is enclosed for you to mark the decisions), you may not know what to do.

Is it worthwhile spending the extra money to buy the shares? Your broker can advise you on this point. He should also remind you that the rights themselves have value and should not be thrown away, even if you don't plan to buy the stock. There is a market for rights in most cases.

At first thought, stockholders tend to credit a company with benevolence when they are offered rights. In more cases than not, benevolence has little to do with it, although few managements admit this.

A corporation needs to raise money from time to time for such reasons as to finance additional growth, enter new markets, launch new products, increase working capital, or build new plants. It figures out the most advantageous way to raise the needed funds. The methods are many—direct loans from banks or insurance companies, the sale of bonds or preferred stocks, the issuance of convertible bonds or preferreds, and the sale of common stock.

Offerings to employees have become very popular in recent years as a way of raising capital and assuring employee loyalty. In fact, more workers have become introduced to stock owning this way than at any time in history. Usually payments are deducted from paychecks, up to 10 percent, and held until the end of the year. Then the company, using a stock price as of a certain date, gives the shares to the employee at that price minus a 15 percent inducement. During the year some interest usually is accrued on the employee's money and is added to the total.

Sometimes a direct sale to its own stockholders appears to be the best. After all, the stockholders can be easily and cheaply reached in this computerized age. Often an underwriting firm acts as a standby to buy up shares not purchased by stockholders.

From certain companies' viewpoints, and that of large stockholders too, the use of preemptive rights can help keep the stock from outsiders' hands by tending to maintain the status quo. Also since the offering price is usually well below the market price, perhaps 15 percent lower, it does create good will among stockholders.

Furthermore some states require that companies incorporated in them *must* provide stockholders with preemptive rights, and some corporate charters contain such provisions.

In recent years many laws requiring preemptive rights have been changed, and so has the attitude of the Securities and Exchange Commission toward permitting companies more flexibility in raising money. There is a feeling that without preemptive rights companies might get higher prices for their new shares, or offer convertibles at lower interest cost or better conversion rates. For example, Eastman Kodak some years ago asked stockholders' approval for sales of securities abroad without preemptive rights.

Despite the trend, some prestigious companies traditionally offer rights, AT&T being the best known. Before the divestiture in 1984, it raised hundreds of millions of dollars through rights offerings to stockholders covering both additional issues of common stock and convertible debentures.

How to Compute the Value of Rights

A quick formula to figure roughly the value of rights follows:

$$V = \frac{C - S}{R + I}$$

V is the value of the right, the unknown which the stockholder wants to find.

C is the current market price of the stock.

S is the price the company has placed on the new stock, usually below the market price, to induce shareholders to subscribe.

R is the specific number of rights necessary to buy one new share. Generally, stockholders receive one right for each share they own.

1 is the mathematical "catalyst" that makes the formula work. Even a mathematician couldn't explain simply why it's essential.

Let's suppose that a stock now sells for $40 a share, and the company offers stockholders new shares at $30, on the basis of 9 rights for each new share. Here is the formula filled out:

$$V = \frac{\$40 - \$30}{9 + 1}$$

$$V = \frac{\$10}{10}$$

$$V = \$1$$

In this case, each right is worth $1. Usually the price doesn't work out quite so evenly. However, rights are quoted in the market—often on the exchanges—and your broker can get you a quotation. The price changes each day, but the formula will show you what you should receive for the rights.

Don't ever throw rights into the wastebasket, for they are worth money. The company, sending the shareholder her rights, will explain how she can obtain the money for selling the rights if she doesn't want to exercise them. She can always sell them through her broker.

Warrants (but Not Rights)

Brokers report that many investors are confused about the differences between rights and warrants.

Most every investor, sooner or later, receives a piece of paper that upon reading turns out to be a right—a right to buy extra shares in the company or to buy debentures (a debenture is a bond). Generally the right must be exercised within a specific period of time, and the company sending out the rights warns the stockholder that the rights have some value and should not be tossed aside.

Warrants are a little different. For one thing, they usually last for a period of years. They were issued in the beginning as a "sweetener." When a company sold an issue of debentures, for example, it also offered warrants to buy shares at a later date at a certain price.

For example, Avco Corporation early in 1969 sold more than $69,000,000 in 7.5 percent debentures with warrants accompanying them. The warrants entitled the bearer to purchase common shares of the company at any time through November 30, 1978, at a price per share of 56. Avco needed the cash at the time to help finance a merger. While Avco common shares were traded on the New York Stock Exchange, the warrants were traded on the American Stock exchange.

Warrants receive no dividends, nor do the holders of them have any rights like stockholders' voting privileges at annual meetings. Furthermore, most warrants are issued in bearer form, which means they are not registered in anyone's name and hence can easily be stolen or mislaid. Furthermore, many investors apparently forget about them, letting the expiration dates pass, at which point they become valueless. However, warrants have a certain speculative charm, especially in the case of volatile stocks or in a booming market.

One fascinating recent application of warrants involved the General Motors Corporation acquisition of EDS, the big computer services company, through an exchange of stock. One of the most unusual deals in recent history, it provided that anyone owning EDS shares at the time of the acquisition would receive warrants guaranteeing a certain return in the future. EDS has a large number of bright young engineers and technicians on its staff who regularly have received stock as an inducement to remain with the company and work productively. To assure that they would continue to participate in the growth of EDS, the plan called for a new type of GM stock, called GM E shares. Everyone receiving 100 shares of GM E in return for their EDS shares would be guaranteed by a warrant that within a certain period the shares would be worth up to $12,500. At present the warrants have no value and cannot be transferred, but they assure that GM will make up the difference between the market price (now around 70 a share, or $7,000 for 100 shares) and the $12,500.

Wall Streeters had never seen an offering quite like this one, and for a while the New York Stock Exchange did not know if it would list the shares, but it finally did. Today you can read the listings—GM's own shares and under it, GM E shares, trading at different prices, paying different dividends.

The Tender Offer

The average stockholder must be aware of a popular maneuver called the tender offer. There's nothing altruistic about it, and the investor should treat it with as much suspicion as if she were a mouse being played with by a cat.

A company or a group of outsiders with acquisition in mind approaches a stockholder with an offer better than the market price for her shares. Along with this, there usually comes a sweet-talking letter, perhaps even followed by a telephone call. The high price is intended to soften the investor. One study indicates that the price offered often runs about 20 percent above the market price for the shares, before the tender offer becomes public.

The stockholder should not jump to the conclusion that she is getting a bonus, or even a little more profit than she expected, for nothing. In fact, if she holds out she could do even better. After all, the outside group is making a bid for the company by means of a tender offer because it believes the deal can be profitable. So the wise investor should try to find out just why the outsiders think they want the shares.

This entails a little detective work. In the case of the typical raiders, it might involve a plan to liquidate the company at a profit, with the company's cash ending up in the raider's hands. Or perhaps the outsiders plan to add the company to a conglomerate they are building—another dazzler in an add-a-diamond necklace. Or perhaps the group has been lured by an incentive as simple as taking advantage of a tax-loss situation. For example, Haven Industries some years ago acquired control of National Sugar, which had accumulated large losses. Still another reason, not usual, but it has happened: a father wants to obtain control of a company and place his son in the presidency.

The acquiring company might have a different and more logical goal, such as getting a foothold in a new industry. Corporations often find it is cheaper to enter a new field by buying an existing business than by beginning a product line.

Another twist for stockholders to consider comes when a company makes a tender offer for *its own* shares, for any of a variety of reasons. The stock might be underpriced, and the company might consider it feasible to buy up the shares for its pension or profit-sharing funds. The company might need stock to use for a merger it has planned. The company might consider the stock much too low-priced and hope to increase the price by indicating it has so much faith in the shares it wants to buy them. Or the company might fear a takeover by outsiders and buy its own shares to cut down the risk of being outvoted at the next annual meeting, as well as to give the stock's price a boost.

There is always a solid reason behind a tender offer, and usually that reason is not volunteered by the group or company making the offer. Therefore the stockholder has to look elsewhere for the answer. Since her money is involved, she should regard the offer with cold cynicism.

What to do?

First, she can read through the company's latest annual report and interim statements for a clue as to why an outside group has become interested.

Second, she should contact her broker; he probably won't have an answer himself but he can obtain some sort of opinion from his research department. In such a case, a second opinion from another brokerage firm is also advisable.

Third, the shareholder can ask her bank what it knows. Big banks not only have investment research departments but they handle trusts and have common funds for investment. If the company involved is well known some of its stock probably appears in the bank's portfolio—in the common trust funds, in personal trusts, or in pension trusts that the bank handles. Sooner or later the bank will have to make a decision about what it plans to do with regard to the tender offer.

Fourth—and admittedly harder to do—the stockholder could contact one of the company's competitors. No one knows better than an aggressive rival what is happening in a company.

Through one of these sources, the investor should be able to find some reason for the outside group's interest. Undoubtedly it involves some hidden values. Under current accounting rules companies can report some assets at cost, rather than present market value. Often, too, there are valuable intangibles—mineral rights, patents, ideas—that might be unknown to the general public.

Remember Xerox and the copying process that made it so successful? And look at Minute Maid frozen orange juice, the pioneer frozen juice company that made a fortune for its backers, among them Bing Crosby. It is such hidden values that a typical stockholder might not realize unless he searches for them.

Stock Certificate Procedures

Lost Certificates

The best advice about losing stock certificates is, don't.

The still-discussed classic example concerns an economics professor who thought he had inherited some railroad preferred stock from his father. No certificate could be found, but the company kept mailing information to the deceased father's home and said he was a stockholder of record.

By the time the estate was settled, the preferred shares of the railroad, in the process of going through reorganization, became quite valuable. So the professor went through the rigmarole of taking out a surety bond and obtaining a new certificate from the railroad. Then he sold the stock for $8,000, divided the money with his sister, and the estate was settled—or so he thought.

When the railroad finally reorganized, a broker suddenly presented a large block of shares, including the "lost" certificate. The surety company contacted the professor and forced him to pay back the $8,000. His father apparently had sold the shares, signing the certificate and thus transferring it to the broker. The professor had to mortgage his house to raise the $8,000.

Each corporation follows its own rules about replacing lost, strayed, or stolen stock certificates, but most are quite similar.

For example, after it hears from a stockholder that a certificate has been lost, a typical company alerts its transfer agent to put a "stop transfer" notice on the account. Then there is a waiting period of about three months, during which the stockholder cannot sell his shares. Also, the stockholder must file an affidavit of loss that the company mails to him, and he must pay for a surety bond.

If he uses the company's blanket coverage, the surety bond premium is 3 percent of the value of the securities at the time of the assumption of liability. Thus, on shares valued at $5,000, the cost of the bonding would be $150. After this procedure, the new stock certificate is issued.

The American Telephone & Telegraph Company asks its stockholders to fill out a notarized "affidavit of loss" and then politely suggests that they wait six months. The wait doesn't have to be that long but a spokesman explained that "we find certificates turn up in most cases." The cost ($1.20 a share in the case of AT&T for the surety bonding) and the psychology of the long wait sometimes induce stockholders to search more thoroughly and turn up the errant certificates. General Motors Corporation uses a similar technique—an affidavit and a surety bond costing about 3 percent of the shares' value.

What most shareholders do not realize is that the surety bond protects the company and its transfer agent, not the shareholder. If the shares show up, as in the case of the professor, the surety company can take civil action against the misguided shareholder. If a stolen certificate is processed, then the action might be against the culprit, possibly on charge of theft and forgery (if he can be found), because to be transferred a stock certificate generally has to be signed by the person to whom it is registered. In some cases, too, the brokerage firm that accepted the stolen certificate and passed it on for transfer could be held liable.

An officer of the Morgan Guaranty Trust Company, a bank that does a large amount of corporate stock transfer work, advised: "The stockholder had better be awfully sure that the certificate is really lost. He can't shrug off responsibility."

Name Changes

Sometimes stockholders worry about a name change, following marriage, for example. However, a bank probably will continue to honor dividend checks under the woman's maiden name for a while until notification has taken effect.

The quickest way to change a stock certificate to the woman's married name is for her to go to her local bank and ask it to guarantee her signatures—both single and married—on the back of the certificate.

The bank should certify that the woman is one and the same person. Then she can mail the certificate directly to the transfer agent. One transfer agent bank reports that it takes about a week once it receives such a certificate to issue another in the married name. However, if a stockholder goes through her broker the process can take much longer.

Signing Your Certificate

If stock is registered in your name you have to sign the back of the certificate when you sell it. At first glance the procedure looks confusing, mostly because of the type of printing used on stock certificates, and the legal language. It's much like endorsing a check.

The certificate reads "for value received . . . hereby sell and transfer unto. . . ." Don't sign your name there. Farther down there is another blank space reading "do hereby irrevocably constitute and appoint. . . ." Here the stockholder should write in the name of her brokerage firm, although if the shares are delivered to the broker by hand, this line too can remain blank. The broker will use a stamper to inscribe the firm's name there. However, if the name of the broker isn't there, it could be "stolen" and negotiated.

Still farther down is the simple, straightforward word "dated" with space for insertion of the date, if you wish, but it isn't necessary.

Then comes the key line, apt to be a quite bare line, and this one requires your signature. Make sure that you sign it exactly as your name appears on the face of the certificate. Naturally, if the shares are jointly owned both owners must sign, just as they must sign a federal income tax return if they file jointly.

If the broker keeps your registered certificates and you order him by telephone to sell, he can send you authorizations to sign, in lieu of signing in person.

Commissions

As we mentioned earlier in the book, the Securities and Exchange Commission deregulated the brokerage industry in 1975 to the extent of allowing firms to charge any commissions they wished on transactions. Previously there was a set rate for commissions.

Rates by the leading brokerage firms have tended to rise for small investors and decrease for large investors with clout. This has stimulated an increase in the number of discount brokerage firms, such as Charles Schwab & Company and Muriel Seibert & Company. Such firms offer little or no investment guidance, but they execute orders quickly and cheaply for customers.

The result has been that many sophisticated investors now use two brokerage firms, as urged in this book. One firm can provide investment advice and research reports—as long as you the investors give it some of your business—while the discount broker offers a way to save money on transactions, especially valuable for people with Individual Retirement Accounts who want to buy and hold securities for a longer term.

19

Planning Your Portfolio

Passages in Your Life and Career

The young in heart and the bold in spirit can do well in the stock market, and so can the temporarily sorrowing widow. Wise planning should be influenced by a full understanding of your own personal needs and careful attention to economic trends. I am going to present sample portfolios tailored to several stages in a woman's life as well as specific suggestions and general advice for thoughtful planning.

The Young Working Woman

Tim Cutler, a young registered representative for Smith Barney in New York City, offers a growth portfolio for a young (married) working woman who has accumulated $50,000. Here yield is not a priority. See Table 19-1.

A recent issue of *The Outlook,* published by Standard & Poor's, suggests four different groupings of stocks, each providing different investment aims. Figure 19-1 illustrates the way Standard & Poor's groups stocks to meet par-

(text continues on p. 225)

Table 19-1. Sample portfolio A: $50,000.

Young, Married Professional Woman

Selection	*Share*	*Cost*	*Comment*
Cash and equivalent	20%		
Asset management account fund (taxable/tax free)		$10,233	Should be drawn down for IRA and collectibles
Fixed income holdings	54%		
Compound interest bonds (tax free)			Preferably in state of residence
$50,000 15-yr Zero's @ 10.5% (insured)		10,225	
$20,000 20-yr "GAIN" @ 9.875% (insured)		6,867	These "flip" to cash payments in 10 years
High-yield/lower quality (taxable) "junk bond" mutual fund (reinvested monthly)		10,000	No reinvestment load
		27,092	
Common stocks	24%		
100 KLA Instruments @ 18½		1,850	Major new optical technology
25 Intn'l Bus. Mach @ 127		3,175	Anchor to windward
100 Federal Express @ 40		4,000	Excellent growth, good management
75 Pub Serv Elec & Gas @ 30		2,250	Reinvest dividends tax deferred
100 West. Union Pr. E @ 8		800	Possible reinstatement of dividend
		$12,075	
Options	1%		
1 Put Upjohn July 90 @ 1.50		150	Drug stocks overvalued
2 Call Gen Elec Sep 65 @ 1.50		300	Good chart
2 Call U S Steel Jun 30 @ 0.75		150	Stock and option undervalued
		$ 600	
	Total	$50,000	

Figure 19-1. Sample stock portfolios based on investment goals.

Group 1: Foundation stocks for long-term gain

These issues are basic building blocks for a portfolio. They offer the prospect of long-term appreciation, along with moderate but growing income. The investor seeking to build an estate should start with stocks from this list, augmenting them with issues from other groups according to one's objectives and temperament.

Earnings Per Share ($) 1983	E1984	E1985	Indicated Div. $	1983-85 Price Range	Recent Price	P/E Ratio	Yield %		Annual Growth Rates—for Latest 5 Years— Sales	Earn.	Div.	▼Price Action vs. Mkt. 11-28-80 to 8-12-82	Since 8-12-82	Listed Options Traded	Last Page Ref.
2.81	3.98	4.05	2.20	44 7/8-33 5/8	42	10.4	5.2	CPC Int'l	2%	-2%	8%	1.35	0.76	..	819
'6.41	'5.89	6.60	2.54	69 -42	59	8.9	4.3	•Federated Dept. St. (Jan.*)	10	9	7	1.85	0.91	..	819
3.40	E3.85	4.30	1.60	50 -24	50	11.6	3.2	Heinz (H.J.) (Apr.*)	11	16	15	1.58	1.61	..	767
9.04	10.77	12.00	4.40	138 1/4-92 1/4	128	10.7	3.4	•Int'l Business Machines	15	16	3	1.29	1.16	C	854
5.22	5.35	4.20	2.60	63 1/4-45 5/8	51	12.1	5.1	Procter & Gamble (Jun.)	13	11	12	1.68	0.68	A	819
3.73	4.10	↑4.10	1.20	78 1/2-34 1/2	40	9.8	3.0	Schlumberger Ltd.	10	9	17	0.55	0.63	C	767
3.62	3.96	4.35	1.34	31 1/4-14 7/8	30	6.9	4.5	•Security Pacific	16	10	10	1.32	1.48	..	767

Group 2: Stocks with promising growth prospects

These stocks promise to enjoy well above average growth rates in earnings per share for the foreseeable future. Although most of the issues command relatively high P/E ratios, the premiums are, in our view, justified. Income is not a consideration here.

Earnings Per Share ($) 1983	E1984	E1985	Indicated Div. $	1983-85 Price Range	Recent Price	P/E Ratio	Yield %		Latest 5-Year Growth Rates Sales	Earn.	No. of Earn. Gains '78-'83	Interim ■Earn. Trend	▼Price Action vs. Mkt. 11-28-80 to 8-12-82	Since Aug. 12, '82	Listed Options Traded	Last Page Ref.
2.86	3.34	3.75	1.40	54 -36 1/8	54	14.4	2.6	Abbott Laboratories	15%	18%	5	+16%	1.51	1.04	Ph	807
3.00	3.45	↓3.90	↑1.88	61 3/8-31 3/16	61	15.6	3.1	•Bristol-Myers	10	14	5	+13	1.70	1.22	C	755
4.42	5.10	↓5.75	2.60	78 1/4-54 7/8	70	12.2	3.7	•Emerson El. (Sept.)	10	9	5	+ 4	1.96	0.71	A	807
1.47	1.74	2.05	0.52	32 3/8-17 5/8	28	13.7	1.9	•Nat'l Med. Ent. (May)	51	29	5	+16	1.08	1.36	A	909
†2.05	†2.76	†3.40	†0.50	49 1/8-22 1/8	37	'15.0	'1.0	•Northern Telecom	17	‡	4	+49	1.62	1.89	T	755
3.85	4.08	4.60	1.92	65 -37 3/4	64	13.9	3.0	Syntex (July)	19	25	5	-3	1.62	0.95	C	807
1.74	2.51	↓2.65	↑1.36	43 1/4-25 1/8	37	14.0	3.7	Thomas & Betts	7	-2	4	+37	1.03	1.06	..	755

Figure 19-1. Sample stock portfolios based on investment goals (continued).

Group 3: Cyclical/speculative stocks

This group comprises stocks selected for high reward potential. It includes emerging and turnaround situations, stocks to benefit from cyclical upswings, and the like. Readers can expect to see more frequent changes in this list than in the others. The risk factor in some of the issues may be high.

Earnings Per Share ($) E1984	Earnings Per Share ($) E1985	Indicated Div. $	1983-85 Price Range	Recent Price	P/E Ratio	Yield %	▼Price Action vs. Mkt. 11-28-80 to 8-12-82	▼Price Action vs. Mkt. Since Aug. 12, '82	Listed Options Traded	Last Page Ref.		Remarks
6.71	7.50	1.60	108 1/2-48 3/8	105	14.0	1.5	1.84	1.60	Pac	854	**Amer. Broadcasting**	Speculation on completion of Capital Cities merger.
9.52	10.35	2.70	66 -35 5/8	66	6.4	4.1	1.02	1.38	..	851	**•Bankers Trust**	Favorable earnings trend; stock remains undervalued.
[2]4.01	6.00	1.40	66 7/8-31 7/8	59	9.8	2.4	0.64	1.92	C	889	**•Boeing Co.**	Pickup in commercial aircraft orders expected.
2.28	2.50	0.92	27 5/8-16 7/8	20	8.0	4.6	1.55	0.97	..	401	**Borg-Warner**	Cyclical businesses to join prospering service lines.
2.60	3.25	1.08	47 5/8-26 1/2	44	13.5	2.5	2.26	1.25	A	899	**•Browning-Ferris (Sept.)**	Growth in waste disposal activity aids prospects.
7.15	↓7.20	1.40	58 3/4-25 1/2	51	7.1	2.7	0.63	1.68	C	947	**•Burlington Northern**	Superior rail, with expanding natural resources base.
1.66	2.15	None	23 3/4-13 1/2	22	10.2	...	[4]N.A.	[4]N.A.	...	947	**•Circus Circus (Jan.*)**	Rebound in Nevada gaming benefiting profits.
[6]2.53	2.75	0.72	44 3/4-22 5/8	28	10.2	2.6	[3]N.A.	0.78	C	401	**Engelhard Corp.**	Favorable prospects for most catalytic products.
6.68	6.85	2.60	53 7/8-31 3/4	51	7.4	5.1	1.24	1.08	...	899	**Interlake**	Good late-cycle momentum; P/E may expand.
2.05	3.15	1.80	34 3/8-24 1/8	31	9.8	5.8	0.77	0.97	...	411	**•Ogden Corp.**	Focus on resource recovery should aid earnings.
2.68	3.30	1.12	39 1/2-20 1/4	31	9.4	3.6	0.99	1.17	...	851	**•Parker-Hannifin (June)**	High level of capital spending helping profits.
4.02	4.75	1.60	57 1/2-34 3/4	45	9.5	3.6	0.93	0.70	C	851	**Raytheon**	Strong growth likely in defense electronics.
6.07	4.50	1.00	41 5/8-24 7/8	36	8.0	2.8	0.82	0.97	Pac	848	**•Reynolds Metals**	Lower aluminum inventories, firmer prices to aid net.
[5]2.65	3.00	1.00	38 3/4-23 3/8	33	11.0	3.0	0.97	1.34	Pac	947	**•Signal Cos.**	Diversified company has sizable earning power.
[7]4.30	5.00	1.85	43 1/8-23 1/2	40	8.0	4.6	0.97	0.96	..	443	**Sonat Inc.**	Positioning itself for future oil services upturn.
E3.05	3.50	1.32	37 3/8-21 1/8	27	7.7	4.9	1.50	0.71	..	412	**•Zurn Industries (Mar.*)**	Increasing resource recovery business to boost profits.

Group 4: Income with inflation protection

If high yield alone were the goal, it would be easy to compile a list of high-grade bonds returning 12% or more. But bonds afford no protection against inflation. While it was hard to beat inflation in recent years, the list below comprises quality stocks that in our opinion offer the prospect of dividend growth sufficient to compensate for the degree of inflation we envisage for the period ahead.

Earnings Per Share ($) 1983	Earnings Per Share ($) E1984	Earnings Per Share ($) E1985	Indicated Div. $	1983-85 Price Range	Recent Price	P/E Ratio	Yield %		Dividend History: 5-Year Growth Rate %	Dividend History: No. of Ann. Incr. 1980-84	Dividend History: 5-Year Avg. Payout %	Latest Increase	Inflation Hedge Ratio††	Listed Options Traded	Last Page Ref.
[8]N.A.	10.17	11.00	↑6.60	84 1/8-62 1/8	83	7.5	8.0	**Ameritech**	[8]N.A.	[8]N.A.	[8]N.A.	5-1-85	[8]N.A.	...	887
4.17	4.22	4.40	3.04	34 3/4-25 5/8	34	7.7	8.9	**•IPALCO Enter.**	7	5	70	4-15-85	1.25	...	887
7.44	5.64	6.95	2.68	56 1/2-33 1/2	48	6.9	5.6	**Mellon Bank**	9	5	35	2-15-85	1.57	...	833
5.02	3.56	5.60	3.32	44 3/8-28	43	7.7	7.7	**•Pacific Lighting**	11	5	58	11-15-84	1.89	...	833
[8]N.A.	8.46	↓9.00	↑5.72	73 1/8-51 1/4	69	7.7	8.3	**Pacific Telesis**	[8]N.A.	[8]N.A.	[8]N.A.	5-1-85	[8]N.A.	...	977
[8]N.A.	9.04	9.65	↑6.00	75 1/2-55	73	7.6	8.2	**Southwestern Bell**	[8]N.A.	[8]N.A.	[8]N.A.	5-1-85	[8]N.A.	...	921
3.14	3.72	3.80	↑2.36	31 5/8-20 3/4	31	8.2	7.6	**TECO Energy**	9	5	59	5-15-85	1.66	...	935
4.75	4.01	4.80	2.92	44 3/4-31 7/8	42	8.8	7.0	**Tenneco**	6	5	45	12-11-84	1.01	A	887
3.97	4.35	4.50	2.28	35 5/8-22 1/2	33	7.3	6.9	**•Wisconsin Elec. Pwr.**	7	5	62	6- 1-84	1.35	...	983

Standard & Poor's Corp.

ticular needs. From week to week it might add and remove certain stocks depending on changed outlooks.

Women with Children in College

Investing needs change with age sometimes or with altered financial needs, and therefore one woman's portfolio can be poison to another.

There comes a period in the life of many married couples, a midway period, when children are suddenly ready for college. It may come when the husband's income level has not yet reached its peak. Most budgets cannot stand the strain of sending several children to college, especially at the same time, without some borrowing. At times like this the husband might think in terms of taking out or increasing the mortgage on his house, borrowing on his life insurance policies, or selling stock.

My advice is this: Borrowing on your life insurance is a good idea because most life insurance policies stipulate that the money can be borrowed at about 8 percent interest, a low rate for these days when bank money costs 15 percent or more. Secondly, consider a home equity mortgage, which is merely what used to be called a second mortgage. It has been readapted today because so many people have a large amount of equity built up in their home because of inflation. Example: a house bought 25 years ago at $35,000 would be worth more than $200,000 today. In mid-1985, mortgage rates had declined to 12 percent and less and home equity rates ran about 12.5 percent. In early 1986, rates were lower.

Don't consider selling your portfolio of stock, but you can winnow out some stocks in which you have good long-term capital gains. Put the same money into high-income stocks, issues of sound companies temporarily low-priced because of the business cycle or because demand for their products is temporarily low. The list of undervalued stocks is a long one and your broker can help you with suggestions. Then, once your child is out of college and the financial burden is no longer there, you can reinvest your money into fast-growth stocks.

If more money is needed than the loans on life insurance and home equity can provide, then consider using your stock as collateral. Brokerage firms allow borrowing on margin accounts, or you can use your stock certificates as collateral on a bank loan. Collateral loans require lower rates of interest than most other types of installment borrowing. And psychologically this is a good idea because it is so hard to save up capital for investment. Debts, of course, have to be paid but people can gear themselves to pay off debts on time while it is hard to set aside funds for building up investment capital. So, don't cash in your chips; keep them and borrow on them.

The Widow

I don't intend to be lugubrious, but all married women should prepare themselves to be widows, no matter what their age or status in life. If they are not married they should prepare themselves for the loneliness of making their own decisions, in a world where opinions are a dime a dozen.

One day a man telephoned me at *The New York Times* with a puzzled urgency in his voice. He was only an acquaintance, virtually a stranger, calling me because I wrote a personal finance column. "My mother has just become a widow, and she has a hundred thousand dollars. How should she handle it?"

The question is ages old, one that recurs almost every day. Brokers, bank officers, lawyers, and, even more often, sons and daughters hear it.

There are many answers, but one interesting approach is to set the question into some historical perspective. Back in the 1920s and again in the 1930s *Barron's,* the financial weekly published by Dow Jones, sponsored contests to gather ideas on how a widow could invest such a sum.

The 1939 winning essay with its accompanying portfolio was submitted by Eugene M. Kaufmann, Jr., who showed the good investment adviser's interest in changing with the times. "Over many years," he wrote, "there has grown a tradition that the only safe medium for conserving principal and returning a safe income to widows are first mortgages on real estate, bonds secured by mortgages and government obligations." Such was the tradition that had gained popularity in the 1920s, when mortgages returned 8 and 10 percent.

All that changed with the Depression and the doldrums of the 1930s. Mr. Kaufmann pointed out that during that period real estate and bonds suffered from government policies he politely called "prejudicial to creditors."

Also, the government assisted debtors by keeping interest rates low. Thus the high bond yields of the 1920s gave way to 3 and 4 percent in the 1930s, and a few years later when World War II began, interest rates fell even lower. Now rates are much higher again but constantly changing.

Looking at such factors, Mr. Kaufmann wrote dolefully: "There is no means whereby we can estimate how long current chaotic political conditions will continue . . . a gradual attrition is the normal fate of most investment funds." The only way out, he suggested, was "a number of well-selected stocks so that the fund can grow. . . . I cannot escape the conclusion that the stock market offers quite as much safety at prevailing levels today as does the bond market," he wrote in 1939. His remarks seem timely today.

He suggested that the widow with $100,000 commit 50 percent of her money to common stocks "whose earnings seem capable of expansion," plus 15–20 percent in cash reserves for buying opportunities, and the remainder in

Figure 19-2. A prize-winning portfolio plan from 1939.

Common Stocks

Number of Shares	*Description*	*Market Value*		*Income*
100	Am Gas & Elec	36 1/8	$ 3,612	$ 160
40	E I duPont	153	6,320	200
100	Gen Am Trans	48	4,800	225
100	Can Electric	34 5/8	3,462	100
50	Ingersoll-Rand	105	5,250	275
100	Int Nickel	48 1/4	4,825	200
100	Libbey-Owens-Ford	47 1/2	4,750	200
50	Owens-Illinois Gl	65	3,250	100
100	Pac Gas & El	33 1/4	3,325	200
50	J C Penney	88 1/2	4,425	212
50	Sears, Roebuck	75 1/8	3,756	150
100	Texas Corp	34 1/8	3,412	200
Total stocks			$51,187	$2,222
Current return				4.34%

Corporate Bonds

Quantity	*Description*	*Market Value*		*Income*
5	Western NY & Penn RR 4s, 1943	106 1/4	$5,312	$200
5	Louisv & Jeff Bridge 4s, 1945	108 1/2	5,425	200
5	Appalachian El Power Co 4 1/2s, 1948	106 1/4	5,312	225
5	Am IG Chemical 5 1/2s, 1949	102 5/8	5,131	275
5	Bethlehem Steel cv 3 1/2s	100 1/8	5,006	175
5	Ohio Valley Water 5s, 1954	108	5,400	250

Cash and Its Equivalent

	Market Value		*Income*
$10,000 U.S. savings bonds, due 9/1/1949	75%	$ 7,500	$ 210
$10,000 U.S. savings bonds, due 1/2/1950	75%	7,500	210
Fed Savings & Loan Assoc share account	100%	1,975	69
Total bonds and cash or equivalent		$48,562	$1,304
Current return			3.73 2/3

short- and medium-term corporate bonds. His portfolio is shown in Figure 19-2.*

How have times changed since 1939?

The 1939 sum of $100,000 is worth only about $15,000 in terms of today's

*It is interesting to note that most of the recommended stocks are still listed on the NYSE. All the corporate bonds and the government issues have matured and been paid off. The point to remember is that a portfolio of securities must not be static, and it must be updated periodically.

purchasing power. So today's widow or working woman inheriting $100,000 has less than the woman in 1939 in terms of today's living costs.

Interest rates today are high again, so that bonds are looked upon favorably for high yields and even appreciation if they are selling below par value.

The widow or retired working woman today, if she is over sixty years old, probably receives a sizable Social Security check and possibly even her own or her husband's corporate pension, which might help compensate a little for the cost of living increases.

She pays higher taxes than in 1939.

Buying common stocks for growth has become much more prevalent and acceptable than in 1939.

Today's investment advisers believe even more firmly that a widow's portfolio should be handled aggressively, with the idea of appreciation through long-term capital gains rather than just reliance on income securities.

The reason is twofold—to fight inflation on its own terms and to save on taxes. Taxes on long-term capital gains, remember, can be less than half as high as taxes on dividends and other regular income.

I once asked Russell Morrison, former president of Standard & Poor's and a long-time believer in growth stocks, to suggest a portfolio for a widow with $100,000. He advised limiting the portfolio to four or five stocks in basic industries offering growth, plus keeping about $20,000 in short-term Treasury issues as a hedge fund for buying opportunities.

His suggestions: Ford Motor, for appreciation and income; a public utility for slow appreciation and income; Union Carbide, a stock depressed in price but with good potential.* "For play she might enjoy some shares of IBM," he added.

The old-time investment adviser probably would say nothing about "play." It wasn't proper in those days to suggest that a woman might have some fun in the stock market! Playing might suggest that men thought she had brains enough to learn about the market, and most of them, sadly enough, did not give us the benefit of such a thought in those days.

More than ever today the stress is on appreciation, even for the widow. To invest even as much as $100,000 is no easy task because brokers and other advisers will come up with so many answers to the questions: What kind of stocks to select? What income to expect? What can be hoped in terms of appreciation? What about inflation rising at more than possibly 5 percent per year? When to sell?

Yet the sum of $100,000 is not large by today's inflationary standards, though it is about what a moderately prosperous businessman might leave a widow.

*Union Carbide is once again a depressed stock because of public reaction to the accidents at the company's plant in Bhopal, India, and at a West Virginia plant.

"As a widow myself it is a problem I can understand," says Mrs. Ione Sutton, a registered representative with Stifel Nicolaus & Co. She talked about a widow with $200,000.

"Asked the question: Suddenly widowed, with two hundred thousand dollars to invest and live on, to maintain a reasonably habitual lifestyle, what would I do? The sum could be from insurance, pension, or an inheritance.

"Well, first, I'd have to assume the money didn't just appear out of the blue without a background—a background of a house, earning capacities which could produce average (or better) Social Security, a sense of ambition for security in the future as part of a past lifestyle.

"What to do with two hundred thousand at sixty or sixty-five is one thing; at age fifty, working and with ten years to go, is another; or, a nonworking mother, wife only, is still another.

"So at this moment, I'm addressing my thoughts to the latter: a housewife having been lovingly cared for by a loving, hard-working husband; having raised the children, now all out on their own; having a paid-for house; a comfortable lifestyle; but no more the monthly income which brought it all about!

"She has maybe Social Security of five or six thousand a year, house expenses (no mortgage) of two or three thousand a year. That becomes a net amount to *live on* of three thousand, or two hundred and fifty a month—not any elbow room! So the two hundred thousand should produce fifteen to eighteen thousand a year, making a total of fifteen to eighteen hundred a month before taxes." See Table 19-2.

Mrs. Sutton also offers ideas for a working person with ten years to go before retirement and $150,000; see Table 19-3 (p. 232).

The Older, Retired Couple

The older couple needing high income probably will concentrate on stocks that offer a good income potential and some possible gains. The market of 1983 and 1984, with bond interest rates high and prices of many bonds well below their par value to reflect 12 percent and higher yields, was a good time, perhaps among the best in history, to accumulate high-return investments that also promise excellent capital gains.

Ironically, inflation that has hurt so many older couples has been good to them in this particular way. The government in its fight on inflation permitted bond yields to rise to historic high levels. It is a situation that probably won't continue forever, but some economists do predict that interest rates will not return for many years to the low levels of 4 percent which prevailed back in the early 1960s.

Table 19-2 Sample portfolio B: $150,000.

Working Woman Age 50, Ten Years Before Retirement

	Selection	*Cost*	*Dividend*		*Comment*
		Group I: Classic growth stocks			
1,000	AT&T (T) @ 21½	21,500	1.20	1,200	Substantial growth in 3 to 5 years
100	IBM (IBM) @ 126	12,600	4.40	440	Steady growth
500	GME (N) (GME) @ 40	20,000	.40	200	Predicated growth due to terms of EDS buy-over (50% in 7 years?)
200	Exxon (XON) @ 52	10,400	3.40	680	No. 1 oil
		$64,500		$2,520	
		Group II: Growth stocks in basic industries			
100	Abbott Labs @ 54 (ABT)	5,400	1.40	$140	Diversified health care products
100	Allied Corp @ 41 (ALD)	4,100	1.80	180	Oil and gas, chemicals, fibers
100	Bristol Myers @ 60 (BMY)	6,000	1.20	120	Toiletries, drugs, vitamins
200	Chevron @ 36 (CHV)	7,200	2.40	480	Major integrated international oil
200	Foxboro @ 28 (FOX)	5,600	1.04	208	Process instrumentation
200	Georgia Pacific @ 24 (GP)	4,800	.80	160	Plywood, lumber, paper, gypsum
200	Hewlett-Packard @ 33 (HWP)	6,600	.22	44	Electronics data measurement and testing instruments

200	Loctite Corp. @ 28 (LOC)	5,600	.80	160	Chemical sealants, adhesives
200	Natl. Fuel Gas @ 28 (NFG)	5,600	1.88	376	Natural gas utility, holding company, pipeline
100	Newmont Mining @ 45 (NEM)	4,500	1.00	100	Nonferrous metals; gold
200	Rollins Environment @ 27 (REN)	5,400	.10	20	Industrial waste disposal plants
200	Wettereau @ 28 (WETT)	5,600	.88	176	Wholesaler to supermarkets
		66,400		2,164	
		Group III: Money market fund			
Balance		$19,100	8%	1,528	
		$150,000		$6,212	

Table 19-3. Sample portfolio C: $200,000

Nonworking Widow

	Face value	*Price*	*Interest on dividends per unit*	*Income*	*Percent yield*
40,000	Municipal bonds	40,000	9.3	3,720	9.3
30,000	MCI Communications cv. 7$\frac{3}{4}$ @ 69	21,000	77.50	2,325	11.1
200	Diamond Shamrock cv. pfd. 4.00 @ 40	8,000	4.0	800	10.0
800	Houston Industries @ 26	20,800	2.64	2,112	10.15
1,000	Kansas Power & Light @ 22	22,000	2.36	2,360	10.7
400	Ft. Dearborn Income Sec. (fund) @ 13	5,200	1.36	554	10.7
		117,000		11,871	10.14
1,000	AT&T @ 21$\frac{1}{2}$	21,500	1.20	1,200	5.6
100	IBM @ 126	12,600	4.40	440	3.5
400	Exxon @ 52	20,800	3.40	1,360	6.5
400	Rollins Environmental @ 26 (waste clean-up plants)	10,400	.10	40	0
		65,300		3,040	4.6
	Balance: Money Market	17,700	7.5	1,328	7.5
		$200,000		$16,239	8.1

Trust Funds and "Prudent Men"

If the money you have to invest comes to you as an inheritance from your husband or parent, and if it is put into a trust fund administered by a third party (usually an attorney or bank officer), you may come face to face with the "prudent man" rule. Since many women inherit money at some point in their lives, either a small amount, such as $10,000, or as much as $1 million, they are likely to become acquainted with the grandfather complex, or the prudent man rule.

For centuries women were dependent on men—grandfathers, fathers, husbands, who were supposed to earn enough to leave their women sufficient money. Even today the average man dies earlier than the average woman. Look at a typical list of premiums for insurance policies and you will see that a woman of thirty buying a policy would pay the same premium as a man of about twenty-six. In other words there is probably a four year or more difference in their calculated life-span. No organizations analyze life-spans more closely than the actuaries of insurance companies.

More often than not, a woman will find that she has little to say about the investment of the money she has inherited, at least if her husband or father is typical and has not been pressured by her to give her more latitude. When she investigates, she will hear the bank officer or lawyer handling her money, often in the form of a trust, speak of the prudent man rule, which goes this way, as defined by the courts: "The exercise of sound judgment and care under the circumstances currently prevailing, which men of prudence, discretion and intelligence would exercise, not in regard to speculation, but in regard to investment, considering income as well as safety of principal."

This legal definition of prudence is a logical outgrowth of the idea that such funds for a widow and children should be safely invested. A trustee violating such an approach might find himself open to censure by a court, and even to being surcharged if the investments went awry.

In the past twenty years even conservative lawyers who draw wills and trust agreements for the men in our lives have begun to realize the importance of providing for investment in growth-type securities to help keep pace with inflation. Even so, the typical trust today probably invests at a 60 to 40 ratio—sixty percent in bonds, forty percent in common stocks.

The woman faced with this situation and wanting more growth in her portfolio should, first, be sure that she reads and understands the trust agreement—the document signed by her husband, father, or whoever, stipulating how the money should be invested; then, if necessary, use her smile and pleasant voice in an effort to convince a conservative trustee to take a few more chances in the portfolio by investing in somewhat livelier stocks—IBM, for example.

Trustees, especially bank officers, like to keep their customers happy if they can do so within the limits imposed by the terms of the trust agreement. Often they will consult with a widow or daughter to find out whether she wants high income or appreciation from reasonably sound growth stocks.

Probably many women will find that their trusts have been set up in such a way that while they cannot decide what stocks to buy, they can express their opinion. Here a little psychology can help induce the trust officer to put the woman's opinion into action.

For the woman stuck with a trust that makes no provision for investment in growth stocks and that is strictly interpreted as money to be invested in superconservative issues, there is an out.

I have one friend who found herself in this situation—a trust invested superconservatively, mostly in bonds, handled by a man who showed no interest in her opinions. So, out of the money she earns, she invests each year in fast-growth stocks, thus getting her capital appreciation and fun this way, as well as moving out of stocks fast when she thinks turns in the market are coming. This reminds me of the teenager who can't drink or smoke at home in front of her parents, so she drinks a little extra and puffs madly at parties outside.

In spite of her unhappiness and sense of frustration at the way her trust is handled and its lack of growth, she has the best of two investment approaches—a sound trust invested in conservative bonds and a few stocks and fast appreciation in her sideline investments.

General Advice on Portfolio Planning

If you can, handle your own investments. Don't put all your money into one or two stocks. Remember the adage about all those eggs in one basket. The exception to this would be the new investor just starting out with either small sums of money invested monthly in one stock to build up the number of shares toward a round lot, or with a small sum for investment all at once—$1,000, $2,000, or maybe $5,000—in which case she might be well advised to split the sum between just two stocks. In fact, an Individual Retirement Account into which $2,000 a year can be put could be a starter. It can be opened at a brokerage firm.

If your money is limited don't buy two or three shares of a dozen stocks, thus scattering your shots and paying relatively high commissions. In fact, even with a portfolio of $1,000,000, a half-dozen stocks or so are enough since they do need some TLC—tender loving care. Buy round lots if possible to cut commissions.

Keep an opportunity fund of cash, perhaps 10 percent of the money available, for any special "buys" that come along. This money can be invested in government securities (if interest rates look desirable) or kept in the savings bank or a money market fund.

Put at least 20 percent of your portfolio in good stocks, which I like to call "pivotal" shares—shares around which you build your portfolio. These are the shares of good, conservative growth-type companies with some appreciation expected. Generally they will be the shares you live with for some years.

Set yourself specific goals for your stocks, to be acted upon without emotion. Jot these goals in your ever-handy notebook when you buy a particular stock, noting the price at which you expect to sell it. Then sell when it has achieved your aim and invest the money elsewhere. Greed for a little extra profit in a rising market has tripped up many new investors. You don't want to play with stocks like paper dolls, because there is no profit in those crisp-looking certificates until you sell.

Do use stop orders to help achieve your aims. Downside orders will help protect you in a fast-falling market; the upside stop orders will ensure unemotional exercise of your plan to sell the stock when it reaches your target point.

Don't overlook bonds as an investment possibility for appreciation if they sell below par value and carry high yields. Also don't forget about convertibles; they can give you a conservative investment with possible conversion into common stocks at a favorable price if the company fares well, and they can be used as very acceptable collateral for loans from banks.

From time to time measure the performance of the stocks in your portfolio against the averages—the Dow Jones and the widely used Standard & Poor's 500, as well as any of the growth stock averages. Do your stocks as a group measure well in comparison?

Don't discuss your investing—success or failures—with other people. For some psychological reason it's bad luck. Even good friends become either envious or bored by talk of your ''killings'' in the market. Discussion of your failures can lead them to derision and you to some self-doubts.

Read continually—newspapers with financial pages, brokerage firm market letters, bank economic letters. Such reading widens your knowledge, piques your curiosity, and stimulates your imagination.

Maintain careful records of your transactions, for tax purposes, for your own edification, and also for your heirs.

Learn how to keep simple charts as described in Chapter 14. They give you a better view of your shares' performance.

If possible join an investment club both for fun and profits. (see Chapter 11). It gives you a chance to exchange ideas and pit your investment knowledge against mutual funds and professional investors.

A growth rate should be formulated in your mind, perhaps 10 percent a year in earnings for the pivotal stocks in your portfolio—the solid, big old growers—and perhaps 15 percent or more for the fast-growth types.

It's possible that in the next four or five years growth rates of some companies classed as fast-growth types will slow down. Certainly many dropped sharply in price in previous declines. Recent breaks probably resulted from some overspeculation plus the belief that the government's attempts to control inflation through high interest rates and discouragement of capital spending might hurt corporate earnings. That was a few years ago before the administration got inflation more under control. In 1985 the stock market has been setting records, but no one knows how long that will last.

What price growth is is a question that will always baffle thoughtful stockholders. To some people IBM has always seemed too high-priced; to others small investments in it from time to time have brought fancy profits. One woman I know put $1,000 in IBM back in about 1946 and today, through splits, her money has grown to more than $200,000. To determine what price you will pay for growth you will have to get help from your broker—or rather the analyst who backs him up.

Don't forget that as night follows day, speculative booms eventually collapse, so try to avoid buying a fast-growth stock at a peak in the market. Perhaps by now you can be more forgiving of analysts when they make mistakes in recommendations and fail to call an exact turn in a market.

Do try to buy a fast-growth stock at a low point in its price during the year. As you know in a single year the price of the same stock can vary widely. At some time during the year the market, as measured by the stock market averages like the Dow, will be battered down by economic or political events. This can give you an opportunity to buy a growth stock you want.

Don't forget the underprivileged or undervalued stocks. These are shares that have had their day in the market for some reason, usually a cyclical downturn in their industry. It often happens in basic stocks like steels, construction, oil, public utilities.

For example, Texas Gulf Sulphur was a solid blue chip company with good earnings. For some time it was so rich that it could afford to pay out about 75 percent of its earnings each year in dividends, because it literally sat atop a huge dome of sulfur that it mined (sulfur is mined by the so-called Frasch process of forcing hot water into the earth and piping up the molten sulfur). Then TGS ran into competition and price cutting from Mexican sulfur and from a smaller but higher-cost producer in this country called Freeport Sulphur. Investors lost interest in TGS, except for a group of faithfuls who thought that sooner or later the company's skilled management would make a find or diversify. One morning they woke up to find that TGS had struck it rich in Canada. The stock price soared, from the equivalent of about 7 in 1964 to 53 in 1967. A sudden growth stock, yes! It was later merged into another company.

For some years the paper-producing industry went through a period when new plant facilities had been expanded so much that demand lagged, but that period ended about the end of 1966. Demand for paper, wood, and such products has soared. An example is Boise Cascade Corporation, which could have been picked up for 16 a share back in 1966 and moved as high as 72 in 1968; in 1972 it lingered around 9–10; in mid-1985 it sold at 56. Thus some investors profited from the upswings in the industry's fortunes.

Table 19-4. Takeover candidates, 1985.

Company (Sym)	*May 1985 Price*	*Book value*	*Takeover price (est)*
Allied Stores (ALS)	$56\frac{1}{8}$	$50	$78
Amsted Inds (AD)	40	34	62
Borden (BN)*	69	53	86
Helmerich & Payne (HP)	$22\frac{1}{2}$	17	36
IC Industries (ICX)	$32\frac{1}{8}$	33	49
Owens-Illinois (OI)	$44\frac{3}{4}$	50	64

*Value of two shares after 2 for 1 stock split in mid-May.

Four Avenues to Growth

Like having your cake and eating it too, there are several digestible ways to approach this idea of growth and more growth to combat inflation and alleviate high taxation.

Number one approach is through investment in sound companies participating in natural growth factors such as rising population (food makers), more usage (cars), and high living standards (cosmetics).

Number two approach is through the fast-growth stocks, sometimes smaller companies that are expanding into new technological fields. These would include computers (IBM); medical technology (Merck & Company); oceanography (General Dynamics); nuclear energy (General Electric). Also, waste removal is a new growth industry. (Growth industries, if the companies are small, are called by some Wall Streeters "emerging industries.")

Naturally there are many more names in each of these categories, and just because they are mentioned specifically here does not mean this is the right time to buy them. But, like nicknames for people, the names of companies can stimulate your thinking. Ask your broker to send you the firm's latest brochures or list of fast-growth industries and the principal companies in them. Some of the big brokerage firms like Merrill Lynch publish elaborate brochures on them.

Number three approach is found in the undervalued, overlooked blue chips that have had a play and might make a comeback. The savings and loan stocks made such a return recently. The steel stocks, now unwanted and unloved by many investors, perhaps will recover someday, and so will other metals-producing stocks, especially gold and silver.

Number four approach might be a little more chancy, but certainly fun—

buy stocks in good companies mentioned as possible merger candidates. In 1985, the interesting game to play was to buy shares of companies that appeared to be likely takeover candidates. In May of that year, a publication called *Smart Money,* issued by the Hirsch Organization, Old Tappan, New Jersey, offered a list of likely candidates (see Table 19-4).

This is the kind of approach that often helps speculators do well in the market. In December 1985, prices were: Allied Stores, $65\frac{5}{8}$, Amsted Inds $43\frac{1}{4}$; Borden, 96, Helmerich & Payne, 20; IC Industries, $38\frac{1}{4}$; Owens-Illinois, $54\frac{1}{4}$. Take a look in the newspaper and see how those stocks have fared since then.

20

Don't Be a Hetty Green

Alias the Joyless Millionaire

The world's best woman investor and the worst possible penny-pinching, husband-destroying female, used number three approach, mentioned in Chapter 19.

Her name is Hetty Green, and she parlayed $1 million into $100 million (probably $1 billion in today's terms) in a relatively short period during her unpleasant life. One observer described her as being so mean that when she got her hands on a dollar bill she squeezed so hard the eagle screamed.

Hetty, in one of her rare terse, unsmiling moments of comment, said: "I buy a good stock when prices are low and no one wants it and hold it until they do. I never speculate. There is a price on everything I have. When that price is offered I sell. I never buy anything just to hold it."

I am willing to believe that she never did, because she bought into some underprivileged railroads (not enough equipment, rights of way, etc.) and proceeded to make them successful or desirable to the railroad empire builders. She was so smart that it became a game for years in Wall Street to try to outwit Hetty Green. Since she lived in a freebooting period when there was no Securities and Exchange Commission to act as umpire, she had to be shrewd to outguess the opposition. Few, if any, businessmen got the best of her.

To her credit, she operated in an era when women in business were scorned.

About the only respectable career available for a woman with intelligence was being a schoolteacher. All the more power to Hetty's success, testifying to the lessons she had learned as a child from her father, who ran a successful import-export business in Massachusetts. In the early part of the nineteenth century the family fortune had been founded in whaling—a shipping business that included that famous old whaler, the *Charles W. Morgan.**

It is easier for a smart woman to make money in the stock market when she has a sizable sum and doesn't have to start from scratch and invest small amounts periodically.

Hetty Green did start with a substantial sum, but she had to fight bitter legal battles to get her hands on the money, and much of that fortune was left in trust, which meant in those days it was handled very conservatively and unimaginatively by the trustees. The wealthy heiress has other problems that we save-and-invest small stockholders don't have. She attracts sycophants like a queen bee around which the lesser bees swarm, all interested in honey. Too much advice can confuse and destroy a woman's confidence. Hetty Green soon learned to trust no one except herself.

If you want to learn more about her go to the public library. Since she lived from 1835 to 1916, her specific investments do not seem pertinent to us today, but her theory of picking undervalued situations and waiting for them to recover is sound. In fact, I think in the future we might find that the go-go growth stocks, by which so many investors were "burned" in 1962, 1969, and more recent years, lose much of their following as investors become more cautious and sophisticated. It is logical that then they will see the value in turning to Hetty's type of undervalued, cyclically or otherwise depressed stocks. Her approach represents a combination of a more sophisticated and yet less speculative investment method.

Please, if you copy Hetty's investment theory, don't model your life after hers, not even for $100 million! She didn't enjoy the money, just the grubby fight for it. She wore one black dress so green with age that newspapers often commented upon it in the articles they wrote. Today, it seems, journalists tend to be much politer about what woman wear. She hated publicity and moved so unobtrusively through the streets that few reporters could catch her. She seldom went to parties, though for a while she was married to a gregarious and successful businessman. When he lost his money in the stock market, she let him fail and then gave him a tiny pension, ousting him from her home. With her son and daughter she lived in grubby apartments in then unfashionable Brooklyn and Hoboken.

Her son limped all his life because she would not pay for a proper opera-

*Last of the big whaling vessels, it now is berthed at Mystic Seaport, Mystic, Connecticut.

tion to save his leg. Her daughter in later years commented bitterly, when asked in court where she had lived at a certain time: "With my mother, if you call that living." For years Hetty apparently walked with pain from a hernia. She supported the offending part of her innards by a little platform of wood worn under her dress. A New York surgeon knew the story because she had invited him to examine the hernia, but when he quoted her a price for the operation she angrily said it was too much and stalked from his office.

Making money is at once a challenge for a woman and a source of security, but this combination should bring more joy than it apparently did to Hetty.

Ideas Worth Looking Into

Successful investing ideas exist everywhere, anywhere around you, if like Hetty you develop an approach and do some searching. As you sharpen your investment talents as she did for so many years, consider some of these ideas.

Companies in Your Neighborhood

Like most women you probably pay by check some basic household bills to local electric light, gas, water (unless municipally owned), and telephone companies. What do you know about them? Do you live in a growing area where their services are in demand? Are they well run? They might be a good source of investment.

There probably are some local industries in your neighborhood, perhaps even some fast-growth types, such as exist outside Boston, or dot the suburbs of New York and some California cities. Don't overlook your local department store where you buy clothes and home furnishings. It can be part of a big chain or it might still be an independent company, perhaps dominated by a local family.

There is also your local bank. It can be a branch of a much bigger bank within the state or owned by shareholders locally. Some banks operate statewide such as in California, where a few big banks have many branches throughout the state; other banking chains are limited to operations in a few counties or smaller areas. Banks can be a fine-growing investment these days because of the move to the suburbs and industrialization of smaller cities. Today banks are expanding operations beyond state lines.

Who better can prowl quietly around an area and learn about local business than a woman with some time on her hands, good local contacts, and the inoffensive curiosity of an innocent? It can be done discreetly by leading questions, by observation, by checking through investment manuals, by asking a local broker.

Many fortunes have been made in local businesses, and many growth opportunities have been overlooked by investors because they were so close to local business they lost perspective. Often the family that has been the founder of a local business, such as a power company or a bank, is prominent in the town or city. If it has done well, there may also be a chance for you in this age of fast expansion.

If you do buy a stock of a local company, it might be preferable to keep it unregistered, that is, in its "street name" (the name of your brokerage firm), just to prevent local people from knowing you own the shares. Or to be even more clever, if you make a sizable investment just have a few of your shares—say ten—registered in your name and then you can attend the annual meeting and receive the material the company sends out. In this way you keep the extent of your interest hidden.

The Products You Use

Still another source of investment ideas, where feminine buying expertise and intuition can help, lies in the stocks of companies whose products you use. Is the construction business increasing in your area? Then it may be about to boom all over the country. It could be a good time to invest in construction stock. You can ask builders or architects you know what products they use, what products have a future.

Who is a better judge of food brands in a supermarket than a woman who each week struggles to keep within her food budget? Has Campbell Soup come out with a new line of foods or new type of soup that you and your friends like? Has one of the packaging companies put out a really more effective baking/boiling plastic bag? Is one supermarket chain capturing most of the business in your community? There must be a reason.

General Foods a few years ago put out a line of gourmet foods, but it flopped because housewives didn't buy in enough quantity, something that shrewd shoppers probably noted. Now some other companies have entered the gourmet food business especially in the frozen food lines, offering specialties like souffles and meals for dieters at luxury prices. Can they succeed? If so, it might be an opportunity for investment in such a field. Certainly Birdseye, the pioneer frozen food line, made a great success, so much so that Mr. Birdseye, its developer, sold out to a big company, retiring with a fortune.

One of the most dramatic successes in post–World War II days involved Crest toothpaste, which, because it contained fluoride to help retard tooth decay, won approval some years ago from the American Dental Association. The other toothpaste makers, especially Colgate, were caught in the embarrassing situation of not having a competitive product ready. Despite Colgate's irate protests and legal challenges, Crest became the biggest volume seller. Why? Women with families wanted to improve their children's teeth (or at least stave off decay more effectively) and save on dentists' bills. Any mother whose child eats candy and drinks soft drinks has to worry about teeth.

The Crusaders and Other Life Improvers

Watch Ralph Nader in action, the crusader who campaigned successfully to make cars safer. Believe me, seat belts and other safety devices probably wouldn't be in cars today if Nader hadn't launched his campaign against tremendous odds some years ago. Remember how General Motors assigned detectives to try to discredit Nader through some flaw in his personal life—and could find nothing? Then we watched the spectacle of the head of mighty General Motors confessing to Congress that this had been done and apologizing.

Unfortunately, part of the blame can be placed on leading advertising agencies because they in some cases advised auto makers not to stress safety since that would make people think that cars were unsafe. This is the kind of attitude of total irresponsibility that sometimes is apparent in advertising.

Today, thanks to Ralph Nader, General Motors, Ford, and all car makers, domestic and foreign, periodically recall cars—sometimes hundreds of thousands at a time—for repairs of unsafe parts. Do you think that Congress would have set up safety standards for cars (and an administrative staff to handle them) if Nader had not campaigned so loudly, and if the death toll from car accidents had not mounted to such appalling totals? Today many states have adopted seat belt laws requiring drivers and passengers to buckle up.

What industries did Nader help indirectly? The seat belt makers, for example; makers of safety locks, especially now that car thefts have been on the increase; emission control devices, which soon will be mandatory in many states; makers of padded panels; makers of collapsible-on-contact highway signs and guards to keep cars from head-on collisions. Chains of service stations have grown up to take care of car repairs following analysis with computerlike devices that can detect a variety of engine troubles.

So watch the crusaders, of which there are always a few at any given moment. If the crusade became effective, it could often lead to new industries for life-improving devices.

Don't be upset if you miss opportunities. I have made some serious boners in investing, not so much in what I bought but in what I didn't buy. The one I most regret missing involves Minute Maid orange juice. Back in the 1940s I worked as a copyeditor on *The Wall Street Journal,* one of the few women in such a job on a New York paper. One day a male reporter came back from a company press conference bearing several cans of Minute Maid frozen orange juice, by then unfrozen from resting in his trench coat pocket. As I was the only woman around the city room of the newspaper at the moment, he invited me to test the orange juice for an opinion before he wrote the story. We stood around the water cooler, and he mixed me some juice in a paper cup. I tested it and said, "Well, it's better than canned orange juice, but it will never replace the fresh."

How wrong I was! How I underestimated the American housewife's liking for the convenience of frozen juice. In those days, I could have bought some shares cheaply, with the glamour of Bing Crosby as an added asset because he was one of the company backers. I should have known that he would make a wise investment, just because I knew he was a shrewd businessman. Today frozen orange juice is big business.

Unfortunately, I "missed" another good investment, too. Years ago I went to Allen & Company, an investment-banking firm, to interview Herbert and Charles Allen about one of their business ventures. While there, I was told of their interest in a company headquartered in Latin America called Syntex, maker of birth control items. "Buy some of the shares," I was advised. My problem as a financial writer has been a psychological one—a cynicism that most financial writers develop. Almost every businessman we interview enthuses over his company. I remember vividly the president of a leading oil company telling me, "Our gasoline is better, Miss Fowler." This came after a statement by me that, after all, oil comes out of the ground, and is refined into gasoline, and the brand name doesn't make much difference. I still believe this.

This explains my cynicism about Syntex and my failure to buy some shares at the time. Such disbelief, when it is ingrained as mine was, should be tempered with logic.

Syntex, to make my humiliation worse, rose from about 1 a share in 1958 to a peak of 124 a share in 1966, adjusted for stock splits.* I could have outdone Hetty Green on that one!

Experiences like these happen to many investors, probably all of them sooner or later. It's sobering, like a cold shower, and jarring, too. Yet an investor can learn from it, developing an instinct for separating shining opportunities from shooting stars.

*The company operates in Panama. Competition has hurt its prospects somewhat in recent years, along with high development costs, and its shares ranged in price from 53 to 79 in 1968 but in early 1972 it was as high as 120. Thus, because of its interest in birth control, skin biology, problems of aging, etc., it once more became a good speculation. Syntex shares sold at 46 after a two-for-one split in December 1985.

Looking Further Ahead

If you are forty-five years old or younger, you are a lucky investor because opportunities abound in the future. The chances are that you will have a definite stake in the year 2,000 because you will still be alive.

Today's oldsters probably grew up on comic-strip characters like Buck Rogers, on Jules Verne's ventures into tomorrow, and perhaps on Aldous Huxley's *Brave New World.* Somehow, today, with Americans walking on the moon, and a scientist named Cousteau and others venturing under the sea to promote the science called oceanography, those earlier flights of scientific fancy seem all too real.

In a book called *The Year 2000,* published in 1967 (Macmillan), authors Herman Kahn and Anthony Wiener speculate on the future with more seriousness and more pertinency than most literary commentators. Working in their "think tank," called Hudson Institute, the authors wrote the book out of a study they did for the American Academy of Arts and Sciences, the Carnegie Corporation, and the Corning Glass Works Foundation.

What will A.D. 2000 bring to the average American, in terms of his way of life and his financial planning?

According to Kahn and Wiener, family income will be much higher by then. So high in fact that a new class may emerge—people who work little or not at all because they have enough money for leisure. Often I hear some of my young business friends say, "If I work ten more years and make 15 percent compounded on my investments I can retire."

It is the kind of aristocratic concept that Europeans have been able to understand in past years, because many of them grew up on the theory that nice people shouldn't work but live on their income from investments. It is also a kind of thinking that generations of American businessmen indulged in not at all, preferring to work vigorously for money until they reached age 60 or 65, a kind of Puritan belief in the sanctity of work and money growth. Most businessmen still like to think or talk of themselves as hard workers, with some even saying they cannot take vacations. I think many more people will work until age 70, now that there are laws against age discrimination.

However, perhaps when today's younger generation reaches middle age it might well relish ideas for little work and much leisure expounded so logically in *The Year 2000.*

The authors project a range of per capita income (disposable income after taxes) of $4,900–$8,947. This range would be for the typical middle-class, middle-management family of four. This group consists of well-paid white-collar workers, technicians, some high-paid blue-collar construction workers, and others. Thus the family would have an income after taxes of four times this per capita amount, ranging from $19,600 to $35,780. Of course, inflation would take a toll. By 1985 these estimates already have been reached in some areas, especially in the case of families with working wives.

The work week, which even nowadays is getting shorter, will become so short by the year 2000 that people will work no more than four days a week and less than eight hours a day. With legal holidays and long vacations, this could result in an annual working period of 147 days and 218 days off.

Filling this leisure time may become a serious problem, as well as an opportunity for investment. Children will be encouraged to develop a wider variety of talents not connected with their possible careers, such as sports, music, art. In fact, the pressure could be so great that going to museums, theaters, and other places of entertainment might have to be rationed. Think of the tight three-by-six-foot spaces available now for individual bathers at some public beaches!

Women, both those with children and those without, will continue to play an increasing role in the labor force. "We estimate there will be an increase in the female participation rate partly because it seems likely there will be an increase in the attractiveness and availability of part-time and intermittent work," the authors suggest. Even now several employment agencies for part-time workers have formed corporations and sold the stock publicly.

The average American family will have more of its relatives alive, which may or may not be a problem. In your area even now you can watch the proliferation of nursing homes to care for the elderly or disabled.

With artificial kidneys, heart devices, and other substitutes for vital organs, people may increase their life spans to 150 years, especially in view of the wide use of diet foods, the stress on proper nutrition (protein, for example) and exercise, plus other health measures like immunization against most diseases. Presumably, with high incomes oldsters will not become a burden to most families.

Perhaps one change that Americans may find hard to grasp is entirely new forms of transportation—a trip down an air street to see a neighbor may be on top of an individual platform (the Army is testing such devices for infantrymen now); a trip to Europe by rocket might take only half an hour, with the Taj Mahal a little longer trip for quiet contemplation. This compares with long-distance trips of two or three hours promised by supersonic commercial plane builders in a few years.

The career woman and the housewife will run an automated home, thanks to computers. They won't need much cash because the local supermarket and other stores will be computerized to accept a credit card. Banks will be equipped to pay their bills almost instantly.

Many Americans will live in Boswash, Chipitts, or SanSan, three giant megalopolitan areas that may well be envied by other nations for their high standard of living. Boswash will extend from Boston to Washington and will remain the financial and governmental center of the country. Chipitts will encompass the Great Lakes area in the neighborhood of Chicago and Pittsburgh. SanSan is the fast-growing region, stretching from San Diego to San Francisco. These areas will hold 80 million, 40 million, and 20 million respectively out of the total projected population of 300 million people.

Land prices almost everywhere will be high as the population expands, and more Americans than now will live vertically—in high-rise apartments or condominiums, even in rural areas.

With all the changes, by the year 2000 there will be many problems to be solved, raised not so much by the better standard of living but by the individual's relationship to the terrifyingly huge, faceless bureaucracy called the U.S. government. To keep up with the future, read *The Kiplinger Letter* and the books written by forecasters like Marvin Cetron, who heads Forecasting International in Arlington, Virginia—books with names like *Encounters with the Future, Jobs of the Future,* and *The Future of American Business.*

As you have read this perhaps you have been able to visualize the opportunities for investment that the future holds. They merit continued reading and scrutiny as they slowly evolve, because change does tend to come slowly or with little sudden jerks.

There are some stories to point up the impact of inflation worth remembering, such as the one the late Dr. Marcus Nadler used to tell his classes in international banking at New York University's Graduate School of Business Administration. To emphasize the terrifying impact of inflation in post–World War II Germany, he told his students this one:

It seems that a German businessman who died before World War I left his fortune divided among his two sons, with the admonition of a frugal German father that they invest carefully and keep their capital. One son dutifully put his money into German government bonds and also worked in the family business. The other son—the prodigal—preferred the lively existence of wine, women, and song with some travel as a chaser.

Then came the war and the ensuing inflation. The family business was bankrupt. The German money, the mark, was devalued so badly that it took a wheelbarrow filled with paper money to buy a loaf of bread and a container of milk. When workers received their pay they rushed out the same hour to buy bread and milk, knowing that by the next day the paper money would purchase less food.

The conservative son found that his bonds were valueless. However, the prodigal son soon made a startling discovery. He could sell the large collection of empty champagne bottles filling his cellar for good prices—postwar Germany needed glass.

The moral of this prodigal son tale is that fixed-income securities do not necessarily enable an investor to keep up with inflation these days, unless of course they have some built-in appreciation possibilities.

A more modern version of the prodigal son story was issued by Harris Upham & Company, a once-prominent brokerage firm whose ace investment analyst, Ralph Rotnem, now deceased, wrote with an imaginative flair.

The story is good enough to print verbatim.

How to Invest for Greatest Profits
or The Lesson of the Seven Brothers
Over the Course of Twelve Years

On December thirty-first of 1959 a father gave each of his seven sons $10,000 and asked them to invest as they saw fit during the next twelve years. On January 1st, 1972, he called them together to compare results. Their methods of investing and the present values of the original $10,000* funds were as follows:

First Son. Extremely conservative—decided not to take a chance on the stock market and invested his money in high-grade corporate bonds which he continued to hold throughout the twelve-year period. Very unimaginative.	$7,030
Second Son. Also conservative but he decided that stocks would do better than bonds in the twelve-year period so he put all of his money in the stocks included in the Dow Jones industrial average. But he was both lazy and unimaginative and just stayed with his original purchases for the twelve-year period.	$13,100
Third Son. Also invested in the Dow Jones industrial stocks but decided to take advantage of the major bull and bear trends and to be invested only when bull markets were	

*These figures do not include commissions, taxes, dividends, or interest payments.

in progress. He bought five times and sold four times during the next twelve years and did the impossible by always catching the major tops for selling and the major bottoms for buying. $51,465

Fourth Son. Invested only in the five groups that he thought would advance the most in the next twelve years. He too did the impossible and chose the correct ones—soft drinks, up 763 percent, cosmetics, up 517 percent, air conditioning, up 496 percent, coals, up 491 percent, and truckers, up 473 percent. $64,810

Fifth Son. He guessed that there would be fads and fancies during the twelve-year period so he would try to be in whichever group was most popular. When a favored group peaked out he would shift the proceeds into the next favorite. He was in vending stocks (up 98 percent) from January 1960 to April 1961, in golds (up 30 percent) to June 1962 when most stocks declined, in airlines to June 1966 (up 570 percent), in savings and loans to December 1968 (up 200 percent), in cosmetics to December 1969 (up 30.6 percent), and in mobile homes to December 1971 (up 117 percent). An impossible but excellent record. $1,466,248

Sixth Son. He invested only in the group that went up the most in each year. $4,749,730

Year	*Group*	*Percentage of Gain*
1960	Canned Foods	48.4
1961	Life Ins.	76.6
1962	Integ. Intl. Oils	13.2
1963	Airlines	99.4
1964	Sulfur	73.8
1965	Radio & TV Mfrs.	132.3
1966	Radio & TV Broad.	26.6

Year	*Group*	*Percentage of Gain*
1967	Bread & Cake Bakers	107.8
1968	Savings & Loans	86.0
1969	Cosmetics	30.6
1970	Coals	53.3
1971	Restaurants	103.0

Seventh Son. He bought only the stocks listed on the New York Stock Exchange that went up the most each year. $29,750,168,400

Year	*Stock*	*Percentage of Gain*
1960	Chock Full O'Nuts	135.6
1961	Korvette	287.0
1962	Natl. Airlines	76.8
1963	Monon Railroad	227.4
1964	Boston & Maine	200.0
1965	Fairchild Camera	447.3
1966	Howmet Corp.	139.8
1967	Republic Corp.	1,290.0
1968	Duplan Corp.	297.1
1969	Japan Fund	111.1
1970	Overnight Transp.	122.7
1971	Winnebago Ind.	462.3

$29.7 billion! That's the power of compounding growth stocks. Unfortunately, Mr. Rotnem never updated these figures, but you get the point.

Good luck! When you make your first million dollars, write me a letter. Of course if it's after the year 2000 I may not be available, unless you have developed extrasensory perception—another growing field.

Index